D1557764

ARMED WITH THE
CONSTITUTION

ARMED WITH THE
CONSTITUTION

Jehovah's Witnesses in Alabama
and the U.S. Supreme Court,
1939–1946

MERLIN OWEN NEWTON

THE UNIVERSITY OF ALABAMA PRESS

TUSCALOOSA AND LONDON

Library of Congress Cataloging-in-Publication Data

Newton, Merlin Owen, 1935–
Armed with the Constitution : Jehovah's Witnesses in Alabama and
the U.S. Supreme Court, 1939–1946 / Merlin Owen Newton.
p.   cm.
Includes bibliographical references and index.
ISBN 0-8173-0736-2 (acid-free paper)
1. Freedom of religion—United States—History.   2. United States—
Constitutional law—Amendments—1st.   3. Jehovah's Witnesses—Legal
status, laws, etc.—United States.   4. Jehovah's Witnesses—Legal
status, laws, etc.—Alabama.   5. Marsh, Grace—Trials, litigation,
etc.   6. Jones, Rosco—Trials, litigation, etc.   I. Title.
KF4783.N45   1994
342.73'0852—dc20
[347.302852]   94-3993

British Library Cataloguing-in-Publication Data available

Dedicated to
my parents,
Johnie Lois Battle and *George Dewey Owen*
my husband,
Wesley Phillips Newton
and
my children,
Linda, Alan, and *Brent Newton*

Contents

Illustrations

Acknowledgments

Coming of age in Clay County, Alabama, during the early days of the civil rights movement, I pondered the local white citizens' attitude toward freedom. It seemed to be a love-hate relationship.[1] I was startled to discover that the views of many friends and neighbors toward Hugo Black had shifted dramatically during the decade following *Brown v. Board of Education I,* decided in 1954. I can still vividly recall my shock when I attended a movie at the Ashland Theatre and discovered that the white response to a newsreel portraying the U.S. Supreme Court had turned hostile. Previously, many local people had expressed their pride in the accomplishments of a former resident of Clay County, cheering his appearance on the screen, but in 1954 the applause gave way to boos and catcalls. In 1957 Black's concurrence in *Yates v. United States,* which overturned the convictions of several members of the Communist party on the grounds that the First Amendment protected their right to advocate abstract doctrine, drew vehement criticism. In the early 1960s, after Black wrote for the Court in *Engel v. Vitale,* overruling an officially sponsored prayer in the New York public schools,[2] the verbal attack on the Alabama justice grew even more shrill. Most of my acquaintances angrily felt that the "local boy" who had gotten their vote for the Senate had abandoned and turned on them, fraternizing with the liberal Warren Court.

I, in response, felt betrayed that these generally decent people, friends and neighbors in whose midst I had grown up, were so intolerant. I had been inspired with their patriotism when they had sent their sons, brothers, and sweethearts to World War II and Korea to "fight for freedom." Although I had known deep down that they did not consider blacks to be equal, I had moved in a segregated world of limited, structured contact between the races, largely unaware of the violent hatred of racism. Young and idealistic, denying the flaws in the world about me, I had painted an inner portrait of Clay County in which gentle, rational, understanding people treated each other with kindness and respect. When the events of the 1950s confronted me with a less perfect reality, I was both bewildered and indignant. Impatient for justice, I concluded that if the local folk could not see the error of their ways, then someone wiser would have to lead the battle in righting the wrongs. Wishing earnestly for a local kindred soul, I came to view Hugo Black as my shining knight and the Supreme Court as his charger in the cause of justice.

My father, an uncommonly wise and forgiving man, did not agree with his neighbors who reacted harshly to Black's stance in *Brown* and *Yates* and *Engel,* but he did not hate them for it. Having personally struggled with the problems of religious bigotry, he had tried to teach me at an early age that no one has a monopoly on the truth, especially in matters of faith. Fiercely independent in his thinking, he was willing to let any ideology be heard. Deeply compassionate and committed to justice, he hated racial prejudice. He understood, nonetheless, the desperation with which people often seek certainty and fear change.

As I attempted to absorb my father's teachings and to understand the defensive reaction of my fellow townspeople, and as my interest in government broadened, I began to recognize that the conflict between stated ideals and actual practice that I had observed in Clay County was not an isolated phenomenon. I became aware that advocates of democracy frequently have great difficulty in applying broad principles, which they accept, to certain specific situations, which they view as threatening.[3] I then felt prompted to explore a larger question: how can a people hold to its ideals?

As I wrestled with political theory, I considered the question of the role of the Court as guardian of individual rights in the United States. I became intrigued not only with the Warren-Black Court but with the broader issue of balance in a constitutional democracy. I wanted to focus on the issues that had forced me to reexamine my idealized view of the world. I sought through history to reenter the world of my youth in order to investigate those questions of personal liberty and dignity that I had not examined closely as a child.

The decision to convert a personal quest into historical scholarship resulted in my study of two U.S. Supreme Court cases that had originated in Alabama during my childhood, *Jones v. Opelika* and *Marsh v. Alabama*.[4] The cases represented First Amendment challenges to the status quo by a small religious minority, the Jehovah's Witnesses, and Hugo Black, voting for the Witnesses, had figured prominently in both. Greatly assisting me in this project were Sarah Woolfolk Wiggins and Tony Freyer, history professors at The University of Alabama who codirected the project (my dissertation). Their expertise and consideration were invaluable to me; quite literally, this study would not have been possible without their assistance.

I was also very fortunate in locating Grace Marsh, of *Marsh v. Alabama*, and Thelma Jones, widow of Rosco Jones of *Jones v. Opelika*, and in receiving their cooperation. Despite advanced age and health problems, both women provided me with memoirs, correspondence, and encouragement and read relevant portions of the dissertation. I am deeply appreciative of their support. I also wish to thank Ben and Betty Eskridge of Montgomery, Alabama, members of a local Kingdom Hall, who responded to my request for information and enhanced my understanding of Witness beliefs.

Many others contributed significantly to this study. I especially wish to acknowledge the help of Dr. Gordon T. Chappell of Huntingdon College, who first made me love history, and Dr. Gerald Capers of Tulane University, who convinced me that I could do historical scholarship. I also thank many persons at Huntingdon College who encouraged my return to graduate school, particularly Dr. Willard Top, academic dean; Dr. John Williams, chairman of my department; and Dr. Donna Whitley, colleague and officemate. I also appreciate the assistance of professional personnel at various research centers: particularly Lynn Kitchens, Alma Surles, and Tim Lewis at the Alabama Supreme Court Library; Director

Ed Bridges and Reference Librarians Michael Breedlove, Norwood Kerr, Debbie Pendleton, Tanya Zanish, and Willie Maryland at the Alabama Department of Archives and History; Jean Holliday, Special Collections, Seeley G. Mudd Manuscript Library, Princeton University; Jeffrey Suchanek, Editor of the Oral History Program, and Bill Cooper, Curator of Modern Political Manuscripts, at the University of Kentucky; David Wigdor and his assistants at the Manuscript Division, Library of Congress; Karen Mason, Reference Archivist, Bentley Historical Library, the University of Michigan; and Mary Ann Hawkins, Archivist, National Archives—Southeast Region, East Point, Georgia. Old friends offered moral support, particularly Dorothy Waters Wilson, Mary Lynn Johnson Grant, Sharon McFadden Ritter, Bobbie Olliff, Steve McFarland, and Ronald Hamby.

The greatest thanks, however, I must reserve for my family. My parents, both English teachers in the public schools of Clay County, encouraged me to enter the academic world. My father first introduced me to tolerance and critical thinking, and my mother taught me loyalty. At eighty-eight, with very limited sight, she read the entire manuscript. My sister, Jeanne Owen Hagedorn, herself the author of an exemplary family history, assisted me with research in Birmingham, Alabama, and proofread the manuscript. My adult children, Linda, Alan, and Brent, expressed interest in my undertaking and cheered me on. But the person to whom I owe the largest debt in this venture and to whom I wish to express the greatest appreciation is my husband and best friend, Wesley Newton, who assisted me above and beyond the call of duty. An accomplished historian, both teacher and author, he gave my endeavor priority over his own interests, patiently bore my complaints, and never wavered in his support and encouragement. The completion of this study, then, depended upon the assistance of many. Any errors, of course, remain my own.

ARMED WITH THE
CONSTITUTION

Introduction

The true test of the substance of freedom, U.S. Supreme Court justice Robert Jackson observed, "is the right to differ as to things that touch the heart of the existing order," for "freedom to differ is not limited to things that do not matter much."[1] The story of *Jones v. Opelika* and *Marsh v. Alabama*[2] is an account of such a testing of liberty in the United States, 1939–1946, and of the constitutional repercussions. To understand the cases, one must place them in the perspective of their legal and political settings. But *Jones* and *Marsh* also tell the story of two powerful personalities whose religious beliefs as members of the Jehovah's Witnesses drove them from nonexceptional backgrounds into moments of national prominence. In Witnessing, Jones, a black man, and Marsh, a white woman, found the means to personal expression in a society that offered them limited opportunities. Witnessing demanded fortitude, dedication, and courage, but it offered the chance to make one's mark regardless of race, sex, or economic status. As a soldier for Jehovah, one counted. The examination of the legal challenges of Rosco Jones and Grace Marsh, then, must also penetrate the worldview of the Witnesses.

Jones v. Opelika and *Marsh v. Alabama* provide classic examples of a conflict between differing societal values. Even when a constitution reflects the fundamental values of the broad community, issues may arise when abstractions are tested in the context of concrete problems; that which was accepted as a general principle may produce unexpected consequences when applied to particular situations. The definition of large concepts in terms of specific controversies may lead to differing interpretations of the basic law. Such variance occurred in the United States in the late 1930s and early 1940s as the nation attempted to determine how the First Amendment freedoms of speech, press, and religion applied to the proselytizing activities of the Jehovah's Witnesses.

The complexities of explication multiply when a constitution aims at equality as well as democracy, rests upon the premise that each individual has certain innate rights, and encompasses a variety of different peoples. Interpretation of the U.S. Constitution—which espouses both freedom and order, champions both majority rule and minority rights, governs a heterogeneous population, and divides power between levels and branches of government—demands a delicate balancing of competing interests. In such a complex constitutional structure, disputes as to *how* to interpret *what* constitutes the fundamental law are often interwoven with debates over *who* shall do the construing. Frequent conflict regarding the role of the U.S. Supreme Court and its relationship to the elected representatives is not unexpected.[3]

While the U.S. constitutional system lessens the likelihood of tyranny by countering power with power, the system inherently resists change because any shift threatens the fragile equilibrium. Unorthodox challenges to community mores may elicit intolerant responses by the power structure or even by an "overbearing majority,"[4] particularly, as Jackson stated, if those demands "matter much." As a constitutional democracy, in which government is not valued in and of itself, the United States must guard against subordinating the end of liberty to the means of order. The state, as Socrates so wisely observed, often needs a gadfly.[5]

The role of critic in the United States during World War II was not easy, for Americans sought stability through uniformity. One who marched to a different drumbeat often marched alone. The fledgling American Civil Liberties Union (ACLU) stood a solitary guard as a national organization dedicated exclusively to protecting the principles of individual freedom. The National Association for the Advancement of Colored People (NAACP), bearing the incubus of racial prejudice, normally concentrated on specifically racial problems, and the leading labor organizations confined their activities largely to bread and butter issues. Women's movements, generally undeveloped, had neither the power nor the focus to champion the singular cause of personal liberty. The ACLU, which was confined principally to urban areas and divided internally in its attitude toward Communist activity, maintained its vigil with few funds and numerous difficulties. With a membership of approximately five thousand in affiliate organizations in less than a dozen states, the ACLU maintained unofficial "correspondents" to secure information and give advice in local matters in a majority of the states and often cooperated with kindred groups such as the NAACP or the Workers Defense League. In the South, where a traditional white male elite clung tenaciously to the reins of power, the ACLU had no chapters, the NAACP walked softly, and the organizations that rose to prominence during the civil rights movement of the 1950s and 1960s were yet unborn.[6]

In those troubled war years, from 1939 to 1946, Rosco Jones and Grace Marsh served as gadflies pestering Alabama and the nation. The litigation to which they were parties originated in Alabama but ultimately reached the U.S. Supreme Court. *Jones v. Opelika* began in the small mill town of Opelika in 1939 and was decided twice by the Court, in June 1942 and then in May 1943. *Marsh v. Alabama* originated in 1943 in Chickasaw, a company town that served shipbuilding interests near Mobile, and was decided by the high court in January 1946. Both cases were successful Witness challenges to the small-town power structure in the state, with the U.S. Supreme Court upholding the First Amendment rights of minorities against the will of the community officials.[7] Harbingers of change, the cases were part of a larger trend to expand individual civil liberties, a movement that grew under the pressures of World War II and eventually crested in the Warren Court era of the 1950s and 1960s. By tracing the steps of Jones and Marsh as the Witnesses carried their crusade through the courts of state and nation, we can do more than look through a window into their lives and into various doctrines. We can also view constitutional history and observe a democratic society wrestling with its own values.

The Witnesses, a small but zealous millennial sect governed by the

Watch Tower Bible and Tract Society,[8] were originally known as International Bible Students or Russellites. Organized in Pennsylvania by Charles Taze Russell in the late nineteenth century, the sect initially attracted a significant professional element as well as farmers, small businessmen, and urban workers. The Bible Students included both sexes and all ages. By the 1930s, under the leadership of Joseph Rutherford, the group had assumed the designation Jehovah's Witnesses and was aiming its message particularly at the poor and underprivileged. The racial composition of the Witnesses in the 1930s and 1940s cannot be precisely determined, but apparently blacks constituted a significant minority, located primarily in large cities and in the South. Witnesses that carried cases to the U.S. Supreme Court were generally white, but Rosco Jones was a prominent exception.[9]

Under the leadership of Rutherford, "a twentieth-century Jeremiah," [10] Witnesses prepared for Armageddon in a nationally orchestrated, aggressive campaign. Responding to Jehovah's command to go forth and preach the gospel, they went from door to door and village to village, carrying His message by preaching orally, distributing literature published by the society, and playing records of Rutherford's sermons. In streets and courtrooms throughout the land they confronted state and local officials whose ordinances hindered the coming of Jehovah's Kingdom. Although, as a rule, Witnesses were personally well mannered, their doctrine was stridently antiestablishment. Believing that prevailing religious, economic, and political institutions were agents of Satan,[11] Witnesses minced no words in denouncing them, provoking heated and sometimes violent reactions. Many endured imprisonment or physical abuse. But using tactics that foreshadowed the early black civil rights movement, Rutherford relied on the courage, discipline, and utter dedication of the membership to keep the ranks filled and Jehovah's banner held high. He used the small army of the faithful to maximize its number, shifting troops to open a new front or to reinforce a threatened flank. While occasionally the Witnesses retreated to regroup, they did not falter.[12]

The Witnesses' legal strategy, guided by the skillful hand of Hayden Covington, a dynamic Texas attorney, aimed to test state and local restrictions on the sect in the U.S. Supreme Court. Covington argued that

First Amendment protection of religious exercise, as well as of speech and press, was applicable to the states through the Fourteenth Amendment's due process clause.[13] In *Gitlow v. New York* the Court in 1925 had officially accepted the interpretation that "freedom of speech and of the press—which are protected by the First Amendment from abridgement by Congress—are among the fundamental personal rights and 'liberties' protected by the due process clause of the Fourteenth Amendment from impairment by the States," a concept known as "incorporation."[14] The full meaning of these freedoms was not established permanently at that time, however, and required clarification as specific cases and different personnel defined the concept under varying circumstances. In 1934, in dicta in *Hamilton v. Regents of the University of California,* some members of the Court suggested that free exercise of religion was also incorporated, but the doctrine needed further support, elaboration, and the test of time.[15] In 1937 the Court indicated in *Palko v. Connecticut* that at least fundamental rights, those "implicit in the concept of ordered liberty," should be incorporated through the due process clause.[16] Covington aimed to strengthen and expand the foundation for religious exercise, relating freedom of religious expression to freedom of speech and press, for the distribution of literature was an inherent part of Witnesses' proselytizing.

Covington's efforts bore fruit in 1938 and 1939. In first *Lovell v. Griffin* and then *Schneider v. Irvington,* the nation's highest court ruled for the Witnesses, basing its decisions on the guarantees of freedom of speech and press.[17] While the high tribunal considered those cases, two separate developments augured well for the Witnesses. First, in 1938 Justice Harlan Fiske Stone began to carve a broader jurisdiction for the Court as the protector of civil liberties. In a case in which the Court deferred to Congress in economic regulation, Stone added footnote four to *United States v. Carolene Products,* stating that although the Court should yield to the legislative branch in economic matters, it should subject to "more exacting . . . scrutiny" legislation that appeared on its face to be within a specific constitutional prohibition, that was necessary to keep the political processes open, or that affected "discrete and insular minorities."[18] Second, Covington found an ideal case in which to raise the religious exercise issue. On Palm Sunday, 1938, Newton Cantwell and his two sons were arrested in Roman Catholic New Haven, Connecticut, for having approached three pedestrians and having asked their permission to play a phonograph record that attacked Catholicism. Although the Cantwells stopped the recording and moved when their listeners angrily told them to do so, they were charged with breach of the peace and with soliciting funds without having first obtained a certificate of approval from a state official whose discretion determined in advance whether a cause was religious or "a bona fide object of charity."[19]

The Cantwells challenged the convictions on both procedural and substantive grounds, maintaining that their freedom of religious exercise, applicable to the state through the Fourteenth Amendment, had been violated. Justice Owen Roberts, writing for a unanimous Court, held for the Witnesses on both counts in *Cantwell v. Connecticut* in May 1940. Roberts maintained that while the state could reasonably regulate the time, place, and manner of solicitation, the state could not use this power to censor religious exercise; he also ruled that the Cantwells' actions had not presented a demonstrable clear and present threat to the peace. Significantly, through Roberts the Court asserted that the Amendment embraced both the "freedom to believe" and the "freedom to act," although only the first was absolute.[20] How to reconcile the two aspects remained an unsettled issue.

Another storm that had been brewing on the horizon of the Jehovah's Witnesses broke on the U.S. Supreme Court only a few weeks after *Cantwell*. Reacting to the courage shown by German Jehovah's Witnesses who had endured Nazi persecution rather than participate in the "Heil Hitler" salute,[21] Rutherford had admonished Witnesses in 1935 to reject patriotic ceremonies, such as flag salutes or standing for anthems, because such rituals paid homage to "graven images." A few months later Lillian and William Gobitis, children of Witness Walter Gobitis, were expelled from the public schools of Minersville, Pennsylvania, for refusing to participate in a compulsory daily ceremony that involved saluting and pledging allegiance to the flag. Gobitis sued in the U.S. courts on the ground that the children's rights to religious expression had been violated, and the case ultimately reached the U.S. Supreme Court. The Court rendered its decision in *Minersville School District v. Gobitis* in June 1940, an opinion that would become a cause célèbre.[22]

Justice Felix Frankfurter spoke for the Court in an 8–1 ruling against Gobitis. Arguing that the case presented a conflict between two accepted values—freedom of conscience and the use of symbols to encourage national security and patriotism—he held that the Court could not over-rule the elected representatives who acted on a legitimate concern for national unity in a time when war threatened. Freedom of conscience did not relieve the individual from public duty, he asserted. In the initial vote in the Court's deliberations, Justice Hugo Black of Alabama had passed, but he eventually decided to vote with the majority. Only Justice Harlan Stone dissented. Stone declared that patriotism could not be coerced and that the very substance of liberty was "the freedom of the individual from compulsion as to what he shall think and what he shall say, at least where the compulsion is to bear false witness against his religion." Joining Frankfurter, in addition to Black, were Chief Justice Charles Evans Hughes and Justices William O. Douglas, James McReynolds, Frank Murphy, Stanley Reed, and Owen Roberts.[23]

The one-sided nature of the decision, particularly the votes of three putative liberals—Black, Douglas, and Murphy—shocked Witnesses and other First Amendment advocates.[24] So too did the wave of persecution[25] of Witnesses that followed *Gobitis;* it was as if those virulent opponents of the Witnesses thought that the members of the high bench had sanctioned an assault. Mob action became commonplace, often en-couraged or at least countenanced by the local officials.[26] Many commentators in academic journals and in the larger press heavily criticized Frankfurter and the liberals who had joined him in *Gobitis.* Frankfurter did not budge, but the liberal trio grew increasingly uneasy about the results of the decision.[27]

In this context *Jones v. Opelika* found its way through the Alabama state courts to reach the U.S. Supreme Court in the October 1941 session. Refusing to apply in Opelika, Alabama, for a license to distribute liter-ature, Jones contended that the right to worship, protected by the First Amendment, included distribution of literature. The Watch Tower So-ciety backed Jones, carrying the case to the summit. *Jones v. Opelika* provided an opportunity for U.S. Supreme Court liberals to make amends for their vote in *Gobitis,* narrowing the ruling against Jones in 1942 to 5–4. The storm of criticism that likened the license to the colonial stamp tax and a shift in Court personnel by 1943 finally led to a reversal of *Jones* and *Gobitis* in favor of the Witnesses.[28] (The Court's increasing protection of personal liberty did not extend during wartime to persons of Japanese ancestry, however.)[29]

In December 1943 in Alabama, Grace Marsh took the Witness crusade for full freedom of religious expression a step further. Maintaining that the property commonly used by the public in the business block of Chickasaw, a company town, should be open for distributing literature, she was arrested for trespassing. After fighting the charge in Alabama courts, she petitioned the U.S. Supreme Court. In January 1946 the nation's highest tribunal upheld Marsh, declaring that a company town could not deny its residents fundamental rights.[30]

By 1946 the U.S. Supreme Court had denounced interference with freedom of religious expression, whether from an intolerant majority, a governing elite, or the power of property. The nation's judicial summit had defended a cantankerous minority, calling to task those who obstructed the right to religious exercise guaranteed by the First Amendment, made applicable at state level by the Fourteenth Amendment. *Jones* and *Marsh* were vital links in the chain of events and the legal philosophy that championed the cause of individual liberty. The decisions represented not only victories for the Jehovah's Witnesses but also turning points in the nation's constitutional commitment to individual rights and indexes of the increasingly activist role of the Court as the guardian of personal liberty.

1

The Setting

It was not entirely coincidental that Rosco Jones, a black man in a mill town, and Grace Marsh, a white woman in a company town, carried Jehovah's banner into test cases in Alabama. The population of the state stood at 2,832,961 in 1940, with the ratio of whites to blacks approximately two to one,[1] but the religious census of 1936 had ignored Jehovah's Witnesses.[2] Witnesses composed an exceedingly small minority in the nation as a whole, but they were almost nonexistent in the South, where Baptists and Methodists predominated.[3] Resistance to the Witnesses was greatest in rural areas and small towns,[4] and the Witness message appealed particularly to those without wealth or power.[5] Although white men controlled the movement, women, in practice, bore much of the brunt of Witness activity because men were the primary family breadwinners.[6] In the black community of the South men were more prominent in Witnessing. Traditionally, serving as a minister afforded one of the few opportunities for leadership for black men and represented one of the few positions recognized as respectable by the white community. A black male minister was more often taken seriously by whites than was a black female.[7] But being a minister of whatever sex or race for the Jehovah's Witnesses required assertive behavior, which elicited the disapproval of the traditional power structure. In the rural South in the late 1930s conformity was the norm. The leadership believed in an organic community in which everything had a place.[8] Religion should be kept in the churches, decent white women in the home,[9] and blacks in a position deferential to whites.[10] The establishment could not sanction an outspoken woman engaged in street preaching. Furthermore, it would not tolerate an aggressive black male.

Rosco Jones was assertive—polite, hardworking, but daring and decisive about the beliefs that he valued. A black man, born and raised in North Carolina, Jones had been forced to adjust to a world controlled by whites that offered him limited opportunities. Although he possessed only an eighth-grade education, he was a responsible worker and a good supervisor, wrote with considerable skill, and thought at length about God and religion.[11] For a long time "the truth," the term that Witnesses use to refer to their faith,[12] had eluded him. Having secured the truth at last, he was unwilling to compromise it.

Grace Marsh was not afraid to speak her mind. Although she was in many ways a traditional white southern woman, she was not timid in expressing her unconventional religious views. The daughter of a Russellite who raised his children in the truth, she had been taught from childhood that the will of Jehovah should be paramount in her life. Surrounded by a large, close-knit family in rural Alabama, Grace finished high school and shortly thereafter married a local farmer. The couple moved to Chicago, and briefly Grace left the faith of her father, but she soon went back to her roots.[13]

Jones and Marsh had thus come to identify with the Witness movement by different paths, but each concluded that Jehovah had chosen His Witnesses to spread His word. He had entrusted direction of His cause to the Watch Tower Bible and Tract Society, and the chosen ones enjoyed the privilege and duty to Witness for Jehovah wherever and however the society directed. When the society decided on a widespread campaign to test the reach of the First Amendment, directing Jones to strengthen the movement in Opelika and Marsh to break the barrier to Witnessing in Chickasaw, the two dedicated Witnesses did not hesitate. That their tasks would be hard was insignificant. What truly mattered was that they preach His truth. Jehovah would aid them, for, they fervently believed, He "always seems to figure a way out."[14]

The power structure in Alabama and in the small communities of

Opelika and Chickasaw, however, also assumed that Jehovah was on their side. The church was part of the establishment. Religion figured prominently in almost every aspect of the southern community, a society marked by two primary, at times overlapping, cultures drawn along racial lines. Sermons, prayer meetings, revivals, and church socials composed an integral part of the lives of southerners, white or black. While southern denominations did not generally support the organized fundamentalist movement, they did accept the fundamentalist doctrine formula that distilled "the Old and New Testaments into a core of beliefs that included original sin, the divine inspiration of the Scriptures, the virgin birth of Jesus, atonement, resurrection, the Trinity, the second coming of Jesus, and a final judgment." In an unstable world, religion was the rock of ages, a haven against the storms of modernity.[15]

Religion also provided a means of social control. Employed to conserve and reinforce the traditional white supremacist culture, religion had long been interwoven in the public mind with the celebration of the Anglo-Saxon heritage, local pride, and the myths of the hallowed southern woman and the contented black. Thus, mores were "accorded a certain divine quality." Fraternal orders—Masons, Elks, Shriners— attracted many of the respectable citizenry. Coupling ritual and loyalty, the brotherhoods served as a form of "communal bonding," reinforcing local mores.[16] Since God's kingdom was not of this world, the existing authorities could defer justice for the downtrodden without an overwhelming sense of guilt. Some suggested, in fact, that the oppressed had created their own oppression.[17] Others were more paternalistic, coupling power with moral responsibility. Such persons, imbued with a sense of noblesse oblige, maintained that those with strength and advantages should be magnanimous, assisting and directing the less privileged: males should protect females, and white leaders should encourage and support clean-living, hardworking, nonthreatening blacks. Although a few endorsed the Social Gospel, the linking of regional patriotism, the status quo, and religiosity was common.[18]

Unorthodox religious interpretations thus threatened the entire social order.[19] In the early twentieth century, nonetheless, traditional religion had lost many of the most deprived in the religious hysteria born of the union of poverty and change. Rejected by the present world, many of the dispossessed found identification in a sense of brotherhood, centering their lives around a highly evangelical faith that emphasized the hereafter. The South became "a hothouse for sects," as Pentecostal, Holiness, and Church of Christ movements filled "the religious vacuum at the bottom of southern society."[20] Because the crusade on occasion united the powerless minorities, producing biracial meetings and sympathy for organized labor activity, the sects stirred a sense of uneasiness in the governing elite. On the whole, however, the evangelicals endorsed old values and confined their activities to the religious sphere.[21] As long as formal religion supported the leaders of society and informal religions advocated *personal* redemption, advocates of the status quo felt reasonably secure. But the Witnesses would be a different matter. They not only accepted unorthodox doctrine but also confronted in courts those who made and enforced the law.

The law was a multifaceted concept in the South. Some viewed it essentially as the local sheriff, but others defined it as the defender of state's rights or the guardian of the community or the embodiment of national ideals. In the abstract the law was revered. "There is but one duty of the official, that is to enforce the law. There is but one duty of the citizen, that is to obey the law," stated a leading Alabama jurist—the same jurist who would write the Alabama Supreme Court opinion denying Rosco Jones relief. A popular theme emphasizing order and heroic qualities held that southerners should follow the example of the early republican Romans, who were virtuous and dedicated to the common good.[22]

Alabamians, like many other southerners, emphasized the valor of their past and distrusted those "outsiders" who had not shared it. Protestants of Anglo-Saxon heritage who had been born in the South were generally not suspect, and local Jews and Roman Catholics were usually tolerated in urban areas as long as the community did not perceive them to be a threat. Something close to xenophobia occurred if members of ethnic or religious minorities suggested change in the basic order, and the nonblack community members closed ranks if outsiders defended blacks. Talk of the glorious "Lost Cause" flourished. Confederate soldiers were revered, and their heirs were rewarded politically.[23] Walter B. Jones, a former Alabama circuit court judge, writing a creed for Alabamians in the *Alabama Lawyer,* declared that the people of the state should take pride in the history written by the gallant deeds of "the sons of Alabama" and pledged to make Alabama "a nobler, purer and manlier state—a better commonwealth for the coming generations."[24]

Ordinary folks living in Alabama in the late 1930s and early 1940s had good reason for wishing for a better commonwealth. Labor in the South as late as 1940 continued to be abundant "at rock bottom prices." Farming remained the primary occupation, employing large numbers of women and children as well as men, with the workers largely unorganized. Farm labor wage rates in Alabama fell well below the national average, and "tenancy covered the land like a winter frost." Early New Deal agricultural programs had provided little comfort to sharecroppers, who lived with malnutrition in filth. The Farm Tenancy Act of 1937, with U.S. senator John Hollis Bankhead II from Alabama as sponsor, established the Farm Security Administration (FSA) to grant loans to assist farmers in owning their own land. Hindered by conservative opposition and insufficient funds, the FSA benefited only a small percentage of the tenants.[25]

Manufacturing, mining, and timber industries provided the bulk of nonfarm jobs. In 1929 Alabama textile mills employed approximately 28,000 persons, divided almost evenly between men and women, but the number fell precipitously as the Great Depression hit. As conditions worsened, the United Textile Workers of America appealed to a significant number of the mill hands in the areas of Birmingham and Huntsville, and an unsuccessful strike that began in Huntsville in 1934 spread quickly to twenty-eight mills in Birmingham and other centers in northern Alabama. Mills remained largely unorganized, however, in central and southern Alabama. In Opelika, the mill town to which Rosco Jones would come a few years later, armed guards turned away "a truckload of union members and organizers." Manufacturers of iron and steel, with Birmingham as their center, hired approximately 30,000 in jobs that paid relatively well in 1929, but the depression of the 1930s seriously affected those workers. Coal mining, focused in the Jefferson-Walker-Tuscaloosa area, employed approximately 25,000 men for an average of 231 days annually in 1929; despite some setbacks in the 1930s, some 22,000 extracted coal in the area in 1944. The United Mine Workers made meaningful inroads among the miners, with several strikes occurring in the 1930s, bringing some gains to those workers. In 1937 the Congress of Industrial Organizations (CIO) signed its first contract with Tennessee Coal and Iron (TCI) of Birmingham, but the power of the corporation extended beyond "the magic city" to the shipyards of Mobile and the company town of Chickasaw, where Grace Marsh would soon challenge the status quo. Lumber workmen, although matching textile workers and miners in number, did not organize to any appreciable extent.[26] Pay was poor, and fringe benefits were few for most working people of Alabama.

Such people had limited impact on the political structure in Alabama. The Republican party had been branded by its association with Reconstruction and posed no statewide threat to the Democratic party. The Populist movement of the 1890s, however, had seriously threatened the Democratic monopoly of power, as many small farmers temporarily left the Democratic fold. But conservative forces quickly reacted and sterilized the system "against the disease of conflict over real issues" by removing the potential power of "all the third partyites and all the niggers." The Bourbons, white landowners of large estates in the south-central section of the state, and business leaders, interested in more efficient government, shared certain interests—order, low taxes, and a low wage scale. Using respectable tools such as the secret ballot, the poll tax, and the revision of the state's constitution—which they justified as measures necessary to stop fraud—and the white primary, they assured the disfranchisement of blacks and many poor whites by 1901. As historian J. Mills Thornton observed, "The levees of power . . . had been carefully and lovingly constructed at the turn of the century."[27]

Alabama's river system and migration pattern, and the nature of its agriculture, made the central and southern sections of the state differ significantly from the northern portion. Except for the wire grass in the southeastern corner of the state, most of south Alabama's agriculture lay in the rich lowlands known as the Black Belt, once the center of plantations worked by slaves. North Alabama, more hilly and less fertile, lent itself more easily to small farming. Three major urban centers existed in 1940. To the north lay Birmingham, with a population of roughly 268,000, the hub of the coal-mining and steel industries. Montgomery, the state capital, housing approximately 78,000, was centrally located.

The port city of Mobile, south of the juncture of the Alabama and Tombigbee rivers, dominated the southwestern tip of the state that lay along the Gulf Coast. Census figures list Mobile at approximately 78,000 in 1940, but the population of the metropolitan area was probably closer to 110,000 and was rising rapidly. Chickasaw, the company town in which Witness Grace Marsh would confront the limits imposed by Gulf Shipbuilding, was one of many rapidly growing suburbs of the port city.[28]

Despite the changes since 1901, the "levees" still held in 1940. North Alabama, with appreciable small farming and growing labor influence, continued to be restricted by the structure established in about 1900. The power of the white elite in the Black Belt had been augmented in the constitution of 1901 by the existence of a heavy black population that could not vote. Refusing to reapportion the legislature as population shifted increasingly to the industrial areas, the Bourbons maintained a stranglehold on the lawmaking body long after their numbers fell. Although the industrial giants, or Big Mules, located principally in Birmingham and Mobile, were more progressive on prohibition and civil service, they continued to share many of the aims of the large landowners. The two sets of power brokers struck a deal, governing the state as a coalition. In that manner the Big Mules and the Black Belt retained near-total control over blacks and limited the voice of the white urban middle class, small farmers, and proletariat.[29] Persons such as Rosco Jones, a transient black man, or Grace Marsh, a white woman with limited status, carried little political clout.

The reaction to World War I, the Great Depression, and the popularity of Democratic president Franklin D. Roosevelt did not break malapportionment or the conservative alliance. But it did foster a split in the state Democratic party. While the Big Mule–Black Belt alliance stoutly opposed increased taxes and the New Deal, a counterwing represented primarily north Alabama, urban labor, educators, and city and county officials and called for expanded state services. In statewide contests, such as elections of the governor or U.S. senators, the pro-Roosevelt wing had experienced some success. Bibb Graves, a comparatively progressive politician, had won the governorship twice, serving in 1927–1931 and 1935–1939. Hugo Black, in 1926 and 1932, and Lister Hill, in 1938, had scored victories over anti–New Deal Democrats in the race for the U.S. Senate. But the conservative wing proved resilient, electing conservative Frank Dixon, the "self-styled Birmingham Brahmin," to serve as governor 1939–1943.[30]

"The Bosses moved uncomfortably through the 1930s." They were "irritated by the New Deal, but their power was secure," states one study of Alabama politics. The state Democratic party leadership pulled away from Roosevelt as fast as possible. Gessner McCorvey of Mobile headed the state party, and his reelection as chairman of the state executive committee in 1943 signaled to anti-Roosevelt Democrats that the party was unhappy with "autocratic New Dealers." McCorvey and his ilk relied on existing values to justify their power: "The best ruled" (as they should, they maintained), selected by "literate white people." The standard campaign approach was to "confer with the 'courthouse crowd' and try to win their support. Then . . . stroll out onto the courthouse steps, make a perfunctory speech, and shake a few hands before moving on to the next county seat."[31]

In the early 1940s the conservative wing of the Democratic party searched anxiously for a strong personality to succeed Frank Dixon. Well-informed politicians considered that Bibb Graves would seek a third term in 1942 and that he would be difficult to defeat. Chauncey Sparks, a "Bourbon from Barbour" County, had served many years in the legislature and had run second to Dixon in the 1938 primary. He worked behind the scenes to gain the endorsement of Dixon and big industry and, favored by Graves's unexpected death, won the governor's office in 1942. Sparks's inaugural address called for "complete racial segregation" and complained that outsiders were attempting to foment trouble. Later, he formally spoke out against equal rights for blacks in the U.S. armed forces. When in 1943 Anne Gary Pannell, president of the Alabama division of the American Association of University Women (AAUW), interviewed Sparks, she conveyed to him that the AAUW supported the appointment of a woman as warden of Julia Tutwiler Prison for Women. Pannell's twenty-minute interview with the governor left her with the impression that he was "unconvinced of the ability of a [southern white] woman to handle the hardened negro [sic] women criminals" and that he feared hiring a northern woman, "who might not 'understand the texture of . . . southern social structure—white and black.'"[32]

The power of a conservative white male elite in the state did not stop with the chief executive and the state legislature. A number of executive offices—lieutenant governor, secretary of state, treasurer, auditor, attorney general, secretary of agriculture and industry, superintendent of education—as well as the three-person public service commission were elective. As late as 1940 all were white, male, Democrat, and predominantly conservative on social, economic, and religious questions. Alabama's united front generally held in the state's representation in the U.S. Congress as well. Unanimously, Alabama's congressional delegation opposed "external intervention in matters of race relations," and as late as December 1937 all except Lister Hill voted against the Fair Labor Standards Act. (An overwhelming number of the operators of southern textile mills—96 percent—opposed a minimum wage of 32.5 cents per hour in June 1939.)[33]

Judges in the state at all levels were elective, normally for six-year terms, rather than appointed, as they tended increasingly to be in the rest of the nation. The judicial structure in 1939 provided for the Alabama Supreme Court of seven persons, a court of appeals of three persons, district (circuit) courts served by one or more judges, and a variety of inferior courts in the counties. In 1969 in a study of the Alabama Supreme Court in the twentieth century, Robert J. Frye noted that the high court experienced "a high degree of consensus," with dissents extremely rare, and concluded that "generally speaking, the Court is one of conservative character, providing reinforcement for many of the conservative points within the state . . . , in a very real sense a part of the political system."[34]

In surveying the history of the court's personnel this same study found "a remarkable degree of cultural and social homogeneity." All were Democrats; a majority had been educated at the University of Alabama; another 25.7 percent had "read law" as apprentices in state firms; and every supreme court justice had received his legal education in the South. South Alabama, especially the Black Belt, was strongly represented, while the more populous centers of the state were underrepresented. Almost half of the justices had served in lesser judicial positions before being elevated to the high court, and more than one-fourth had come from

The Alabama Supreme Court met in Montgomery's Judicial Building at the time of Jones v. Opelika *and* Marsh v. Alabama

private law practice or from teaching law at the University of Alabama. The justices divided almost evenly among Baptists, Methodists, and Presbyterians, with Episcopalians and the Church of Christ lightly represented. No one of Roman Catholic or Jewish faith had served.[35] No female or black served on the supreme court until well after Frye's 1969 study.

An analysis of the characteristics of the nine men serving on the Alabama high bench who participated in considering action in at least one of the two Witness cases of this study confirms the general picture of the Frye report. Methodists and Baptists were dominant, with Presbyterians a weak third. All had been born in the state; two came to the court from the small towns of south Alabama, two from Montgomery, one from Birmingham, one from Tuscaloosa, and one each from the small north Alabama towns of Florence, Cullman, and Scottsboro. Two-thirds had studied law at the University of Alabama. Other similarities marked the justices' backgrounds. Five of the six who heard the *Jones* case were quite elderly, though by the time the court decided not to hear Marsh's petition in 1944, two had been replaced by significantly younger men. Of the nine, four were sons of Confederate veterans, and two were grandsons. Three were members of The Thirteen, an exclusive Montgomery literary group; three belonged to the Knights of Pythias, a select fraternal order with chapters in various Alabama localities; three were Masons; and the three younger justices shared overlapping membership in social and legal fraternities. One justice was married to the daughter of a colleague on the high bench.[36]

During the period when the Alabama Court of Appeals considered the *Jones* and *Marsh* cases, the court consisted of three persons, also elected on a partisan basis, all white male Democrats. The justices on the intermediate appeals court averaged approximately ten years younger in age than those on the Alabama Supreme Court, but again they were born and educated locally, socially prominent, and of Baptist, Methodist, Presbyterian, or Episcopalian faith. The same justice wrote the appeals court opinions in both *Jones* and *Marsh*.[37]

Circuit (trial) court judges were elected by district, and their characteristics may have varied in different parts of the state. The blood in the veins of William B. Bowling, the district judge who tried Rosco Jones, ran a little less blue than that of the appellate jurists, but it was clearly respectable. The son of a Confederate veteran educated in the public schools and at Jacksonville (Alabama) State Teachers' College, he had read law in LaFayette, in Chambers County, a relatively poor county in east-central Alabama. Settling there, he married a local woman and served for many years as a solicitor for the Alabama Fifth Circuit Court. A Mason, Knight of Pythias, and very active Baptist, he had served in the U.S. House of Representatives 1921–1929 before taking the position of circuit judge, the post he held for almost the remainder of his life. At the time that he heard the case against Jones, the judge was sixty-nine years old.[38]

David Henry Edington, the circuit judge who heard the case against Grace Marsh, more closely resembled the judges of the higher state courts. Although born in Mississippi, he had attended school in Alabama and received many honors, as well as B.A. and LL.B. degrees, from The University of Alabama before settling in Mobile. The son of a Confederate veteran and a Presbyterian, he was also active in Democratic party and community affairs. An attorney in a Mobile law partnership for over thirty years, he concurrently worked as a recorder in city court and in 1938 became circuit judge for the district. He made public statements that blacks were inferior, that women should not serve as jurors, and that wrongdoers should simply learn to walk "the right road." He was sixty-two years old when he heard the *Marsh* case.[39]

The actions taken against both Jones and Marsh began in inferior court. Under Alabama law, cases appealed from an inferior court to the circuit court are tried de novo, that is, anew, with no transcript of the previous case considered. In Jones's case his first trial occurred in the municipal court, known then as the recorder's court. Records of the proceedings are unavailable, and who presided remains uncertain. In Marsh's case the judge of the County Court of Mobile, Tisdale J. Touart, made the initial ruling. Touart, a member of an established Mobile family of Confederate lineage and local political standing, differed from the usual Alabama politician in that he was Roman Catholic. In the Mobile area, however, Roman Catholicism was good politics, for the early Spanish and French influences had made it the preferred religion.[40]

Opelika, the small east-central Alabama town into which Rosco Jones carried the Witnesses' standard, was peopled predominantly by Baptists and Methodists. It also contained Presbyterians and members of the Church of Christ, with a light sprinkling of Lutherans and a few Roman Catholics and Christian Scientists. Churches were usually segregated, as were all other formal institutions. Jehovah's Witnesses did not appear in the newspaper religious section. Thelma Jones, Rosco Jones's widow and partner in the Witness crusade, remembers a total of seven Witnesses, black and white, in the broader Opelika community in 1939.[41]

The town had been incorporated in 1854. Originally located in Russell County, Opelika became the county seat of newly created Lee County when the county lines were redrawn in 1866. The little town developed slowly as a stop on the railroad between Montgomery and Columbus, Georgia. The community benefited from its proximity to Auburn, seven miles away, the site of the state's mechanical and agricultural college, Alabama Polytechnic Institute. In 1925 the locale had acquired a new dimension with the establishment of Pepperell Mills, a textile manufacturing plant. By 1938, when Rosco and Thelma Jones arrived in Opelika, the municipality's residents numbered approximately 8,000. The population conducting business there was larger, however, swelled by persons from adjoining rural areas attracted by the town's services as county seat and center of ginning operations. A municipal commission governed the little city, with John S. Crossley, a moderately successful local businessman, as mayor. The other more influential commissioner was John L. Whatley, popular owner of a dairy, who succeeded Crossley as mayor a few years later. Cal S. Ellington completed the city governing board[42] but apparently was the least powerful of the commissioners.

Foreign affairs excited little concern in Opelika, for the depression dominated public attention there, as it did elsewhere in Alabama and in the nation at large. A strong disillusionment with World War I and its repercussions had convinced the majority of citizens that the United States should not become involved in problems outside its immediate interests. Adolf Hitler's totalitarian regime in Germany was viewed almost beneficently by champions of order and as a counterweight to Joseph Stalin's power in the Soviet Union. In 1933, when Hitler had begun the systematic persecution of Jehovah's Witnesses after they refused to take part in salutes to the Führer, citizens took little notice. Even in the latter years of the decade, as European war threatened, they joined the majority in state and nation in advocating neutrality. They were concerned with matters closer to home.[43]

A brother of one of Commissioner Whatley's high school classmates, William S. (Bill) Duke, served as the city attorney and was only thirty-one years old when he began representing Opelika in the *Jones* case. A graduate of Alabama Polytechnic Institute who had been admitted to the bar in 1930, the city counselor had studied law under his father, Lum Duke, and had begun his practice in an established family partnership, Duke & Duke. The Dukes were on close terms with one of Opelika's most eminent families, that of Thomas Drake Samford, son of a former governor of Alabama and brother of an associate justice on the Alabama Court of Appeals. The elder Duke had been born in Auburn and had attended Alabama Polytechnic Institute. He had read law and had begun to practice in nearby LaFayette but settled in Opelika in about the turn of the century. Like Duke, Thomas Drake Samford had attended Alabama Polytechnic Institute and joined Alpha Tau Omega social fraternity; both were Masons and members of the Knights of Pythias. For several years after Duke settled in Opelika, Samford and Lum Duke practiced as attorneys in the same firm.[44]

Chickasaw, Alabama, the site of the arrest of Witness Grace Marsh in 1943, existed as a company town in a state of flux during World War II. Specific records as to its religious makeup are unavailable, but one may assume that it was akin to Mobile, where the traditional Protestant denominations prevailed but Roman Catholicism carried significant influence. Witnesses had made a few inroads into the Mobile community by 1943 but faced a particular obstacle in Chickasaw because of its status as a company town. An unincorporated village of approximately 4,000 to 5,000, Chickasaw was located about three miles northwest of Mobile's industrial center, and the lives of its people often intertwined with those of the larger community. The demand for shipbuilding during World War I had led TCI to develop the area to provide homes and other necessities for its employees. In 1921 Chickasaw was a boom town and included 1,138 family units and a "business block" complete with several stores and a post office that served approximately 10,000 people. In the early 1920s, however, as the shipping program was completed, the plant largely ceased operations, and TCI rented many of the residences to the general public. TCI maintained the terminal with repair yards for barges and riverboats. In 1939–1940 the demand for shipbuilding resumed, and TCI sold the shipyards and accompanying land to Chickasaw Development Company, which in turn sold the property to Gulf Shipbuilding Company, a subsidiary of Waterman Steamship Company. During World War II approximately 15,000 persons were employed daily in the shipyards, and Chickasaw experienced rapid growth, as did Mobile generally.[45]

Emory B. Peebles, a University of Alabama graduate who had moved from his native Pickens County, Alabama, to Mobile in 1919, became the controlling figure in Chickasaw. He served both as vice president of the Gulf Shipbuilding Corporation and as a director of Waterman and held offices on numerous other boards of leading businesses in the area. A Presbyterian, he was active in Mobile's civic life and served as chairman of the Mobile County Board of Tax Equalization. Francis Inge, another University of Alabama alumnus, served as a director for Waterman and as its chief legal counsel. Inge came from a prominent Mobile family, moved in country club circles, and belonged to the Episcopal faith.[46]

Rosco Jones and Grace Marsh lived outside the power structure of Opelika, Chickasaw, and Alabama. Although both were native southerners, they had no prominent connections, were not highly educated, and owned almost nothing. Before becoming a full-time evangelist, Jones had worked as captain of a dining crew in a hotel; Marsh's husband drove a bakery delivery truck and had previously worked as an auto mechanic. As practicing members of the Jehovah's Witnesses, the Jones and Marsh families did not believe that they should vote, for government was viewed at best as an essential evil and voter participation as unnecessary. (The Joneses would have faced impossible difficulties had they tried to do so in Alabama.) The religious faith in which they were active owned no extensive communal property in Alabama, attracted few wealthy individuals as members, and depended primarily upon out-of-state attorneys in Witness-related lawsuits.[47] But status, wealth, and political power mattered little to Rosco Jones and Grace Marsh. Jehovah had chosen them to carry out His mission, and His instrument, the Watch Tower Bible and Tract Society, had instructed them to assert their constitutional rights to preach His word. They did not flinch. With Jehovah their comfort and their advocate, they would fear no evil.

2

The World of the Witnesses

Grace Waldrop Marsh "came into the truth" as a young girl. She was a rare phenomenon in the early twentieth century—a child of a second-generation Bible Student.[1] Born in 1906 in Randolph, a rural community near Montevallo in central Alabama, she grew up surrounded by a family highly dedicated to the principles preached by "the pastor," Charles Taze Russell. Her father, Joseph Waldrop, subscribed to the religious magazine, the *Watchtower,* which Russell edited, and every night he read aloud from the Bible to the family, using the periodical as a guide to the scriptures.[2] At times he would read from other books or pamphlets that the pastor had written about God's divine plan. Then he would kneel with Grace's mother and the six children in prayer around the fireplace. Because no other followers of Russell lived nearby, every week Grace's father drove his family ten miles in a horse-drawn wagon to the home of his father, Sim Waldrop, known for his "strange religion." There the children attended an informal Sunday school, and a locally elected elder led the small adult congregation in a Bible study. Occasionally, a traveling preacher, called a pilgrim, visited, attracting others from the community. On those special days, Grace Marsh recalled, the group moved to a "little unpainted frame building known as the Waldrop school house." A row of benches down each side of the room seated approximately twenty people. Wood boxes seated the overflow crowd. On one of these occasions in 1910 her mother was baptized in a nearby creek.[3]

Other special days that Grace remembers from her childhood included Christmas, Easter, and Halloween, holidays that the Waldrops celebrated in the traditional manner. Later, after Russell's death, the Watch Tower Bible and Tract Society banned the observance of the holidays because the society had determined that the holidays were pagan in origin. The Waldrops moved in 1920 to Robertsdale, a small town in southwest Alabama, carrying their faith with them.[4]

Kneeling with her father in front of the fireplace, or listening in Sunday school at her grandfather's home, or sitting on a wooden box when the visiting pilgrim preached, young Grace Waldrop reacted to righteous example and graphic words. Her mind drank in biblical images of Eden and Satan and of Christ's sacrifice. Her admiration of her father and the values that he had instilled in her strengthened her to ignore the taunts of classmates at the local school who often ridiculed her, calling her family "old Russellites." In her mind Russell was a wonderful prophet, and she tried to imagine what he was like. In 1916 she attended an assembly in Birmingham, Alabama, with her father. She remembers the thrill of seeing the pastor at last: "Brother Russell was there. I can see him now standing on the platform with a little stick in his hand pointing to the PHOTO DRAMA OF CREATION and explaining it to us. . . . I remember someone asked a question on Revelation. His answer was, 'I cannot answer that because it has not been fulfilled yet.' This was truly a milestone in my life."[5]

Russell, reacting against the stern doctrines of Calvinism, had explored a variety of Protestant evangelical teachings before 1879, when he emerged as the leader of a new religious movement. Accepting only portions of traditional Protestantism, he developed a doctrinal structure that relied heavily on prophecy and rejected the concept of hellfire yet focused on the "concept of the imminent End of the World." God had created man to live in an eternal earthly paradise, but Adam had forfeited Eden's bliss by willful rebellion, yielding to Satan and condemning sinful man to the sleep of the grave. But a loving God offered Adam's heirs a second chance by placing perfect life in Mary's womb. Christ, a flaw-less being but not the incarnation of God, made ransom for mankind, "atoning with a perfect life what Adam had squandered." Still, however, man defied God's will, as even Christ's instrument, the church, succumbed to Satan. The decadence to which modern mankind had sunk was unparalleled, a clear signal that God would soon be vindicated. He would cleanse the earth at Armageddon, and then Christ would reign for a thousand years until the Last Judgment.[6]

Russell believed that he had been chosen by God to warn mankind and to carry the "present truth" to those who would listen. To spread his teachings in the 1870s and 1880s he had not only founded an organization, the Watch Tower Bible and Tract Society, and published and edited the *Watchtower* magazine, but had also preached orally to those who would listen. He traveled widely and supplemented personal appearances with printed sermons, carried in many newspapers. In 1912 he combined slides and recordings to produce the "Photo-Drama of Creation." The audiovisual tool, which was eventually made into a moving picture presentation, appealed particularly to young people such as Grace Waldrop and Thelma Thomas.[7] By diverse means Russell effectively carried his gospel to thousands.

Essentially a beneficent man, the pastor preferred a loving God to a vengeful one and persuasion to coercion. His dynamic personality and his conviction that he had been given a divine mission nonetheless inevitably meant that he imposed many of his ideas on his followers. By the time Grace Waldrop studied with her father, "verse-by-verse Bible Study" had given way to topical studies directed by Russell. Doctrinal schism and controversy regarding his personal life marred but did not destroy the pastor's career.[8]

His stature benefited from the advent of World War I in 1914, which seemed to verify his chronological interpretation of the coming of Armageddon. At that point Russell asserted that the time had come to speak out against the wrongs of government, even to refusing to support the nation's effort should it become involved in war. Although in failing health, he continued tours and speeches, convinced that his prophecy would be fulfilled by 1918. But in October 1916, not long after Grace Waldrop had seen him in Birmingham, he became suddenly quite ill while on a train tour of the Southwest. He died unexpectedly, without a successor. His death, the extreme unpopularity of his teachings after the

United States entered the war in 1917, and the failure of the Apocalypse to arrive by the appointed date seriously threatened the movement.[9] Many of his followers groped in the desert of uncertainty and yearned for a Moses to lead them.

"Judge" Joseph Franklin Rutherford, Russell's former attorney, became the new prophet, making his own particular mark on the movement. A man who had been reared in poverty,[10] he had learned early how to fight. Through "hardfisted church politics" he quickly battled his way to the top of the Watch Tower organization, driving out those unwilling to submit to a more tightly run society. Although the schism developing from the events of 1917–1918 resulted in an immediate loss of supporters, Rutherford stayed the course. Imposing an iron discipline, he soon gained almost total control over the goals, literature, method of organizing, and finances of the Watch Tower establishment. Then, having vanquished his opponents within the faith, he unified his followers by a hard-hitting attack on the enemies beyond it. He excoriated "the church, nominal, Catholic and Protestant," and the other institutions of the world as the instruments of Satan. Specifically, he singled out for condemnation those who had supported participation in World War I.[11]

The establishment responded. In January 1918 Canada banned Watchtower publications, and the U.S. Justice Department charged Rutherford and seven other directors of the society with sedition under the Espionage Act of 1917. Sentenced to prison and denied bond, they were transported in July 1918 to the federal penitentiary in Atlanta, Georgia. The society's New York headquarters closed, the remaining staff moved to the Pennsylvania office, and it appeared for a time that the *Watchtower* would be silenced.[12]

But Rutherford's opponents had miscalculated greatly. Persecution was like mother's milk to him. Wearing a pink carnation in his lapel at the trial, he declared after being sentenced to twenty years, "This is the happiest day of my life." In prison, emulating St. Paul, he kept contact with his flock through weekly letters published in the *Watchtower*, which the faithful kept alive. He organized Bible studies among the prisoners. Emboldened, he mapped plans for a companion journal, the *Golden Age*. In January 1919 the society met in Pittsburgh and reelected the imprisoned directors, and in March, U.S. Supreme Court justice Louis Brandeis ordered that they be released on bail. In May 1919 an appellate court overturned the convictions, and a year later the U.S. attorney general dropped all charges.[13]

Those Bible Students, such as Grace Waldrop's family, who were loyal to Rutherford and the society in the trying period 1916–1920 accepted the new style of leadership. No one personality should be venerated, they reasoned, for Jehovah had many ways to work His will. He had tested them by allowing Russell's error in computing the exact time of Armageddon, but they did not doubt that the Apocalypse was near at hand. Jehovah had sent a second prophet to fortify them. Rutherford prepared the faithful by speaking dramatically at a "reunion" convention in Cedar Point, Ohio, in 1919; returning the headquarters to New York; purchasing a press for the society's increasing publications; and expanding the proselytizing program. In 1922, to a convention of 20,000, again at Cedar Point, he proclaimed that preaching should not be limited to colporteurs or full-time evangelists but should include everyone who "appreciates the truth." "Advertise, advertise, advertise the Kingdom!" he cried. And he set the example. In personal appearances throughout the land and abroad and from WBBR, the Watch Tower Society's radio station on Staten Island, he preached passionately to thousands. He also broadcast his message of Armageddon and the millennium in a fiery bestseller, *Millions Now Living Will Never Die*. Finally, the chief advertiser kept check on the promotional efforts of his underlings. Increasingly, the society directed local preaching activities through catechetical publications and service directors.[14]

The judge's message reached Rosco Jones, who longed for certitude. As a child growing up in North Carolina around the turn of the century, Jones had been troubled about religion. His parents, Arthur and Florence Jones, took him and his nine younger siblings to Sunday school regularly at the Baptist Church in the rural black community of Good Hope, near Raleigh, but his father "didn't allow" him "to accept the religion the preachers were preaching." In 1914 his parents were reconciled with the church, and Rosco became a member at age nineteen, but he still had reservations about the clergy. His doubts intensified in France in World War I, although he still believed in God. He experienced a terrible ordeal when he moved into position behind the front-line trenches:

Going up toward the front line, we passed the big guns. . . . We were told not to get afraid because all those guns would start shooting before midnight. . . . behind us and the shells exploding . . . ahead of us, the earth was almost as bad as a cradle to stand upon.

I made a promise to God that night that if God would let me get back to the U.S.A. and show me what He would have me do, I would do it as long as I live. . . . I also asked God to not let me kill anybody; if I did, I don't know it.

He credited God with protecting him by making him a battalion scout, working largely alone, sketching maps, or relaying messages between commanding officers and the front line. When he returned home after the war, he told his parents of his promise to God but was dismayed to find that "the clergymen had captured" his father. By then a "full-fledged Baptist deacon," the elder Jones accepted the war as positive. Although both father and son wanted Rosco to become a preacher, they differed strongly as to what that vocation meant, and Rosco left home.[15]

In 1922 after he settled in Richmond, Virginia, Jones married a local black woman, Thelma Thomas, the youngest of ten children born to John and Emma Thomas. Thelma was especially close to her mother, who had been widowed when Thelma was only five months old and who had lost seven of her children. Before the marriage the couple agreed that she "should respect him as a husband," and he promised to care for not only his wife but also her mother for as long as she lived. When, after several years, the union produced no children, Thelma expressed concern that she should see a doctor, but Rosco replied that if God wanted her to have children, she would have them, and if He did not, then He must have another purpose in mind for her. Thelma accepted his counsel and busied herself with employment in a large apartment house and with the care of her husband and mother. When a traveling evangelist from the Watch Tower Bible and Tract Society called at the house during the holiday season in 1924, offering religious literature, Thelma Jones thought of her husband's interest in religion. She purchased a book, *Deliverance*, from the colporteur and gave it to Rosco for Christmas. After reading the book hurriedly, however, Rosco discounted it as the work of a fool.[16]

Rosco Jones continued to work as captain of a dining room crew at the

William Byrd Hotel in Richmond, but he remained troubled about religion. He attended church regularly, "looking for something" that he "never found in there." He felt that he "had been called to preach," but he wanted to preach the truth and he did not know what the truth was. Then sometime before August in 1926 he received a letter from his brother, Leroy, who lived in Washington, D.C., filled with talk about God's kingdom. Fearing that Leroy was "getting mixed up with some kind of Holiness outfit," Rosco concluded that he should invite his brother to come down to visit, a decision that would mark a turning point in his life. His brother arrived with a Watchtower publication about seven o'clock on a Saturday night, and in the words of Rosco Jones, "we started arguing. I said to him, 'Wait, let us have a word of prayer!' He answered, 'No, let us stick to our Bibles now, and pray later.'" Rosco was suspicious of the Watchtower book—he had seen one earlier. But Leroy persisted. "They sat up all night," Thelma Jones remembered, "discussing the scriptures and by morning Rosco was in the truth." Hungry for more information, Rosco Jones gave his brother seven dollars and asked him to send him "everything the society had ever written" when he returned home.[17]

Filled with the zeal of the convert, Jones began immediately to share his newly found truth. Rejected by the church officials whom he approached, Jones was told that he would lose his mind if he "continued to mess with that Russellite stuff" and that he should stick with a regular church in which he could make money. Scornful of the attitude of those clergymen, Jones determined that he would preach the true Bible, the Watchtower version, "without the money either in or outside of the church." Expressing his thoughts bluntly, he gained few converts at first. But as he began to receive Watchtower publications, he initiated Bible studies with several persons. A few weeks later he visited Leroy in Washington and gained a sense of camaraderie with other Witnesses. He and Thelma soon began to follow the Witness practice of referring to others in the faith as "the friends" and "the brothers and sisters." Joining the men who went out to distribute handbills, Rosco observed their techniques of proselytizing. As a standard practice, the colporteurs carried Watchtower publications in a book bag as they walked from house to house or on public streets. They asked for small donations to cover the cost of the literature but gave it away to interested persons who made no contribution. Jones also noted that the most effective brothers were those who could cite scriptures to reinforce their message. Eager to utilize these procedures when he returned home, he used his wife's sewing bag as a satchel and began to write out "house-to-house" sermons. He also learned that a class of white International Bible Students existed in Richmond, and he soon began to attend their meetings, where he was welcomed. Convinced of the rightness of his faith, Jones was baptized by "the brothers" in the James River in August 1926.[18]

During the 1920s, while Judge Rutherford consolidated his power in the society, Grace Waldrop matured and established her own life. In 1925 she married Herbert Marsh and moved to Chicago. Two years later she gave birth to a son, whom she named Joseph Harold. No longer under her father's immediate influence, she began to drift away from the stern lifestyle that the religion of the Bible Students demanded. Although her father regularly sent the Watchtower publications to her, she did not read them. For a time she "sought to be popular with others" and considered attending one of the more widely accepted churches.[19]

But in 1930 a shocking experience brought her back to the faith of her childhood. Hearing a ruckus, she ran to the window and was amazed to see the proprietor of the apartment house in which she lived behaving violently. Her landlord, a person whom she respected and considered to be good and religious, was throwing down the steps a man who carried a bag with religious literature. She quickly "recognized" the books as the same ones that her father had sent her earlier. When she protested the landlord's behavior, he informed her "that he was kicking an imposter out of his home" and that if she asked the man into her apartment she could no longer live there. She promptly invited the evangelist into her home for a cup of tea, listened at length to him, and obtained from him the address of the local meetinghouse. Herbert and Grace Marsh attended the meeting the following Sunday and were thrilled to meet Judge Rutherford, who happened to be visiting at that time. Restored to the faith of her fathers, Grace Waldrop Marsh decided to return to her old hometown, Robertsdale, Alabama. Although Herbert Marsh had not "yet fully embraced the truth," he supported his wife in her belief, and the family returned to Alabama.[20]

Rosco Jones had also become fully committed to the life of the Bible Students by the early 1930s. He had completed only the eighth grade, but seminary training was not a requirement for Witnessing, a lay ministry that identified itself with the example of Christ's "unlettered" apostles. A large man, Jones did not go looking for trouble, but if it found him, he was not one to dodge it. On several occasions the demands of his faith conflicted with what was expected of him at the William Byrd Hotel, but he decided early to place Jehovah's dictates first. Elected an elder not long after his baptism in 1926, Jones thought it very important that he attend the regular Watchtower Study on Sunday evenings. When he approached his supervisor to make arrangements to leave in time for the seven o'clock meeting, however, the "bossman" responded angrily, reminding him that Sunday evening was a busy time. He shouted at Jones, "If you leave here at 7 o'clock to go to church, you don't come back. Get yourself another job." Jones went to church but returned to work at the hotel the next morning. His employer did not speak until the following Wednesday, when he called Jones into his office. The supervisor then told Jones that he had been a good worker for twelve years and that he should think twice before allowing his new religion to ruin his reputation. When Jones continued to leave work on Sunday evenings, however, the superior did not interfere.[21]

A second disagreement some time later resulted in a heated exchange between the two men. As captain of the dining room crew, Jones was expected to distribute forms for contributions to the local community chest among his subordinates; the hotel corporation had indicated that a day's wages should be required of all employees. Convinced that "false" churches were behind the drive, Jones decided that he could not in conscience make a contribution. On that part of the form that read, "I pledge," he wrote "Not giving" and signed his name. He then placed all the forms on the supervisor's desk. According to him, the following sequence of events resulted:

> Everybody was watching to see what would happen. . . . He called out, "Jones, you didn't give anything to the Community Fund boy. If you weren't able to give anything, you could have told me, and I would have given something for you." I told him . . . my reason for not giving . . .

[was that the Fund was not truly Christian, but a racket]. He ran out the front door and went all around the block and came back in the front door. . . . He shouted, "No, we are not going to fire Mr. Jones. We are not going to run him away from here because he is a damned fool."

After that his employment at the hotel proceeded smoothly, and he worked there until he decided to go into full-time proselytizing in 1933.[22]

Soon after his baptism Jones began trying to convert friends and family. He had no luck with his parents. He visited them in North Carolina in the summer of 1927, carrying Watchtower literature, which he distributed in the old home community. His mother and father disapproved of his disputing doctrine with the speaker at the local Baptist revival, a cousin, and were offended when he told the deacons that they were hypocrites. In Richmond, he participated in organizing a "colored ecclesia," or separate meeting of blacks. The group was torn by schism regarding differences in the approaches taken by Russell and Rutherford, with Jones siding with the "present truth," taught by the Watch Tower Society since Russell's death in 1916. He won his wife and seven others to the faith in 1928, although Thelma was not baptized until 1934. Under Jones's leadership the converts began distributing Watchtower literature each Sunday. The sisters alternated in preparing Sunday night meals for the eight, while the remaining seven "worked the territory near the home" where dinner would be served. After dinner the group sang hymns, such as "All the Way My Savior Leads Me," from a green Kingdom (Watchtower) songbook before attending the Watchtower Study, which met without charge at Mrs. Price's funeral home.[23]

During the following year, encouraged by his brother Leroy, Rosco Jones and Irving Jackson, a fellow black friend in the faith, worked as pilgrims for thirty days out in "the rurals" of Orange County, Virginia. (Evangelists usually traveled in pairs, or in sets of pairs, both for morale and for practical purposes.) Jones found the work so satisfying that when he returned home, he told his wife that he wanted to devote his life to spreading the good news. He would not take her away from her aging mother, but after her mother's death he wanted her to come with him. If she did not wish to go, however, he would leave her the house and furniture. Years later she recalled the experience. "I took the matter to

Jehovah God in prayer, and asked him to make me willing to go with my husband," she asserted.[24]

She accepted the association's patriarchal view of society. Men were to care for both the physical and spiritual needs of the family. Wives were "expected to be subject to their husbands, to keep the family home clean, to care for the children, to dress modestly—although in the common garb of the larger society in which they lived—and to participate in the preaching work and those areas open to them within the congregation." Women were forbidden to serve as elders, were required to cover their heads in the services, and were not allowed to give public talks before the entire congregation. It was quite acceptable, then, for Rosco to take the initiative in family decisions and to encourage Thelma to involve herself heavily in house-to-house promotion of the society's literature. His earlier conclusion that Thelma should not seek medical advice when the couple had no children fitted in well with his later identity as a dedicated follower of the Watch Tower Bible and Tract Society. No worldly obligations or family relationships should take precedence over "the agreement to do God's will." Under Rutherford's leadership the society looked upon sexual attraction as lust and preferred that persons remain single. If, however, desire tormented them, then marriage was the second best alternative. Under the circumstances of the Joneses, then, working together in long distance, full-time proselytizing was quite appropriate. Rosco's concession that he would delay full-time commitment until after the death of his wife's mother might well have met with disfavor in the high echelons of the society, but it was a compassionate compromise that he chose to make and something his wife never forgot. "I appreciated it very much he did not take me away from my mother until after she died," she wrote in 1991. They continued to care for Thelma's mother until her death in 1932, but they also made plans to build a house trailer.[25]

In July 1931 Rosco and Thelma Jones attended the national assembly of Bible Students in Columbus, Ohio. There on July 26 Judge Rutherford, in "a bold strike of genius," made the dramatic announcement that clearly confirmed that he had significantly modified the following of Pastor Russell. "It was time," in the words of the semiofficial Witness history, to make it clear "who was who." As Rosco and Thelma Jones and other excited Bible Students listened intently, Rutherford declared,

"By the grace of the Lord Jesus Christ and our heavenly Father, we joyfully receive and bear the name which the mouth of Jehovah God has named and given us, to wit, Jehovah's Witnesses." Separating in that manner those who continued to accept Watch Tower guidance from those who looked to pre-Rutherford dogma, the judge gave distinction and prominence to the faithful.[26]

From that time forward, the term "Russellite" began to recede, and "within less than twenty years the name Jehovah's Witnesses crowded out every other name" for the devoted who adhered to the tenets of the Watch Tower Bible and Tract Society. In the months that followed, Rutherford continued to build the power of the central organization, extending more and more control over local elected leaders. Within less than a year after the judge had given the Witnesses their new name, a letter appeared in the Watchtower questioning the need for the continued service of elders, since "The Lord Himself" had now "taken over Zion." A dual organization "from the 'throne down' and from the 'ranks up'" seemed not in the "best interests of the kingdom." The judge was laying the foundations for theocratic rule.[27]

"Filled up with the new name" and the thought of full-time evangelical work, the Joneses returned happily from the 1931 convention. Thelma's mother died during 1932. In June 1932, Rosco, with the help of Roosevelt Mitchell, a fellow Witness, began building a trailer. By September 1933 they had "everything all lined up" to begin their full-time evangelizing a thousand miles away. Shedding tears as they parted from their close friends within the Richmond congregation, the Joneses and Mitchell began a three-day trip, pulling their trailer to Allendale, South Carolina. There they joined Leroy Jones and his wife, Nellie, and another Witness, Sister Ethlyn Glynn. The six had beef stew for supper and prepared for field service the next morning. They were committed to a life of hard work and little money; they were prepared to do battle with Satan. Convinced that Jehovah had charged them to warn the uninformed or face eternal destruction, they felt impelled to evangelize at all costs. Like other Witnesses, they saw themselves as part of a great crusade.[28]

Rutherford directed Jehovah's army as his soldiers prepared for Armageddon. Adopting military terminology, congregations became "companies," their directors were redesignated "company servants," and pilgrims—those such as the Joneses who devoted themselves to full-time proselytizing activities—were renamed "pioneers." In the struggle to overthrow the devil, the judge guided Witnesses into a belief system that increasingly portrayed Jehovah as a wrathful God who must be vindicated. In 1914, Rutherford explained, Christ began his heavenly kingdom and purged Satan from heaven. Thus restricted to earth, Satan intensified his evil plan. Christ, although invisible, remained on earth; at the appointed time he would lead the forces of Jehovah against Satan at Armageddon, extending his kingdom to earth. Christ and the 144,000 "anointed ones," also known as the Bride of Christ and the "little flock," would rule as associate kings, during the millennium, fulfilling Jehovah's prophecy.[29]

Although Watchtower literature did not specify who would constitute the anointed, it assumed the inclusion of Christ's apostles and their modern counterpart, the Witness leadership. The number was derived from the Book of Revelation 14:1–3 and was thought to consist only of those who had been tested on earth and proved their fidelity to Jehovah. At death or Armageddon, whichever came first, the 144,000 would ascend to heaven for a spiritual existence with Christ. Russell's teaching had implied that all dedicated Witnesses would constitute the Bride, but by the 1930s, as Witnesses living and dead exceeded 144,000, Rutherford made adjustments. Only a Remnant of the anointed were then living, he declared; the mass of Witnesses, present and future, he designated the Great Multitude. Unlike the "little flock" of the anointed, the "other sheep" would not reign in heaven with Christ, but they could look forward to conditional immortality on earth. The task of those Witnesses living at the time of Armageddon who were not the Remnant would be to cleanse, restore, and repopulate the earth during the millennium. During that thousand years, those who had not willfully disobeyed Jehovah, such as Old Testament saints, would be restored, in an orderly manner, to earth. The former dead would be resurrected to life not in their original bodies but in perfect form "dependent upon God's memory" of their essence. Those who had died ignorant of God's wishes would be given the opportunity through restoration to earth to learn obedience. The end of the millennium would bring final judgment. Those who remained steadfast to Jehovah and yielded not to Satan's last efforts would be granted perfect life on earth (Eden) forever, but those who succumbed to Satan would suffer permanent death.[30]

Rosco and Thelma Jones and Grace Marsh thus accepted a theology that deviated from traditional Christianity. They did not believe in the Trinity or the full deity of Christ, the immortality of the soul, the resurrection of the body, the existence of hell, or universal atonement for man's sins by Christ's death. All Witnesses were considered ordained ministers, and any adult male Witness could perform baptism, which was only an outward sign of dedication and submission to Jehovah. Marriage was not a sacrament. Paradise for all but the 144,000 "anointed" was to be a renewed Eden, not a heavenly city. Celebration of the Lord's Supper was performed annually, with only the Remnant, which was self-defined, partaking of the host. Ironically, as the Joneses and Marsh accepted Rutherford's attack upon Roman Catholicism as the "Whore of Babylon," they relied upon Watchtower literature that resembled a catechism. They embraced the doctrine that man must perform good works and yielded gladly to an authoritative hierarchy. They followed Jehovah's instruments, Judge Rutherford and the Watch Tower Bible and Tract Society, as willing soldiers in an offensive against established institutions.[31]

As Rutherford directed his army into the 1930s, his control within the Witness movement grew increasingly more authoritative and his verbal assaults on the outside world more strident. He rejected the terms "religion" and "church" as agents of Satan, "a snare and a racket." He armed his troops with the *Watchtower* and the *Golden Age (Consolation)*, pamphlets, and testimony cards identifying them as ordained ministers of the Gospel. He directed them to make return calls if one proselytizing effort did not bring results. When clerical and business pressures forced him off the air, he provided phonographs and records and eventually sound cars. He expanded the use of conventions to rally and fire the faithful. He instructed them to concern themselves only with God's kingdom and to refuse to honor laws that conflicted with those of Jehovah.[32]

The harsh and abrasive tactics of the judge alienated some of the Bible Students but brought a heightened sense of identification to others. The Joneses and Grace Marsh clearly ranked among the latter group. Pioneering meant going into "outlying or even hostile areas," granted at best a

small stipend that did not cover many expenses. They purchased literature from the Watch Tower Society at reduced rates and exchanged it for
whatever they could. With the depression dominating the economy,
times were particularly hard as Rosco and Thelma Jones became practiced pioneers in South Carolina and eastern Georgia in the early 1930s.
Most days they ate only two meals. Breakfast usually consisted of whole
wheat bread or cereal made from wheat that they had ordered from
Virginia for one dollar per bushel and ground on a hand mill. The sisters
often cooked a late supper, from items such as chickens, eggs, milk,
butter, peanuts or peanut butter, and home-canned goods that they had
received in exchange for religious literature. They accepted almost anything of any possible value, including Octagon Soap coupons, which
could be redeemed in quantity for a little cash. Part of the time they
traded Watchtower publications for overnight board, which afforded the
added benefit of a second opportunity to Witness. Each Monday the
brothers carried any surplus chickens and eggs to Augusta, Georgia, for
sale to restaurants. The cash that they received primarily paid for gas for
the field service the following week, but if any money was left, they
bought fish or stew meat. As they put more miles on the car and pulled
the trailer through the rough terrain from Athens to Atlanta, car repairs
became a major expense. But the Joneses adjusted. When Leroy and
Nellie Jones gave birth to a baby boy, Rosco and Thelma gladly added
babysitting to their regular duties.[33]

In addition to sustaining themselves physically, the four (five) pioneering Joneses, Roosevelt Mitchell, and Ethlyn Glynn experienced several
other major problems. In 1934 in Savannah they competed with Roman
Catholics and the "divine healing religious outfit" of a Bishop Grace. The
healing group built two-story prayer houses; the top floor, called "up
in the mountain," was for loud singing and dancing, while the lower,
"down in the valley," provided a sawdust floor "for rest when one was
overreached with the spirits." Despite the attractions, however, Rosco
Jones maintained that the healers could not "stand up against the truth."
The high porch of "a Catholic old folks' home for colored people"
almost proved more damaging to Rosco Jones. After he was pushed
down the steps by a priest when he attempted to convert the patients
sitting on the veranda, Jones reacted momentarily to what he described as

the devil's prompting and started up the steps "to get the priest." But Jehovah prevailed when Jones heeded the "good advice" of the janitor, who advised him to leave. The next day, according to the Witness, the priest apologized when some of the "white brothers" accused him of hitting Jones because he was black. When these events were recounted to the Watch Tower Society, the association instructed its members not to go into Catholic institutions.[34]

Other challenges included finding the most effective preaching methods and locating a meeting place for significant numbers. Each of the pioneers carried a testimony card, which identified that person as an ordained minister of the Jehovah's Witnesses. The Joneses found that this identification usually gave them entrée in house-to-house calls in communities where hostility to the Witnesses was not already present. Once given a hearing, they then attempted to interest the audience through personal testimony, through literature, by playing a recording of a short talk by Judge Rutherford, or by some combination of the three. In personal testimony these evangelicals began by asking rhetorical questions about the world's problems or biblical themes and then provided answers, usually citing scriptures with references to the *Watchtower, Golden Age,* or other available Watchtower Society pamphlets or books. In the 1930s, as the Joneses worked their way through Georgia, Watch Tower policy placed less stress on personal sermons, encouraging its ministers to rely more heavily on the Rutherford recordings, 78 rpm discs of four-and-one-half minute talks, which were played on portable black phonographs that the society made available for ten dollars. The pioneers could slowly recover their investment at the rate of "a nickle [*sic*] a set-up" subsidy if all went well, but often problems occurred. Rosco Jones's phonograph was stolen at least once, and one belonging to Grace Marsh was destroyed. The hand-cranked machines were heavy, particularly for small persons such as Thelma Jones, and were later replaced by lighter automatic brown ones.[35]

In addition to house calls, the Joneses, like other Witnesses, employed the congregational technique. Such proselytizing entailed attracting a crowd and locating a suitable place to assemble. The pioneers depended primarily on word-of-mouth and advance handbills to advertise a specific meeting, but in Atlanta in 1934 they also used sound equipment. The sites varied. The Witnesses used what was available—a borrowed or rented schoolhouse, church building, funeral parlor, furniture store, or an individual home or yard. An early experience in the Joneses' pioneering convinced them that the use of church buildings was unwise; after they had advertised for two weeks and gathered a large group for a lecture, the established religious leader entered to claim the crowd. The Joneses and interested persons then retired across the road to a private yard, while the sheriff sat in his car between the two groups, averting potential violence. At the large meetings the pioneers usually featured longer recordings of Rutherford sermons. They also used the assemblies as additional opportunities for distributing the association literature.[36]

In the fall of 1934 the six pioneers proceeded to Atlanta, where they found fifteen "colored people in the truth" already working the black community. Without funds and with cars in disrepair, the Jones party parked its trailers and walked four miles one way each day to the territories in the towns around Atlanta and soon organized a congregation. They purchased vegetables and fruit from a vendor for a nickel per bucket. When the weather turned very cold, they found it necessary to break the long walk from their trailer to the territories. A railway station, located at approximately the halfway point on their daily journey, provided a shelter to which they retreated temporarily to warm themselves. By late winter Rosco and Thelma Jones decided it was time to move and requested that the society assign the two of them some rural territory to work.[37]

Their departure for the rurals was delayed, however. They received the news that a white Witness, Brother Brown, had been arrested in Griffin, Georgia, and sentenced to ten days in jail for preaching. The society called the faithful to rally to his support in a zone assembly. Rosco Jones recalled, "The next Sunday morning there were several hundred Witnesses assembled out in the field in Griffin." After the Witnesses had been given hot coffee and doughnuts, they received field instruction that they should not enter any home: "Do your talking at the door." Resisting "the Devil," Jones knocked at the doors of three homes but refused all invitations to "come in." As he completed his proselytizing at the third doorway, he turned to see a waiting police officer who told the Witness, "Come on. . . . You are under arrest." The Jones party of pioneers joined many other Witnesses in jail, although Thelma Jones and Ethlyn Glynn were the only black sisters. Imprisonment did not faze Rosco; when his cellmate became too agitated to eat, Jones ate both dinners. The incarceration proved to be short-term, with all the Witnesses quickly released, for the "city appeared to be very glad to get rid" of the evangelists. The liberated Witnesses, anything but intimidated, lined up two abreast and walked as a group to the local auditorium for "a fine encouraging talk" and prayer and then went home.[38]

In the early spring of 1935, Rosco and Thelma Jones were assigned ten rural Georgia counties, and they decided to leave the trailer in Atlanta and to camp in the car. They worked the rurals for several weeks, then took temporary leave to attend the national convention of Jehovah's Witnesses in Washington, D.C., in June. The society gave them three cities to proselytize as they worked their way north: Anderson, South Carolina; Charlotte, North Carolina; and Lynchburg, Virginia. En route they stayed in the homes of other Witnesses or interested black persons with whom they conducted Bible studies. The convention brought a happy reunion with friends from Richmond whom they had not seen for almost two years and provided stimulation as they shared Witnessing experiences. Judge Rutherford electrified the assembly with accounts of the fortitude of German Witnesses who endured persecution by the Third Reich because they refused to pay homage to the Führer and specifically to perform the "Heil Hitler" salute. The German brothers' experiences should inspire their counterparts throughout the world, the judge declared; to salute a flag or stand for an anthem was to venerate graven images.[39]

Inspired by the fellowship of the convention, the Joneses returned to rural Georgia, leaving the trailer in Atlanta for the summer. Each day they drove the car, heavily laden with books and produce, to a new location, locked it, and then worked the neighborhood on foot. Sometimes they were invited to spend a night or more in a home, where they would lead Bible discussions well into the night for all who were interested. On other occasions, however, Thelma cooked hoecake cornbread and perhaps chicken on a "stove" that consisted of two bricks under which she made a fire, and they slept in the car, putting burlap bags at the windows as screens against sand flies.[40]

Insects were not their most serious problem. A greater threat stemmed from conditions born of racism and exploitation. Rosco recalled events that began as he rented a room with a black family:

> The sun was about an hour high. . . . Sister Jones and the man's wife were in the kitchen cooking, and I was sitting on the porch. I saw the sheriff's car drive up and stop. . . . Two men with sheriff badges got out of the car, and began asking questions. "What is your name? Where did you come from? What in hell you doing loafing all over this county meddling the niggers like you been doing for these past three weeks?" . . . I reached in my shirt pocket and gave him my testimony card and then reached in the book bag and gave him the territory assignment letter.

Jones's audacity or Jehovah's intervention produced a miracle. The official, who later identified himself as the sheriff, read the material and responded favorably, saving Jones from the local chain gang and earning him the sobriquet "Daniel" in the black community. His new appellation carried more honor than the nickname "Horse" that some of the brothers had previously given him, but it stemmed from the same roots— Jones's daring and dedication.[41]

As the winter of 1935–1936 came, the Joneses, "naked and broke," returned to Atlanta in worn-out shoes to move their trailer. Thelma fretted that Rosco faced a winter in the country without long underwear and with only one pair of trousers. As they drove up to the trailer, a fellow Witness shouted, "Hello Horse. . . . Man, you been gone all the summer, I know the brothers will be glad to see you. Come on down to the Kingdom Barber Shop." Jones accepted the invitation, visiting and sharing experiences. Although he mentioned nothing about his clothing needs, his fellow Witnesses presented him with enough shoes and clothes—including long underwear—to last him for three years. (Thelma Jones's memoirs did not mention her clothing problems, but it is likely that she had similar difficulties and that the sisters helped meet her needs. Like the Pentecostals, the Witnesses cared for their own.)[42]

After eight days in Atlanta, the couple began the trip back to the rurals to their first destination, Crawford, Georgia. A broken car axle and a flat tire on the trailer complicated their journey, but Atlanta friends assisted them. By nightfall they had parked only three miles short of Crawford in the yard of a black family. They had spent all their money moving, and the only supplies they had were lard and flour, leaving the prospects for breakfast the next morning rather bleak. Just before dawn, however, they heard a knock on the trailer: their local host had brought them an extra rabbit that he had just found in his trap. As a member of a faith that tended to see the Hand of God in everything good, Rosco said to his wife, "See how Jehovah provided breakfast for us before we got out of the bed." With such spiritual and nutritional support the couple felt renewed and strengthened.[43]

Working in the farming communities brought a variety of experiences. Rosco gardened and made boxes to catch rabbits, and Thelma raised chickens for sale as well as for dinner. On one occasion their fowls were stolen, but Rosco confronted the thief and retrieved the chickens. The couple usually began work at seven in the morning, with Rosco working one road and Thelma, another. Thelma Jones recalled that in the spring of the year both man and wife were in the field, often as much as two miles away, but the children would direct her to them. She would find them at work, "the man plowing and his wife dropping corn. . . . I would ask permission to play the phonograph. The man would stop plowing when Brother Rutherford began talking. Even the mule would look around to see what was going on, as Brother Rutherford would say 'Is Hell Hot?'" Reaching homes that lay across a creek required special skills. If there was only a foot log without a hand pole, Thelma Jones explained, "I would throw my book bag across the creek, stride across the foot log like you horse back ride. . . . This was much closer than walking down the road." The day's work ended at six in the evening, but it took time for the couple to walk back to the car, for them to drive to the trailer, and for Thelma to prepare supper. They sometimes did not get to bed before midnight.[44]

As black itinerant ministers the Joneses had a delicate task proselytizing blacks without alienating the white community. Paternalistic whites could be won over if they recognized that the Joneses were not attempting to change racial mores; such whites might prove supportive when they observed the couple's serious, conscientious lifestyle. Less secure whites, however, were likely to feel threatened by any black outsider, especially one who was literate and drove an automobile. When the Joneses went from Crawford to the other side of Oglethorpe County, a white landowner offered them a place to park the trailer. Late in the afternoon of their first day, however, a second white man, named Foster, came and told Rosco Jones that they would have to move before dark because they were too close to him. Local blacks begged the Witnesses to leave, warning them that Foster was "the meanest man in the county." But the Joneses decided to stay. Early the next day, as they prepared to go out in the field service, a tall white man carrying an axe handle came to the trailer. The intruder informed Rosco Jones that if he were not gone by noon, Mr. Foster would have him given "the whipping of his life." To this threat, Rosco Jones replied, "Well, Mr. Foster will have to have his last Negro whipped. I think I will stay here and be Mr. Foster's last Negro whipped." The messenger tried to persuade Jones to go, but then he spotted a Watchtower booklet entitled, "Government." The booklet convinced the visitor that Jones was a government agent, an FBI man. After that experience, the big landowners sent groceries and good wishes.[45]

Racism reared its ugly head in still another encounter, but again the Joneses survived. In the spring of 1936 they headed for Smithsonia, Georgia, despite warnings by blacks that it was mean territory. Reputedly, the community was "an old chain gang place owned by a white man called Captain Smith," who bought "all the colored men that were sentenced to the chain gang" to work on his farm. The Joneses decided not to take their trailer, lest it attract too much attention. They had been informed that several black families lived at Smithsonia, and they hoped that one of the black homes would provide lodging for the night. When the Witnesses were within a few miles of their destination, their car ran out of gas. Rosco stayed with the car while Thelma walked about a quarter of a mile to a service station, carrying an empty gasoline can.[46]

As Rosco waited for Thelma's return, he observed the scene. On the right side of the road, a white man was plowing in a big field, coming toward the road. On the left, three young white men were drinking, "picking a guitar, dancing and singing." The youths called Jones "old nigger" and told him to dance for them. When he replied, "I don't dance," they taunted him to drink and then to preach or pray. Jones further asserted, "No, that would be a mockery." One of the youths commented to the teaser, "You ain't having no fun off of that nigger." About that time, however, the white man who had been plowing reached the road, and he sent the youths on their way after convincing them that they should help push Jones's car. He then befriended the Witness couple by filling their car with gasoline and allowing them to park in his yard. He further advised Rosco to go out proselytizing only after dark, though "Sister Jones could work the whole neighborhood. Nobody paid much attention to Negro women walking about in the neighborhood that time of year." Following this counsel, the Joneses "teamed up and got it worked."[47]

But racial customs did not always operate to the Witnesses' disadvantage. As the Joneses continued to work in rural Georgia and east Alabama in the late 1930s, they were at times befriended by whites who saw them as good influences because of their sedate lifestyle and hard work. U.S. senator Walter George allowed them to park their trailer on his property near Vienna, Georgia. Generally, they confined their initial activities in an area to the black community, but some whites would listen to their ideas. A congregation of white sisters in Hawkinsville, Georgia, called on the Joneses at their trailer, asking Rosco to conduct a funeral for one of their number. Although some "hoodlums" followed and observed them in a threatening manner, the white women asked Jones to bring his phonograph and ride with them to the service. He agreed and reported conducting a "successful" funeral.[48]

Despite the strong unwritten code that prevented blacks from assuming a leadership role in the white community, diplomacy and decency occasionally combined to overcome certain aspects of segregation. Some whites were ashamed of the abuse of the Witnesses by fellow whites and sought to make amends, and the black Witnesses sometimes disapproved of the habits of some other blacks. In Russell County, Alabama, in 1937 a white woman agreed that the Joneses could park their trailer on her property and loaned them thirty-five dollars to pay a fine so that they would not miss the national Witnesses convention in Columbus, Ohio. In Seale, Alabama, Rosco Jones stated he found that whites more nearly shared the Witnesses' attitudes than did blacks. More whites "got in the truth," he observed, adding, "The colored people believed more in spell binding, adultery, fornication, stealing, and anything that was lowdown and dirty." One white family of some wealth was converted. When the family went away for extended visits, they left the Joneses to run their grocery store and auto repair shop. Even more unexpected, the white woman also began to accompany Thelma Jones in proselytizing activities.[49]

In the period from 1933 through 1938 the Joneses handled most of their difficulties alone or with informal assistance from fellow Witnesses or other well-wishers. Their major problem with authorities in the early years stemmed from white concern that Rosco was "meddling the niggers." Usually, this fear was allayed when it became apparent that the Joneses were clean-living preachers who did not challenge the local racial customs and who limited their activities to the spiritual realm. Local law enforcement personnel on occasion even offered assistance. The Witnesses were, nonetheless, highly vulnerable, particularly if they were perceived to be more than isolated itinerants largely confined to the black community. In Griffin, Georgia, in 1935, it was the arrest of a white brother that had set off the zone assembly in which the Joneses had participated.[50]

If the local white power structure decided to move against the Joneses or other Witnesses, the means existed to do so. In 1936 in Gainesville, Georgia, the Witnesses were forced to call on the society for help. Rosco had been arrested for "buying junk without a license" after he had traded a Bible for an old stove. Informed that he must come up with $150 and threatened with work on the chain gang, Jones asked his wife to contact the Watch Tower Society, and a Witness lawyer from Macon, Georgia, came to arrange bond. In Russell County, Alabama, in 1937 a patrolman arrested Rosco Jones for failure to use flares and flags while repairing a flat on his pickup truck. When asked what kind of work he did, Jones replied that he was a Jehovah's Witness. "You will need Jehovah to witness for you," the patrolman responded. Jones was tried that evening and told to pay a $35 fine or work six months on the chain gang. Intervention by the white woman on whose place they had parked the trailer and a change of heart by the judge saved Jones on that occasion, and he and Mrs. Jones were able to attend the national Witnesses' convention as they had planned.[51]

Grace and Herbert Marsh were also present at the 1937 convention in Columbus, Ohio. Grace, assisted by her son, had been active in Witnessing since her return to the faith, but after hearing Judge Rutherford in 1937, she determined to become a full-time pioneer. Herbert, although not then fully in the fold, agreed that they should arrange immediately to auction everything that they owned and use the proceeds to buy a trailer. They parked the trailer in Robertsdale, at Grace's parents' home, and she prepared for pioneering.[52]

In 1938 Rosco and Thelma Jones, Grace Marsh, and countless other dedicated Witnesses followed Judge Rutherford as he charted a new course. In that year the Watch Tower Bible and Tract Society officially adopted the concept of the Theocracy, establishing a network of districts, zones, and circuits and requiring regular reports to the central office. The campaign to save the great multitude before Armageddon required tighter organization. And as the tempo of the Witness movement increased, it provoked more intense opposition. The failure of local officials to protect the evangelists encouraged individual and mob action against the Witnesses, and authorities on occasion found ostensibly legal means of harassing Witnesses.[53]

In order for the kingdom to advance, Rutherford determined, Witnesses must find a shield against the escalating resistance. As a lawyer, he logically turned to the law. The society decided to arm its people with the aegis of the United States Constitution, and Witness Hayden Covington of Texas, a spirited and charismatic attorney, was brought to Bethel to direct a national legal campaign. The plan was that Witnesses would confront local authorities with the First Amendment, which, Covington was convinced, the U.S. Supreme Court would hold applicable to the states through the Fourteenth Amendment. Legally, they would establish the good news. To accomplish its goal, the society would provide a bevy of regional attorneys who would be waiting in the wings to assist those Witnesses who ran into trouble with the law.[54]

The success of the battle, nonetheless, depended upon the intense dedication of the lay membership. The faithful would have to probe on many fronts; when one member fell, another would have to come forth to take up the banner of Jehovah. Rosco (Horse) Jones had already proved his mettle to his brothers, but he would prove it to the world in Opelika,

Alabama, in 1939. Grace Waldrop Marsh was also preparing to follow Jehovah's charge wherever it might lead. By 1943, when that command led her to Chickasaw, she was ready.

3

Jones v. Opelika

Rosco and Thelma Jones began pioneering in the rural area around Opelika, Alabama, in the fall of 1938. Without their trailer, which had been vandalized in Seale with most of its contents stolen, and with a badly run-down car, they had to find a place to stay from which they could walk into the outlying areas. A few Witnesses were already in the Opelika-Auburn area—three black brothers, two black sisters, and two white sisters—but they were not active. Thelma Jones called on the white woman who acted as company servant (congregation director) and through her met the other white Witness, Sister Cooper. Mrs. Cooper immediately assisted the Joneses, locating a room for them in the home of a black person who had once worked for her and paying the fifty-cents-per-week-rent. A few weeks later, after she happened to observe the Joneses walking some ten miles out of Opelika, she also helped them get a car to work the rural county.[1]

While many of their evangelical activities were aimed at persons in the rurals who had had no prior contact with the Witnesses, the Joneses also cultivated the Opelika congregation for Kingdom work. After six or seven weeks they succeeded in efforts to establish regular attendance at the Sunday night Watchtower Bible study. On Sunday evenings they would begin walking about an hour before the meeting, stopping along the way at "the homes of the people who claimed to be in the truth and would get one or two, then go on to the next house and get two or three," until they built a crowd of about fifteen. Often a police squad car stayed parked across from the meeting place until the members dispersed, but the police did not interfere.[2]

As the Opelika congregation became established, Rosco and Thelma Jones began trying to expand the Witnesses' following within the city. Some time before the Joneses' arrival, a "zone servant" (district director), Brother Tujon, had visited the Opelika congregation. When he had inquired why the sisters in the truth had not been working the city, they had told him that Opelika offered too much resistance. Tujon had replied that through God's grace the city would be worked, because the Bible commanded that "the 'good news of the Kingdom must be preached in all the earth' (Acts 1:8)."[3] The Joneses intended to follow the commandment through house-to-house activity in the black community.

They ran into stiff opposition. Thelma Jones found one street on the south side of town to be especially rough; each time she worked the area, she was cursed repeatedly by an elderly woman and was laughed at by the woman's neighbors. About two weeks later, when Thelma was scheduled to return to the difficult street, Rosco Jones worked it for her. He described what happened:

> It was a very chilly, sunshiny morning. The old lady was behind the house washing in the sun where it was warm. I said to her I have a record here I would like to play for you. She said, "You want me to hear a preaching record?" She took an empty tub and turned it upside down and said, "put your phonograph on there." As the record was playing, she was looking down on it . . . , crying. I thought she was angry, looking for her to curse and show off as soon as the phonograph stopped, but she asked me . . . [to call my wife.]

She then asked the Joneses to forgive her, explaining that the neighbors had pushed her into cursing them. They forgave her, and, in Jones's words, "The lady got in the truth."[4]

The success of the Joneses in gaining adherents rankled some of the "sanctified" ministers in the Opelika area. When one of the black ministers failed to persuade Rosco to stop carrying the phonograph into the community, the anti-Witness black clergyman sought assistance from a white preacher. On a Saturday morning late in 1938 or early in 1939, Jones was conducting a Bible study in a downtown secondhand furniture store owned by Mr. Bud Williams, when a white minister entered and turned to Jones. The Witness recounted what followed. "He . . . said, 'You see I am a white man. . . . As a white man talking to a colored man about the Bible I want to tell you something.' I said, 'Tell me something about the Bible?' He answered, 'Yes, you see, I am a white man.' I said, 'No, I [do not] want to discuss the Bible with you on those terms. . . . let the Bible speak for itself.' . . . He stood there and looked at me for a few seconds. Then he shouted, 'To hell with you, who in hell do you think you are?'" According to Jones, the clergy increased their pressure after that incident, conspiring to push the Joneses out of Opelika.[5]

In the spring of 1939, the Joneses were living in Auburn at the home of Winnie Glaze, a black sister who worked as a cook at Alabama Poly- technic Institute. Their primary activity by that time centered in Auburn, but they went to Opelika on Saturdays to do street work. Normally, they walked the seven miles each way, with Rosco carrying the black pho- nograph, but occasionally they rode the train. About that time the Watch Tower Society suggested to the colporteurs that they "make a small sign board with a banner attached" to display two booklets, one on each side. On Saturday, April 1, Rosco Jones prepared the stand, "an upright piece of timber, braced at the bottom to keep it erect, and cross-pieced or boxed at the top," five to six feet high, with two Watchtower booklets, *Face the Facts* and *Fascism and Freedom,* attached to the boxed area. Across the sign were the words, "Get your 2 copies, only 5 cents." He or Thelma Jones positioned the stand on the edge of Ninth Street, a busy thoroughfare in downtown Opelika. Rosco apparently left Thelma with the stand and their two book bags while he walked to the U.S. post office about three blocks away.[6]

Within a short time both Rosco and Thelma Jones were arrested sepa- rately. The exact sequence of events is not clear, but apparently Thelma's arrest occurred first. She remembered standing on the sidewalk, not blocking the street, holding the banner. The chief of police came and asked what she was doing. She responded that she was "preaching the good news of God's Kingdom." The chief then told her that she could not do that and told her to accompany him to the jail. "Since I could not carry the banner, my book bag, and Rosco's book bag," Sister Jones later recounted, "I gave the Chief of Police the banner to carry. As he and I walked through the city of Opelika on our way to the jail, everyone was looking and reading what was on the banner." By the time the chief and Thelma Jones reached the jail, Officer O. B. Broadwater had located her husband and also brought him there.[7]

Rosco Jones recalled the details concerning his arrest: "I was on my way . . . to get a post card to write my brother in Atlanta. . . . I had a dozen of those books under my arm, in my hand, out in the open; I didn't have no bag; I heard someone say, 'Hey you.' . . . It was a police officer in an automobile. I says, 'Are you talking to me?' He says, 'Yes, I am talking to you. Come here. Get in this car.' I said, 'Am I under arrest?' He said, 'Yes, you are under arrest.' " After checking with another officer, who recounted that the chief had already taken Thelma Jones to headquarters, the arresting officer, Broadwater, drove Rosco Jones there also.[8]

At police headquarters the couple, bookbags, and stand were reunited. Official records of what then transpired are unavailable, but probably officials wished to end the matter quickly. A minor charge was frequently dropped if the accused had no previous offense, threw himself/herself on the mercy of the court, and promised not to repeat the transgression. According to the Joneses, the city was not at all subtle about the matter. Rosco Jones states that the policemen first offered to release the couple for five dollars, to which Jones replied that he did not have the money. Then, when the policemen found that the Joneses lived in Auburn, an officer called Paul took them and their bags to the railroad station twenty minutes before the next train to Auburn and told them to do what they liked but to report back to the jail at five o'clock. The Witnesses interpreted this action to mean that the officers were hoping that they "would get on the train and leave town." When they returned to the station at five, Rosco Jones explained, the policemen were angry and locked the couple in separate but adjoining cells that were quite filthy. The Joneses remained in the jail over the weekend.[9]

Rosco Jones's trial in recorder's court occurred on Monday, April 3, 1939. As no official record of the municipal court proceeding can be found, the only available evidence stems from the recollections of those involved in the proceeding, and I had access only to Rosco Jones's written memoirs. Jones remembered the experience as one in which he and righteousness prevailed except with the judge. The Witness was found guilty of soliciting without a license and was sentenced to pay a $50 fine or serve ninety days in jail; he asked for an appeal. During the three or four days before the "brothers outside" had the opportunity to contact the Watch Tower Society and before the association could arrange to make bond, Rosco and Thelma Jones remained in jail, reinforced by the support of some white Witness children from the rurals who were also jailed for standing on the corner and of some colored brothers who "saw to it that [the Joneses] . . . had plenty to eat." An appeal bond of $125 was filed on April 8.[10]

The feature story in the *Opelika Daily News* on April 3, 1939, dealt with the visit of Franklin Delano Roosevelt to the city on March 29, when the president had stopped in Opelika en route to Warm Springs, Georgia. The front page focused on a picture of Mayor John S. Crossley greeting the president. The local paper also carried accounts of mixed economic developments that directly affected the area—ginning in 1938 had been less than half that of 1937, cotton consumption in the mills was in decline, agricultural specialists recommended Johnson grass for grazing cattle—and items of personal interest, from details of the meetings of the local ladies' garden club to the upbeat observation that Mayor Crossley was recovering nicely from an appendectomy. Holy Week religious activities made page six, but page two carried the Bible Thought for Today, which read, "Trust ye in the Lord forever: for in the Lord Jehovah is everlasting strength: Isa. 26: 4." On the following day the periodical carried an account of the national coal strike, warned Lee County farmers against overplanting, and gave extended coverage to community religious activities. The newspaper on April 4 also described a 4-H rally and band parades, advertised *Jesse James* and *Fast and Loose* as the attractions at the local movie theaters, and reported the distress of the Daughters of the American Revolution that pranksters had pulled concrete cannonballs from the base of the local Confederate monument and rolled them down the street. But nowhere in the town's daily paper on April 3 or 4 or at any time during the next month was there any mention of the arrest, trial, or sentencing of Rosco Jones in recorder's court on April 3 on the charge that he had violated the city ordinance by selling books without a license. On April 12 the periodical did report, perhaps purely coincidentally, the formation of a new secret organization, the Alabama Council of Accepted Americans, the stated purpose of which was "to teach the virtues of democracy and Americanism." The council defined itself as a secret fraternal organization that was not tied to the Ku Klux Klan.[11]

The failure of the local press to cover the incident likely reflected the priorities of the city officials as well as those of the subscribers—the arrest and trial of Jones in the police court was nothing to get excited about. To the established white society of Opelika, Rosco Jones probably appeared to be an ordinary poor black man attempting to peddle the papers of an obscure religious cult, as other poor blacks regularly hawked fresh berries or turnip greens. Whites in many southern communities similar to Opelika tolerated or even welcomed peddlers, provided the seller's manner was appropriate and the merchandise desirable. A flexible and selective enforcement of license requirements allowed officials to overlook or implement regulations as they saw fit. Vendors with deferential mien and desirable fresh produce had little difficulty marketing their wares; others were viewed as nuisances that could be controlled by intimidating warnings by law enforcement officials, arrests, or, if necessary, conviction in municipal court. The possibility of a fine or jail sentence normally removed any threat to the status quo. At least when the city first arrested Rosco Jones, the officials were not aware of the looming battle. Two years later, as William S. (Bill) Duke argued Opelika's case against Jones before the U.S. Supreme Court, the young city attorney referred to the Witness as "a street vendor" in a case involving "a plain, ordinary municipal business privilege or license tax."[12]

The distinguishing characteristic in the *Jones* case was, of course, the religious issue. Someone or something drew the attention of the police to the Witnesses, possibly some of the traditional clergymen.[13] Once the attempt to enforce the law against Jones began, the city officials apparently felt obligated to carry through. The difficulty for Opelika was that Jones did not scare easily; a mere fine or jail sentence did not dispose of him. Even after the recorder's court ruling and the resulting decision of

Jones to appeal to circuit court, the city did not realize that this poor black man had both the legal resources and the will to fight his conviction on constitutional grounds. It would have to learn the hard way that truly dedicated Witnesses—regardless of sex or age or status or race—would not be frightened out of what they considered their religious mission. The struggle was joined.

Whether or not Rosco and Thelma Jones had originally planned to begin a test case, the time and circumstances of their arrests fitted well into the Watch Tower Bible and Tract Society's legal strategy. In 1938 the U.S. Supreme Court had ruled in *Lovell v. Griffin*[14] that a city ordinance prohibiting the distribution of printed matter without the permission of the city manager violated freedom of press, and in 1939 *Cantwell v. Connecticut*[15] was pending before the high court. Witness Attorney Hayden Covington was attempting through *Cantwell* to gain the Court's ruling that the First Amendment protected religious expression at the state level as fully as it guarded freedom of press. The Joneses, dedicated Witnesses, were accustomed to hardship and to following the Watch Tower Society's instructions obediently. If their convictions could be used to further the larger cause, they reasoned, then their convictions must be part of Jehovah's divine plan.

Witness Attorney Grover Powell was one of several regional counselors who assisted the faithful ones involved in the campaign to defend and establish legally the good news. Born in Tennessee in 1893, he had received an LL.B. from Cumberland University in Lebanon, Tennessee, in 1914. By 1939 he had begun practice in Atlanta, and in that year he responded to the call of Rosco Jones and prepared his case for trial in the Alabama Fifth Circuit Court. Jones's appeal from recorder's court in April had placed his case on the circuit court docket for mid-May.[16]

Powell and Jones took the city by surprise, however, by sending subpoenas to the local clergymen. The audacity of a black man, represented by an out-of-state attorney, to command the appearance of the local clergy in court certainly was unexpected and unsettling. The summoning introduced elements of drama, furthermore, stirring public attention and official concern. By this time someone had informed the local newspaper, which reported on May 10 that "practically all Opelika ministers, white and colored," were "quite perplexed" at having been summoned as witnesses by Jones in a city ordinance licensing case. The paper speculated that because "the negroes [*sic*] are said to belong to a religious sect known as 'Jehovah's Witnesses' and some who have read their literature say it contains 'Fascist doctrines,'" the ministers might be asked to testify that the literature was "only religious tracts." Unsure and disturbed, the city needed time to react and regroup. Duke countered the Witnesses' move with a request for a delay and a motion to transfer the cases from jury to nonjury docket. On May 15 Judge W. B. Bowling of the Alabama Fifth Circuit Court granted the transfer. The cases were set to be heard by Judge Bowling on November 2, 1939.[17]

During the interval before their case would be heard in circuit court, the Joneses moved in August 1939 to Columbus, Georgia. They continued their Witnessing in Opelika for some time after the trial in recorder's court. On one occasion Rosco was playing a recording of Judge Rutherford's talk on the porch of a home at which he regularly called when an officer approached him and said, "Aren't you the same fellow they had in jail" several days for proselytizing? Jones responded, "Yes, I am the same man." Frowning, the officer then looked at Jones and said, "I will be God dam [*sic*]." The woman at the house where Jones was Witnessing laughed and commented, "You are getting away with him."[18]

Jones also asserted that he "got away" with a municipal judge during this interval. He and Thelma Jones were arrested several more times in Opelika, he stated, and finally the judge asked Sister Jones to explain why the couple persisted. After she justified their actions as responses to God's command to spread the gospel even against a local government that stood as a barrier to that sacred duty, the judge turned to her husband and said, "Rosco, you have cost this city a plenty. . . . If you will give me $20, I will let you go." Jones refused the offer, stating that, among other reasons, he did not have the money. At that point, by Jones's account, "the judge's eyes blared. He shouted, 'I just don't understand it. . . . You have been arrested about six times and raised a $1,000 bond every time. If I find you guilty, you would raise another $1,000 bond.' Then he shouted, 'I am going to take the initiative to dismiss this case, and I hope I don't ever see you anymore.' It looked like the judge was trying to make me laugh, but I wouldn't. I thanked him."[19]

When Circuit Judge Bowling heard Rosco Jones's case in Opelika in November 1939, the *Opelika Daily News* took note. Despite the news about the war in Europe, the case made the first page. "Unique Case Calls Pastors Here as Witnesses," the left-hand column headline read, and by the term "witnesses" the paper did not mean the followers of the Watch Tower Bible and Tract Society. Referring to Rosco and Thelma Jones as "negroes [*sic*], said to be members of a group known as 'Russellites,'" the *News* recounted the appeal from recorder's court, identified the counselor from Atlanta, and opined, "The ministers were summoned as witnesses by the defense in an effort, it is believed, to prove the books being distributed by the defendants were religious literature." The paper's assumption regarding the purpose of the subpoenas of the ministers was mere speculation. The press's inaccuracy resulted from failure to investigate the doctrines of Jehovah's Witnesses; a reflex reaction to the title of one of the pamphlets, *Fascism and Freedom;* and secrecy by the defense as to its motivation in calling the non-Witness ministers.[20]

Essentially, the city argued that Jones had, within the twelve months prior to the beginning of prosecution, sold books in the city of Opelika without first procuring the required municipal license. Jones was charged with being a book agent, a transient book agent, a transient dealer of books, and a transient distributor of books, all in violation of the ordinance's licensing specifications. Jones through Powell demurred and called for dismissal of all charges on the grounds that the charge against Jones set out no offense against the city; the defendant's procedural rights guaranteed under the due process clause of the Fourteenth Amendment to the U.S. Constitution had been violated in that he was arrested without a warrant; and the ordinance was invalid because it violated the due process clause of the Fourteenth Amendment in that it denied or unduly restricted freedom of press and was arbitrary and unequal in practice, making licenses "subject to revocation in the discretion of the City Commission, with or without notice." Judge Bowling denied the defendant's demurrer.[21]

The city of Opelika opened with a certified copy of the license schedule for 1939, an eighteen-page typewritten document, introduced as an exhibit for the plaintiff. Adopted by the city commission in 1938, the ordinance required a city license for almost every potential occupation. The license could be acquired by payment of a fee but was "subject to revocation in the discretion of the City Commission, with or without notice to the licensee." Fundamentally a commercial license ordinance, it dealt with fees that ranged from $1 annual charge to $200 and with a great variety of occupations, covering a wide range of working persons, from those employed in bootblack stands and one-chair barbershops to fertilizer manufacturers and attorneys. The sections relevant to the city's complaints against Jones dealt with stands on public streets or sidewalks and with the sale of books or periodical literature, by transients or other book agents. A license for a stand could not be obtained without the written permission of the city commission. Although in recorder's court Jones had been charged only with "violation of city ordinance of Opelika," he was informed when the case was called for trial in Circuit Court of the new charges, that " 'he did sell books,' 'as a book agent,' 'as a transient agent,' 'as a transient dealer,' 'as a transient distributor.' " Apparently, the city's only hard evidence regarding the stand was that Thelma Jones had been found with it on Ninth Street and that Rosco Jones admitted that he had built it. If the city could not place Rosco Jones with the stand, then the case against him would have to be based on something more—that he had been engaged in a business of selling literature.[22]

The city then placed the arresting officer, O. B. Broadwater, on the stand. The policeman testified that he had arrested Rosco Jones after observing Jones with pamphlets:

> The defendant was walking on the sidewalk, holding the books . . . , offering them for sale. . . . He was holding the books up; he may have had some more books in the other hand. . . . I asked him if he had a license; he said [no]; . . . I said, "Well, you are violating a City ordinance. I will have to carry you down." . . . I then carried him down, . . . and locked him up. . . . as to whether I told . . . [him] that he was under arrest, I supposed he had sense enough to know that.

Broadwater maintained that Jones had freely stated in recorder's court that he had made the stand and had placed it on Ninth Street. He could not remember just who had been present when the defendant made such statements, he declared, but he thought that perhaps there had been one other policeman, Mr. John Crossley, and maybe counsel for Jones. He identified the stand and declared that the pamphlets attached were the same or similar to those that Jones had been carrying at the time of his arrest; the stand and pamphlets, *Face the Facts* and *Fascism or Freedom,* were introduced as plaintiff's exhibits. Jones's attorney, Grover Powell, objected to the introduction of the exhibits on the grounds that they had been seized without a warrant.[23]

Under questioning from Powell, the officer stated that he was not sure that he had heard Jones say anything when he first observed him but that the defendant had been holding the booklets over his head, indicating that they were for sale. Broadwater testified that he had heard Jones later on the day of the arrest and that the Witness had said substantially, "two copies for five cents." Powell asked whether Broadwater had not assumed that Jones was offering the booklets for sale because of the sign on the stand; the policeman replied that he had seen "Thelma" and the sign before he arrested Rosco Jones but that seeing them was not what caused him to conclude that the defendant was trying to sell the literature at the rate of two for five cents.[24]

When the prosecution rested after Broadwater's testimony, Powell moved for dismissal, modifying the reasons from those stated in the demurrer. He maintained again that Jones's rights had been violated by the city's arresting him without a warrant and that the complaint did not state facts constituting any offense under the law. Powell expanded the earlier points regarding the invalidity of the ordinance. It was invalid on its face and as applied because it violated the due process clause of the Fourteenth Amendment in that it unduly restricted freedom of speech and press and undertook to license the printed page, was too vague and indefinite, was applied in an arbitrary and unequal manner, and unduly restricted freedom of worship, conscience, and religion. The court denied the motion.[25]

Powell attempted early in the trial to introduce the issue of free exercise of religion. When Duke objected, Jones's attorney explained to the court that the religious question was "a very important part of the case" because the U.S. Constitution made Jones "exempt from the provisions of the ordinance . . . on the ground of freedom of religion." He hoped to show that Jones was "a regularly ordained minister of the Gospel, that his activity at the time in question was in furtherance of his work as such minister," and that the city was attempting to interfere with his free exercise of religion. Judge Bowling was not impressed; he stated, "I do not see that the matter of religion is involved in the question of the violation of this ordinance." Similarly, the court overruled Powell's motion to introduce subject matter of the pamphlets in question, maintaining that the contents were irrelevant, that the only issue was whether Jones was selling without a license. Bowling stated that he had not "heard any testimony to the effect that . . . [Jones] was worshipping . . . [but] merely offered books for sale. If he was [sic] selling First Readers it would be the same thing." When Rosco Jones took the stand in his own behalf and began to explain how he worked as a minister, Duke objected. Powell again argued that Jones's activities in question were religious in nature, that distributing religious literature and accepting voluntary contributions was a customary "method of preaching . . . practiced by others beside the defendant" in Opelika, and that he had been arbitrarily "singled out" because of his particular faith. The court excluded the religious points as evidence but allowed them in the record for whatever purposes the defense wished to make thereafter.[26]

Rosco Jones's testimony disagreed with Officer Broadwater's version of events. Jones denied having stated that he brought the sign to Ninth Street or that he had offered any books for sale. When an attorney had asked "who made that sign . . . , I told him I did. He asked me did I bring it to this town. I told him I didn't. . . . He said, 'Tell about that sign on the corner.' I said, 'I don't know. They got my wife. Get her.'" Jones agreed that he had made the sign and prepared the lettering on it. When Jones was asked if he had at any time proposed to sell any books, his attorney advised him that he did not have to answer any question that might tend to incriminate him, but the court intervened, stating that such was "not the rule in Alabama." Jones then stated that he had worked the rural area around Opelika but had heard no witnesses say that he had distributed literature in the city and that he did not remember selling any within the police jurisdiction. He testified, "I wouldn't swear that I haven't done that but I don't remember it; I will say it like this: I am the man and does the walking; . . . I work the Columbus route. . . . I know where the sign says City limits; it is way down the road by some little colored houses on the left hand side of the road going toward Columbus." He also worked the route from Opelika to West Point, Georgia, he declared, and all other roads leading out of Opelika, beginning at the city limits. He emphasized, however, that he was "not engaged in the book selling business anywhere." Jones evaded a direct statement that he had never solicited within the city limits but made it clear that he was not a commercial salesman.[27]

Attorney Powell then began to use his "surprise weapon." He called for ten ministers within the city limits of Opelika to take the stand in turn. His first witness was to be Dr. Stewart Melvin Baker, pastor of the Trinity Methodist Church. The following exchange then took place between Powell and the court:

> Mr. Powell: May it please the Court, what we desire to prove is that they use literature too in connection with the propagation of their faith . . . yet there is no objection made to it. . . .
>
> The Court: You think then because the City fails in *in* [sic] its duty to prosecute Dr. Baker there should be no insistence that it ought to prosecute your client?
>
> Mr. Powell: If he was [sic] the only one that would not be true; but if that is followed as a rule and the exception is made then I think it would be.
>
> The Court: . . . the law should be administered to all people . . . [equally]. But the mere fact that the City of Opelika . . . prosecute[d] in some instances but . . . [not] in others, would not be a defense . . . for violating the law.

Temporarily, nonetheless, the Court overruled Duke's objection and allowed Powell to question first Dr. Baker and then Dr. Norman McLeod of First Methodist Church of Opelika.[28]

Powell then began to build his case that the city was discriminating against Jones. Both Baker and McLeod admitted that they pastored churches within the city limits, that they distributed devotional literature, and that they took voluntary offerings in Sunday school and church services. McLeod also stated that he "considered the literature an essential part of the Christian work," that he had "no special license to distribute literature in the church," and that he knew of no instance in which a minister had been arrested for such distribution. Judge Bowling then inquired whether the defense expected to prove that the other ministers summoned by the defense had also distributed literature without interference. Powell stated that it did. Duke & Duke then conceded that the other pastors would testify in a similar manner to Baker and McLeod but contended, nonetheless, that such testimony would not amount to evidence that the city had acted in a discriminatory manner. The judge then granted Duke's motion to exclude all of the ministers' testimony. Noting that his statement would probably be excluded also but that he wanted it in the record, Powell asserted that he proposed "to recall the City authorities and prove by them that no case has ever been made or ever offered to be made against any other class of religious belief except Jehovah's Witnesses." Duke objected, "If he wants to call them as his witnesses. We object to calling them as our witnesses." When Powell stated that he would call them in rebuttal, the judge told him to call his next witness.[29]

Powell then attempted to bring to the stand four persons who would vouch for the good character of Rosco Jones. The first, Will Samford, testified that he resided in Opelika, had known Jones for about one year, and considered the defendant to have a good reputation for truth, veracity, and sobriety. When Powell asked whether, on that basis, Samford would believe Jones under oath, Lum Duke objected. The court sustained the objection, observing that Jones's character had not been impeached and stating that Alabama law ruled as inadmissible testimony regarding veracity unless one's character had first been attacked by the adversary party. "You cannot put a man on the stand and let him testify and then put somebody else on the stand and let them [*sic*] testify that [*sic*] believe him on his oath." He also struck down the testimony as support for the contention that Jones was engaged in ministerial work, sustaining Lum Duke's contention that the fact Jones was a minister was without conflict but immaterial.[30]

The testimony having concluded, Powell again moved for dismissal and asked that the defendant be discharged. Judge Bowling denied the motions. He then stated that after hearing the evidence he found Rosco

Jones guilty of violating the city ordinance and assessed a fine of $50 plus court costs of $103.50. Jones through Powell gave notice of appeal, and Judge Bowling set the appeal bond at $200.[31]

The *Opelika Daily News* carried a factual account of the trial on November 3 and rendered no editorial opinion. The paper correctly identified Jones as a "Jehovah's Witness" and accurately explained the reason for calling the ministers. The *News* noted that Powell "claimed 'discrimination' against his client" and concluded that the defense was trying to "establish . . . that other ministers distributed religious literature and charged for it." The paper also reported that the "case against Thelma Jones was continued by agreement pending the outcome of the appeal."[32]

Rosco Jones was delivered to the sheriff following his trial and was placed in the county jail. The sheriff, W. J. Linch, was identified by Jones as a former highway patrolman, the same man who had arrested Jones for failure to have flare and flags when he first moved to Seale, Alabama, in 1937. The official sat outside the cell and listened as Jones began to discuss the Bible with the other convicts, the Witness recalled. At supper-time three men who appeared to be cooks came in, pushing a food truck, and began to call names and hand trays to the answering prisoners. After the cooks had given trays to everyone except Jones, the Witness was told he would not receive one, to which he responded that it was unlawful to "lock a man up and don't feed him." The sheriff then unlocked the door and called Jones out, the Witness recounted, telling him, "You know one thing preacher, you are going to find yourself in the Chattahoochee River if you don't change you goddam [*sic*] way of preaching." When Jones asked, "You think so?" the official replied, "I am telling you." He then told Jones that his bond had come and directed him to a door at the bottom of the back steps, telling the minister that he might go. Jones opened the door and stepped out in the backyard, and the sheriff closed the door behind him. Alone in the yard, Jones realized:

> I was in the yard with four or five vicious dogs. . . . The fence was a high wall all around with a wire fence on top. There was a steel door on the back that opened on to the street. . . . I decided that my only hope of getting out of there would be out that steel gate. I looked at the dogs. They

were watching me. I started walking. . . . beat them to the gate . . . fell outside pulling the gate shut behind me . . . I went around to the front of the courthouse and found Sister Jones waiting for me. . . . I met a man downtown that evening. . . . He said, "These people here are trying to kill you."

Jones probably attributed his good fortune to Jehovah's intervention. But even a Daniel should not tempt the Lord. Shortly after the incident with the dogs, the Joneses began to work in Columbus, Georgia, where they had no trouble with the law or the clergymen.[33]

On December 1, 1939, Powell petitioned for a new trial for Jones, setting forth multiple reasons why the request should be granted, but on December 19 Bowling again denied the petition. On February 29, 1940, the defense filed a bill of exceptions in order to carry the case to the Alabama Court of Appeals. The assignment of errors drawn up by Grover Powell, Jones's counsel, stated that the court had erred in denying the petition for dismissal because the complaint was invalid, particularly when applied to a minister whose distribution of literature was collateral to his primary purpose, preaching. He maintained that the charges that Jones sold books and was a dealer denied the defendant freedom of speech, press, and worship, contravening the Fourteenth Amendment to the U.S. Constitution. He further argued that the court had erred in excluding expert testimony from the ministers vital to Jones's defense, in presenting charges different from those made in recorder's court, and in denying the defendant a jury trial and then a motion for a new trial. Duke stated in response, "There is no error in the record."[34]

The Alabama Court of Appeals heard arguments in *Jones v. Opelika* on November 19, 1940. The three-judge panel was composed of a presiding judge and two associate justices whose backgrounds varied greatly from that of Rosco Jones. All were Alabama natives of prominent families, educated in the state and active in state politics, and they had interlocking social ties. Presiding judge Charles R. Bricken of Luverne was seventy-one, but associate justices James Rice from Tuscaloosa and Robert T. Simpson, Jr., of Florence were in their fifties. Robert Frye's 1969 study of the Alabama Supreme Court stated that the customary practice in effect made each opinion a one-man decision. "Once an assignment has been made," he concluded, "there is very little communication between a justice and his associates concerning the case; the operating assumption is that the case is the particular justice's 'baby.'" The writing judge is responsible for the briefs and transcript, as well as writing the opinion. Voting follows the writing of the opinion, and "dissenting opinions are virtually non-existent." No comparable study of the Alabama Court of Appeals prior to the reorganization of the judicial system in the 1970s is available, but a typewritten booklet sponsored by the Alabama Legislative Reference Service in 1954 observed that any two justices on the three-person body could make a decision. Quite possibly the decision actually rested with one justice, as in the state's highest tribunal.[35]

In the court of appeals ruling in *Jones v. Opelika,* in fact, only one name was cited in the secondary appellate court's decision. James Rice wrote the opinion in *Jones,* finding for the Witness. What was there in his background that made him favorably inclined to Jones's cause? Certainly, Rice "belonged" in the Alabama elite community. He was a bit eccentric, perhaps, riding a bicycle regularly to work, and his training in chemistry set him apart, but he moved in the socially correct circles. In rendering the *Jones* decision James Rice probably confined himself to the law on the subject. Relatively young, analytical, and active, he likely kept abreast of legal trends. No First Amendment case involving the Jehovah's Witnesses had reached the upper echelons of the Alabama court system at that time, and recent precedent in the U.S. Supreme Court had found for the Witnesses in related cases. Only two years earlier, the highest court in the nation had unanimously ruled against the city of Griffin, Georgia, where Rosco and Thelma Jones had joined the brothers and sisters in jail in 1935. The key to the decision, *Lovell v. Griffin,* had been the fact that those who would distribute literature of any nature had first to obtain a written permit from the city manager, which left the right to freedom of press dependent upon the goodwill of an official.[36]

Rice's opinion contained only three pages and relied heavily upon *Lovell.* Finding Jones's claim that he was an ordained minister of the Jehovah's Witnesses undisputed in the testimony and that "the sole purpose of the pamphlets" he had distributed had been "to set forth the gospel of the Kingdom of God as he believes and preaches it," the justice accepted the Witness rationale that he had not applied for a license because he considered such an application to be contrary to Jehovah's commandments. Rice further approved the argument that the ordinance was invalid as applied to Jones because it was in conflict with the due process clause of the Fourteenth Amendment to the U.S. Constitution in that it abridged freedom of speech, press, and religion. He called attention to the arbitrary power granted the city commission under the ordinance:

"All licenses, permits or other grants to carry on any business, trade, vocation or profession for which a charge is made by the City shall be subject to revocation on the discretion of the City Commission with or without notice to the licensee. No license shall be issued to any . . . stand for the sale of any product . . . unless written permission be granted by the City Commission of . . . Opelika. . . . (Italics supplied by us.)" He then declared that he was "unable to distinguish the principle implied" in the Opelika ordinance "from that involved in the ordinance of the City of Griffin, Georgia," which the U.S. Supreme Court had overturned in *Lovell.* He found it no more objectionable legally to require all who wished to distribute literature, freely or with charge, to first obtain a written permit from the Griffin city manager "than there is here, in, while pretending to provide a general license ordinance, providing as a matter of fact, that the license is held at the sole, unbridled, and complete discretion of the City Commission of Opelika." The Court of Appeals of Alabama ordered the conviction by the circuit court reversed and Jones discharged.[37] The Joneses probably felt doubly vindicated in that they had been active in both Griffin, Georgia, and Opelika, Alabama.

Duke[38] applied for a rehearing on March 31, 1941, maintaining that the court of appeals had erred in holding the ordinance as applied to Jones to be invalid. On April 22 the appeals court in a per curiam statement denied the application. The city of Opelika on May 1, 1941, petitioned the Alabama Supreme Court for a writ of certiorari directing the court of appeals to affirm the circuit court decision. The Alabama high tribunal met after adjournment and on May 22, 1941, granted the petition and reversed the judgment of the Alabama Court of Appeals.[39]

The Alabama Supreme Court consisted of a chief justice and six associates. As Robert Frye's study noted, the usual procedure was for one justice to be responsible for each case, with the other members almost always voting to confirm his opinion. Since no judicial papers that might provide clues to the reactions of individual justices in the Witness case are available, it is impossible to be certain that this method prevailed in *Jones v. Opelika*. Existing records reveal that one ailing justice, Thomas Knight, did not sit on this case at any time. The six who participated in the case were Chief Justice Lucien Gardner and Associate Justices Virgil Bouldin, Joel Brown, Arthur Foster, J. E. Livingston, and William H. Thomas. Only Livingston, who had joined the body the previous year, was under the age of sixty-five. The average age of the other five voting in *Jones* was more than seventy, and their average tenure on the high court was twenty-one years. The men were active in interrelated social organizations and Democratic party functions, and the majority were direct heirs of Confederate veterans.[40]

Associate Justice William H. Thomas (photo 2) was assigned to write for the court in *Jones v. Opelika*. Court procedures in assigning opinions were shrouded in secrecy but involved statutory provisions, rules of the court, and custom. The usual procedure in cases coming to the supreme court from the court of appeals was for the clerk of the court to distribute assignments among the justices on a rotating basis. If, however, the case came to the court on a writ of error, it could be the result of an individual justice's ruling "in vacation." The *Jones* case came to the Alabama Supreme Court after its adjournment. Possibly, Thomas's selection was a random choice, but that is unlikely.[41]

Thomas's influence within the Alabama Supreme Court was formidable, and his ties with persons involved in Rosco Jones's conviction were legion. Almost seventy-four years old when the *Jones* case reached the high tribunal, Judge Thomas had shared twenty-seven years in that body with Chief Justice Gardner, and their close association had been reinforced by mutual participation in a highly exclusive men's literary club in Montgomery, "The Thirteen." Thomas's younger brother, Jonathan Render Thomas, had been appointed the clerk of the supreme court in 1938.[42]

Judge Thomas, furthermore, had grown up in Chambers County, where he had read law under Judge James Dowdell of LaFayette and where he had practiced for a time as a partner with William James Samford, father of Thomas Drake Samford. Lum Duke, father of the

The official Alabama Supreme Court portrait of
William H. Thomas, taken in 1916

Opelika city attorney who handled the case against Rosco Jones, had also read law in Lafayette and had been a partner in Thomas Drake Samford's firm. W. B. Bowling, the circuit court judge whose decision against Jones had been reversed by the Alabama Court of Appeals, had also read law and practiced in LaFayette. Thomas's one child, Georgia Thomas Varner, resided in Tuskegee, Alabama, which, like Lafayette, fell within a twenty-five-mile radius of Opelika and within the Alabama Fifth Judicial Circuit. It would not have been strange for the elderly justice with so many ties to the scene of *Jones v. Opelika* to have been approached "in vacation" by the representatives of the city; once the court agreed to hear the case, Thomas's assignment to the case would have been natural. His longtime associate, the chief justice, or his brother, the court clerk, would almost surely have considered Thomas's interests in assigning the case, and no evidence indicates that the justice attempted to recuse himself.[43]

Other factors may have contributed to Thomas's reaction in the case. A man of scholarly inclination, he had pursued a study of the classics at Emory College (later, Emory University) in Atlanta, Georgia. He considered the law a sacred trust and the Ciceronian man of honor an ideal. He was greatly concerned over "contempt for law and authority" and logically would have looked askance at deliberate challenges to local ordinances. He criticized the abuses in the system that lightened the penalty on the wealthy and laid it heavily on the poor and powerless, but he did not attack the law itself. He argued that the common good should be the paramount consideration of the law and deplored "technical constructions" that limited "the power of trial courts in such a manner that the rights of the public are . . . construed away, in the safe-guarding of individual liberty."[44]

Thomas held a paternalistic view of blacks, maintaining that prejudice existed in all races. He was concerned about injustices to blacks but also maintained that much of the time such wrongs were righted, since the white southerner was the black man's "truest friend." He viewed the granting of the franchise during Reconstruction to the "unprepared negro [sic]" as a serious error. The justice also strongly supported the traditional southern white Methodist religious position. He was quite active in promoting the Young Men's Christian Association, participated in the Sunday school program, and wrote for the church's mouthpiece, the *Christian Advocate,* on at least one occasion.[45] One can with some justification speculate that the diatribes of the Jehovah's Witnesses against organized religion, especially when delivered by a black man, well may have offended him.

Whatever his reasons, Thomas did write *for* Duke and Bowling and Opelika and *against* Rosco Jones in the Alabama Supreme Court decision on May 22, 1941. The thrust of his argument was that the court of appeals had erred in relying on *Lovell v. Griffin.* That case, he asserted, was "not decisive" of *Jones v. Opelika.* In *Lovell,* he stated, "the ordinance prohibited the distribution of literature of any kind at any time, at any place, and in any manner without a permit from the city manager," thus constituting censorship, whereas in *Jones,* the license was nondiscriminatory and "imposed for police protection and public order." He equated the Opelika license law with a New Hampshire ordinance requiring a permit for "the use of streets for parades" that had been upheld earlier in the year by the U.S. Supreme Court in *Cox v. New Hampshire.* Judge Thomas also referred to *Schneider v. Irvington,* in which the U.S. high tribunal had distinguished the commercial distribution of literature from that freely circulated. Rosco Jones, Thomas maintained, had been a peddler engaged in commercial activity. The fact that Jones was a minister was irrelevant, the jurist stated, for the Alabama Code under which the Opelika ordinance took place allowed no exemption. The Alabama Supreme Court reversed the judgment of the court of appeals and remanded the case to that court. Jones was ordered to pay court costs.[46]

The ruling did not attract the attention of the state press, and even the Opelika paper reported the ruling with a secondary headline and no editorial. Later that year, however, the organ of the state Baptists, the *Alabama Baptist,* clearly denounced the actions of Rosco and Thelma Jones with the following statement: "The so-called Jehovah's Witnesses are not helping the Lord's case before the bar of public opinion . . . [but] are inviting a popular reaction which will reduce their field of activity to the narrow measure of a rail on which they may be taken for a ride. . . . [The insistence that] "freedom of worship" permits them to evade commercial regulations . . . invite[s] revulsion."[47]

In July 1941, Rosco Jones through counsel petitioned the U.S. Supreme Court for a writ of certiorari to the Alabama Supreme Court, and the national body responded affirmatively on October 13. Thus, the battle was joined in the national arena, with Witnesses Joseph Rutherford and Hayden Covington representing Jones in an effort to expand the reach of the First Amendment to nondiscriminatory ordinances that in effect taxed the distribution of ideas. The skirmishing between Jones and Opelika within Alabama did not end in 1941, however. William Duke, assisted by a Washington firm, won the preliminary struggle in February 1942, arguing successfully that the U.S. Supreme Court should deny certiorari on jurisdictional grounds. The issue had not been finally settled, Duke maintained, since the Alabama Supreme Court had remanded the case to the state court of appeals.[48] Grover Powell, as counsel for Rosco Jones, initiated the technical formalities of petitioning the Alabama Supreme Court for a rehearing, which the court refused. The state's highest tribunal then "issued a mandate to the Alabama Court of Appeals with direction to affirm the judgment of the trial court." On March 9, 1942, the court of appeals rendered the mandated judgment, affirming Jones's conviction by the Fifth Circuit Court in Lee County, and on March 17 denied Jones's petition for a rehearing. Powell then filed a motion with the Alabama Supreme Court to review the new judgment of the court of appeals. By April 9, 1942, the petitioner had exhausted all legal remedy within the state when the Alabama Supreme Court affirmed the March rulings of the state court of appeals. The way was then clear for rehearing by the U.S. Supreme Court. On April 25, 1942, Hayden Covington filed Jones's petition to the national tribunal to vacate the previous dismissal for want of final judgment and to restore the cause to the docket for a consideration on the merits of the case.[49]

While their battle was being carried to the highest court of the land, Rosco and Thelma Jones had continued their Witnessing. After establishing a "very nice congregation" in Columbus, Georgia, they attended the annual national convention in the summer of 1941, held that year in St. Louis, Missouri. They found the fiery speech of Judge Rutherford as inspiring as ever, not realizing that he was giving his last public appearance. On December 7, 1941, Rosco Jones remembered, they moved to LaGrange, Georgia. It was, he stated, "a very tough city for Jehovah's Witnesses. . . . [Some had been sentenced] to work on the streets . . . for thirty days. When we . . . [arrived], everybody was afraid of us. . . . The police . . . warned the people if they let us visit them, . . . their homes . . . [would be] burned down. There were only two houses in which we could have Bible studies." To avoid double arrests, the Joneses worked separately; if one failed to return home, the other would be able to notify the Watch Tower Society. Despite such precautions, Rosco Jones recounted, Sister Jones was eventually arrested, and he was beaten badly by nine policemen, who referred to him as "a dam Jap [*sic*] looking son of a so and so."[50]

Rosco and Thelma Jones continued the fight in the trenches of LaGrange in 1942 and 1943, secure in the belief that Jehovah would ultimately triumph. They were pleased that Hayden Covington, also confident and armed with the U.S. Constitution, continued the struggle that they had initiated in Opelika, Alabama, before the U.S. Supreme Court.

4

An Uneasy Supreme Court

*J*ones *v. Opelika* was a critical link in a series of cases that the Witnesses carried from state courts to the U.S. Supreme Court. Defining freedom of expression as *fundamental* to liberty, the Witnesses asserted that the Fourteenth Amendment restriction that "no state shall deprive any person of life, liberty, or property without due process of law" incorporated the First Amendment protections. Hayden Covington, the brilliant attorney directing the Witnesses' legal strategy in 1939, probed in community after community to. determine local limits. Rosco Jones tested the bounds in Opelika, Alabama, at a pivotal stage in the Witness campaign and at a time in which dissension and realignment marked the U.S. Supreme Court.

Jones and the city of Opelika approached the case from quite different perspectives, but the two parties agreed on one point—neither would yield voluntarily. The city would have preferred to overlook Jones's infraction if he would "go and sin no more," but when the Witness insisted that he had the constitutional *right* to distribute the pamphlets, the Opelika officials saw the challenge as one that must be met. The case presented "squarely the question of the right of a municipality to license persons who wish to sell material on the public streets." Because Opelika had prosecuted Jones under a comprehensive ordinance that imposed license fees on almost all potential occupations, the municipality argued that the only legitimate issue was the right of the city to regulate commercial activity.[1] Both the Alabama Fifth Circuit Court and the Alabama Supreme Court had ruled in favor of the city, dismissing the First Amendment claims of the Jehovah's Witnesses as irrelevant and excluding testimony regarding religious practices. Grover Powell and the Alabama Court of Appeals, on the other hand, had maintained that the very nature of the Witness belief system dictated that its followers should distribute religious literature without a government license and, thus, that the municipal requirement violated Jones's constitutional rights. Powell had asserted that the ordinance under which the city's complaint had been filed had no application to the facts and was invalid as applied to Jones, an ordained minister, contravening the U.S. and Alabama constitutions.[2]

Powell had in specifications of error also maintained that Jones's constitutional rights were denied because he had been arrested without a warrant, refused a trial by jury, and presented with a different set of charges without prior notification when his case was called for trial in the Alabama Fifth Circuit Court. The Alabama Court of Appeals had not ruled on all of the exceptions but had overturned the lower court decision on the grounds that the ordinance as applied violated Jones's freedom of speech, press, and religion, emphasizing the arbitrary provision that allowed revocation of licenses "on the discretion of the City Commission with or without notice to the licensee."[3] It was freedom of worship protected through guarantees of free speech and a free press that the Witnesses pursued; once the Alabama Supreme Court ruled against those liberties, Rosco Jones took steps to petition the U.S. Supreme Court.

The Court that heard *Jones v. Opelika* in 1942 was divided severely. Although seven of the nine justices were "liberal" appointees of Franklin Delano Roosevelt, their measure of agreement in accepting New Deal economic legislation did not extend to questions of personal liberties. The effects of the 1930s controversy regarding the role of the judiciary continued to be felt. The reaction against the "nine old men" who had scuttled state regulation of business by substantive interpretation of the due process clause of the Fourteenth Amendment and overruled national legislation by narrow construction of the U.S. Congress's tax and commerce powers had convinced several of the justices that generally the Court should defer to the popularly elected representatives. Others, however, thought that such judicial restraint should be restricted largely to economic matters.

Harlan Fiske Stone, a progressive Republican appointee who was elevated to the position of chief justice by Roosevelt in 1941, fell into the second category. Disturbed by the rise of totalitarianism in Europe, he was concerned that racial and religious hatred threatened civil liberties in the United States as well. In 1938 in footnote four of a decision in which the Court deferred to the Congress in economic matters, *United States v. Carolene Products,* Stone had begun to carve a broader jurisdiction for the Court as the protector of civil liberties. As World War II descended, Stone's concerns intensified, for the emotions stirred by war led to demands for conformity. During World War I Stone had served on a committee dealing with conscientious objectors and had experienced firsthand the dilemma of reconciling personal rights with majoritarian exigencies in a democracy at war. The Court, removed from the people by lifetime tenure and armed with the Bill of Rights and the due process clause of the Fourteenth Amendment, could, he hoped, stand as the constitutional guardian of individual liberties, protecting a fearful public from its own worst impulses.[4]

In 1940, even before the nation entered World War II, the very intolerance that Stone had feared had manifested itself not only in the enactments of elected representatives but also in the chambers of the U.S. Supreme Court. The catalyst in a confrontation between chauvinism and nonconformity had been a family of Jehovah's Witnesses. In 1935, reacting to the courage of the Witnesses who had refused to salute Adolf Hitler, Judge Rutherford had urged Witnesses attending the national convention in Washington, D.C., not to venerate graven images. Among the Witnesses who listened by radio to Rutherford was the Walter Gobitis family of Minersville, Pennsylvania. In October 1935, two of the Gobitis children, William and Lillian, had recounted to their parents that the public school authorities had been displeased when they refused to take part in the daily ceremony of saluting the flag. The parents had backed their children's action despite an opinion by the state attorney general that the community could require children to participate. After the local school board passed a resolution making the pledge of allegiance compulsory, the superintendent had expelled the Gobitis children.[5]

Walter Gobitis had responded, suing to enjoin the school authorities from mandating the salute as a condition of attendance on the grounds that the requirement violated the children's guaranty of religious liberty. After Gobitis won in U.S. district court and in the federal appeals court, the Minersville school board successfully petitioned the U.S. Supreme Court for a writ of certiorari. In June 1940 the Court ruled 8–1 against the Witnesses in *Minersville School District v. Gobitis*. Only Harlan Fiske Stone dissented.[6]

Justice Felix Frankfurter, a former Harvard professor of law who had assisted in the shaping of the Social Security Act and national legislation regulating public utilities, wrote for the Court. An Austrian immigrant of Jewish descent, Frankfurter loved his adopted country passionately and placed great store in its democratic processes. Although concerned for the exploited and closely associated with liberal causes, he believed in a meritocracy and had great "faith in . . . the good sense . . . and . . . benevolence of the country's old elite," men such as Oliver Wendell Holmes, Jr., and Franklin D. Roosevelt. He had, above all, a "romantic attachment to something called the rule of law" and had tended to view his appointment to the Court in 1937 as an opportunity to use his skills in "artful balancing" and to "educate" other justices and the public at large.[7]

Frankfurter had written the *Gobitis* opinion, seeing it as a means of establishing leadership on the Court. The case, he asserted, presented a conflict between "two rights," the right of the individual to freedom of conscience and that of the community to encourage national security through patriotic symbols. No right was absolute, he stated, and the need for national unity was a legitimate concern, especially in light of the war in Europe. Contending that religious *belief* was guaranteed, but that a distinction existed between *conviction* and the *action* such scruples might inspire, he maintained that freedom of conscience did not relieve the individual from public duty. Although the justices might personally think the required ceremony unwise, the Court must act with judicial restraint with regard to the decision of the elected school officials, to whom "no less than the courts . . . the guardianship of deeply-cherished liberties" was committed. It was not up to the Court, he stated, to become "the school board of the country."[8]

The votes of Chief Justice Hughes and Justices James McReynolds and Stanley Reed were not surprising. Hughes had opened debate in the conference with an opinion favoring the school board on grounds of judicial restraint. McReynolds, whose appointment dated to 1914, was a known conservative. Reed of Kentucky, who had joined the high bench as a Roosevelt appointee in 1938, had defended New Deal legislation before the Court as solicitor general but was considered generally moderate to conservative on issues of individual rights. Thus his ballot for the compulsory salute did not raise a stir.[9]

The vote of Owen Roberts, while at first glance surprising, was not truly startling. Although earlier that year he had written for a unanimous Court in the pro-Witness case, *Cantwell*, by 1940 Roberts had come to be considered somewhat unpredictable. His mercurial record in reversing himself during Roosevelt's attempt to pack the Court in 1937 had identified him to critics as the "switch in time that saved nine" and to defenders as an independent thinker.[10]

But Frankfurter's opinion and the supporting votes of Justices Hugo Black, William O. Douglas, and Frank Murphy brought an uproar in the liberal community and distress to the Jehovah's Witnesses. *Gobitis* represented a setback, particularly in light of the one-sided vote. Black, Roosevelt's first nominee, had been known to support the New Deal even to the point of backing the president's Court-packing effort. Once on the Court, he had quickly established himself as a champion of personal liberty, diminishing fears spawned by his earlier political ties with the Ku Klux Klan. Although Black had not endorsed Stone's footnote four formula, thinking that it allowed too much judicial discretion, he had moved toward much the same end by advocating a "return to first principles in order to fashion broadly based new constitutional interpretations." Like other liberal justices, he was willing to assume an activist role in protecting equality and personal liberty from state action, but he felt such interpretations must be justified by some specific constitutional guidelines. He argued instead that the framers of the Fourteenth Amendment had intended the measure to guarantee equal protection of the laws and apply all of the protections of the Bill of Rights.[11]

Douglas and Murphy also had been expected to vote in support of the First Amendment rights. Douglas, who had worked his way through Columbia Law School, taught at Yale, and headed the Securities and Exchange Commission, had been in 1939 Roosevelt's fourth appointee to the high court. Because in his first year as a justice he had voted frequently in First Amendment cases to uphold free expression, his vote against Gobitis shocked liberals. Frank Murphy of Michigan, who had joined the Court only a few months before the *Gobitis* decision, had been well identified as a "fervent libertarian evangelist." A Roman Catholic committed seriously to the principle of religious freedom, he had championed the cause of minorities through membership in the American Civil Liberties Union and the National Association for the Advancement of Colored People and had attempted to strengthen civil liberties during his tenure as Roosevelt's attorney general. Uncomfortable and a bit uncertain as the freshman member of the high bench, however, he was awed by the arguments of Frankfurter and Hughes regarding the importance of local autonomy and the need for judicial restraint. Thus, he, too, voted against Gobitis.[12] The decision did not augur well for Jones's case.

Stone's powerful dissent in *Gobitis* declared that patriotism could not be coerced and that the very substance of liberty was "the freedom of the individual from compulsion as to what he shall think and what he shall say, at least where the compulsion is to bear false witness against his religion." The author of footnote four argued that the Court should guard the rights of "a politically helpless minority" to "freedom of mind and spirit." Stone was disappointed that he could not win any other justices to the cause but even more distressed by the expression of "religious bigotry and fanatical, unthinking patriotism" that followed in the wake of the decision.[13]

The expulsion of Witness children from public schools became commonplace, and efforts to force individual Witnesses to salute the flag abounded. Vigilantes undertook massive assaults on Witnesses throughout the land, burning their homes, destroying their literature, and physically abusing them, often encouraged or at least overlooked by law enforcement officials. Rosco Jones was beaten in LaGrange, Georgia, during this period, and Grace Marsh's son, Harold, was expelled from school in Mississippi. Frequently, communities that had previously ignored the Witnesses began to pass restrictive ordinances or to enforce existing ones selectively. But the Witnesses persisted. Within the next two years the U.S. Supreme Court ruled that the state might require a permit for parades and upheld the conviction of a Witness who had used "fighting words" against a city marshal.[14]

In 1941, while Jones readied his U.S. Supreme Court certiorari petition, key changes in personnel occurred in the high tribunal. The chief justice, Charles Evans Hughes, retired from the Court, and Roosevelt elevated Stone to the leader's position. He then appointed Robert H. Jackson, who had succeeded Frank Murphy as attorney general, to fill the vacancy. Jackson was a complex personality, whose emphasis on individual liberty presented him with a paradox in judging whether the Witnesses' rights were infringed by societal demands. The justice valued freedom for the "inner self," prizing the singularity of the individual over the class or group. A person should have the right to be left alone, to retreat unto himself or herself without being roused to the door by an uninvited evangelist, he maintained. When Witnesses' proselytizing invaded the privacy of others, that religious expression should yield, he asserted. Yet the question of the Witnesses' rights was complex, not limited to proselytizing, as the flag salute controversy demonstrated. Ultimately, Jackson would work to resolve the dilemma created by the public demand for a ceremony that violated the Witness children's "inner selves."[15] James McReynolds also retired in 1941, and the president named James Byrnes of South Carolina to that position. Byrnes was conservative on social issues.

The Court that agreed to hear *Jones v. Opelika* in 1942, then, consisted of predominantly Protestant white males, with one Jew (whose roots were ethnic rather than religious) and one practicing Roman Catholic. Six identified themselves as Democrats, two as Republicans, and one as Independent (Frankfurter). Roosevelt had appointed all but the two Republicans and had elevated one of them to be the chief justice. The jurists ranged in age from forty-four (Douglas) to seventy (Stone), with the average over fifty-seven. Regardless of the statistics, the Court consisted of strong, often competing characters. Stone presided under the belief that the justices should express themselves freely, and they did. Dissension became the order of the day.[16]

Such an array of powerful personalities demanded much of the attorneys who argued cases before the Court. When the Watch Tower Bible and Tract Society decided to carry Rosco Jones's case to the summit, it brought out its heavy artillery, Joseph W. Rutherford and Hayden Covington. Judge Rutherford's was the first signature as counsel for Jones in July 1941, but Covington was the primary attorney. By the time the case reached oral argument in February 1942, Rutherford was dead. Through haranguing, prodding, and inspiring, he had built in his followers an "iron-like character" that allowed them to endure the persecutions of the 1930s and 1940s. In spite of the tension heightened by World War II and the aftermath of *Gobitis*, the Witnesses' cause did not falter. By the time of Rutherford's death, the Watch Tower Society had become organized to the point that a combination of personalities could cooperate in governing and assure that no internecine struggle weakened the ranks as they prepared for Armageddon. The governing troika consisted of the dynamic Covington; a quiet but skillful organizer, Nathan Knorr; and a biblical scholar, Frederick William Franz.[17]

Knorr had earlier been designated the judge's hand-picked successor. By the time of his graduation from high school in 1923, after reading the Watchtower literature, Knorr had converted from the Reformed Church in his hometown of Bethlehem, Pennsylvania, to the Witnesses. Soon thereafter, he had been invited to live at Brooklyn Bethel with the society's leadership. Upon assuming the presidency of the society in 1942, he emphasized loyalty to the organization above that of any personality and instituted the policy of anonymous authorship for all Watchtower publications. He established theocratic ministry schools to prepare Witnesses who were "capable of doing their own talking" in door-to-door canvassing. He also founded Gilead, an international training center— which Rosco and Thelma Jones would attend in 1955—in South Lansing, New York. Less concerned with doctrine, he left dogma to Frederick William Franz, the society's most accomplished theologian, and the ongoing legal battle in the hands of the capable, committed, and charismatic Hayden Covington.[18]

The attorney from the Lone Star State was himself a star. Born in Hopkins County, Texas, in 1911, Covington had attended San Antonio Bar Association School of Law (later St. Mary's University), had been admitted to the Texas bar in 1933, and had become "a preaching Witness of Jehovah" the following year. During the next six years he had been admitted to the bar in New York and in ten U.S. district courts and ten U.S. courts of appeal. A man of immense energy and dedication, Covington exuded confidence, displayed daring, and embraced hard work. "To Hayden Covington, the tall, Texas tornado with sea-green eyes, the dignity of the United States Supreme Court" should not impede the legal process, an observer for *Newsweek* concluded in 1943 after seeing Covington in action. He described the attorney's performance as follows: "A precedent-buster extraordinary, the 6-foot lawyer erupted into the austere chamber in a bright green suit with padded shoulders and a red plaid tie. Locking his hands behind his back and bending his body into a right angle, or tucking his thumbs into his green vest and lifting his head, he roared, 'Jehovah's Witnesses are plain people who derive their authority to preach the truth from Jehovah himself, not from organized wealthy groups. . . . They don't preach in a dead language.'" The reporter concluded that Covington stood "flat on the Bill of Rights" in arguing his cases and sincerely believed that the issue was "mob rule versus constitutional rights for all citizens." [19]

His friend and fellow civil libertarian, Roger Baldwin of the ACLU, revealed much about the Witness attorney in a note to the counselor in the fall of 1942, following his reading of Covington's latest brief in *Jones v. Opelika*. In that brief Covington was pushing hard for the full incorporation of the First Amendment through the Fourteenth—placing its liberties in a position superior to the licensing power of municipalities—and almost daring the Court to see the justice of his cause and to respond righteously. Baldwin wrote,

My dear Covington:
That's one of the hottest briefs I reckon the Supreme Court has ever had before it.
If you don't get jailed for contempt, you may win.
Yours,[20]

Covington, one may speculate, was Rosco Jones's kind of man.

Covington's first task in petitioning the U.S. Supreme Court for a writ of certiorari to hear *Jones* was to try to overcome William Duke's argument that the high tribunal lacked jurisdiction because the judgment rendered by the Alabama Supreme Court was not final. Citing precedent, Duke maintained that the Court had "always made the face of the judgment the test of its finality, and refused to inquire whether, in case of a new trial, the defeated party would stand in a position to make a better case." The heart of the matter, Covington asserted, was the substantial federal question that the Opelika ordinance ran afoul of the due process clause of the Fourteenth Amendment of the U.S. Constitution. The Alabama Supreme Court had "disposed of the whole case on the merits and directed the Court of Appeals to enter a judgment affirming the Circuit Court's judgment. . . . and left nothing to the judicial discretion of that Court or of the trial court." Because the federal question had far-reaching implications, affecting "the fundamental personal and civil rights" of all Americans, he declared, timing was of vital importance, lest this "alien theory" (counter to a pristine interpretation of the Bill of Rights via the due process clause) take root, with the "devastating consequences" of reducing the guarantee of a free press to "the sole prerogative of the rich."[21]

After the Court granted certiorari on October 13, 1941, Duke filed the respondent's brief for the city of Opelika, again stressing that the nation's highest tribunal lacked jurisdiction because the matter had not been finally settled in the state. He declared that after Jones's conviction, Witness attorney Grover Powell had set forth some thirteen specifications of error in the petition to the Alabama Court of Appeals. The intermediate appellate court had considered, however, only the assigned errors that "charged the unconstitutionality of the Opelika ordinance." Nowhere did that court opinion refer to any of the other assignments. The Alabama Supreme Court, he added, had "neither considered nor denied any assignments of error other than those covered by the Court of Appeals," reversing the appellate judgment and remanding the case to the appeals court for further proceedings. Nothing in the record justified Covington's claim that the Alabama Supreme Court had disposed of the whole case on its merits, Duke argued, and under those circumstances, the "rule" that the U.S. Supreme Court might not "be called upon to review by piecemeal the action of a state court" applied, and "the judgment should be found to lack that finality that is a *sine qua non* of review."[22]

Covington, in Jones's reply brief, addressed Duke's argument, declaring that it was very hard to understand how the city could "seriously say that the judgment of the Alabama Supreme Court" was "not a final judgment." In the Alabama intermediate appellate court, Jones had "urged only two points supported by two specifications of error." No other stipulations were even considered. The Witness attorney then concluded, "On the strength of the Alabama Supreme Court's decision in the case at bar, the Alabama Court of Appeals *affirmed the conviction of Thelma Jones,* wife of the petitioner, *in a companion case* where the assignments of error and the facts were identical." It was thus clear, he argued, that the judgment in Rosco Jones's case was considered to be final. Despite Opelika's "tenacious efforts" to prevent the Court from considering the case's merits, clearly those efforts were only devices to obstruct the real question and should be repudiated as "frivolous and without merit."[23]

Despite Covington's efforts, however, Duke and the city of Opelika prevailed on the issue of jurisdiction. The Court heard arguments on February 5, 1942, and in a per curiam opinion four days later ordered the writ dismissed "for want of final judgment." Covington began the procedures required to return Jones's case to the U.S. Supreme Court docket. He applied for additional time in which to file a motion for rehearing to allow Jones to petition the Alabama Supreme Court once more. The Court granted the extension, and in the month from March 5 to April 5, 1942, the state courts delivered final judgments against Jones, affirming the trial court ruling.[24]

On April 25, Covington then filed a supplemental transcript of the Alabama judicial proceedings with the clerk of the U.S. Supreme Court, asking that the court restore Rosco Jones's cause to the docket. He requested that the briefs and argument previously submitted, except for those portions pertaining to the jurisdictional question, be continued in the cause. At that point the U.S. Supreme Court agreed to reconsider, addressing itself to the federal questions presented.[25]

During the fall and winter of 1941–1942, between the October 1941 grant of certiorari and the February 1942 dismissal of *Jones,* the Watch Tower Bible and Tract Society built allies. The ACLU, guardian of individual liberties, had supported the Witnesses in *Gobitis* and publicized the persecution of the Witnesses in 1941. As Rosco and Thelma Jones prepared to leave Columbus, Georgia, the society corresponded with Clifford Forster of the ACLU regarding the Union's interest in *Jones* and other Jehovah's Witnesses' First Amendment cases. Forster had contacted Osmond Fraenkel, a member of the New York firm of Goldsmith, Jackson, & Brock, who recommended that the Union file an amicus curiae (friend of the court) brief in Rosco Jones's case. The ACLU Board of Directors in New York met early in December and agreed to participate. Fraenkel would compose and sign the brief. During the remainder of December 1941 and in early January 1942 extensive correspondence to coordinate ACLU efforts with those of the Watch Tower Society transpired; the ACLU also exchanged several letters involving legal courtesies with William Duke and his assisting counsel in Washington, D.C., Hogan & Hartson.[26]

The ACLU made efforts to strengthen its brief by gaining the endorsement of prominent Alabamians. On December 8, 1941—the day after Rosco and Thelma Jones had moved to LaGrange, Georgia—the ACLU sent inquiries of possible support to two established Alabama lawyers, Douglas Arant and James A. Simpson. Arant, a recognized Birmingham attorney, had risen from rural poverty and retained a sense of empathy with the underdog. He chaired the Special Committee on the Bill of Rights of the American Bar Association in 1941, a panel that had presented an amicus brief for the Witnesses in *Gobitis* the previous year. Although eventually his committee decided to concentrate its strength by not joining the *Jones* case, Arant was sympathetic to the suit.[27]

Simpson's role is more complex. Raised in Tennessee by a populist father with socialist sympathies, he had reacted against government programs and become a staunch advocate of laissez-faire. He became the esteemed counsel of Birmingham industrialists, was active in state politics, and served in 1941 in the Alabama legislature. He despised the New Deal, Hugo Black, and Lister Hill and would later run a racist campaign against Hill. As late as 1941–1942, however, this champion of coal and

steel barons apparently retained a streak of idealism and/or independence. In the 1920s he had publicly stated that he desired to represent
"white and black, Jew and Gentile," and had opposed the Ku Klux Klan.
In the 1930s he had led a fight against courthouse politics in Alabama
and had championed a state merit system. By the early 1940s his opposition to the Klan and the courthouse politicians and his antipathy for
Franklin D. Roosevelt merged as both local politicos and Klansmen were
attracted to Roosevelt's economic programs.[28]

Simpson had built an attitude of autonomy, which may have prompted
his willingness to consider the ACLU request. At any rate, he responded
positively within two weeks, agreeing to join the brief. Arant was "de-
lighted" with Simpson's decision and wrote to the ACLU suggesting, "It
would be a very fine thing if Mr. Simpson could be induced to make an
oral argument in behalf of the petitioner in the Opelika case." On January 19, 1942, as the date for oral arguments approached, Forster of
ACLU wired Covington, asking if he would be willing to give part of the
time for oral argument to Simpson or Fraenkel. When the case was
argued on February 5, however, Covington decided that he should use
the full time. By that date Rutherford had died. Although Covington
elicited the support of the ACLU, he apparently felt that Rutherford had
entrusted him full responsibility for the case.[29]

The February hearing turned out to be a false start, but it laid the
groundwork for a later consideration on the merits of the case. Covington chose to subordinate all the other issues to the broadest and most
essential to the Witness point of view—those urged as the grounds for
overturning Jones's conviction in the Alabama Court of Appeals—the
First Amendment freedoms for press and religion. Duke and associates
stressed that the ordinance neither deliberately nor inadvertently restricted freedom of religion or of press. The true purpose and significance
of the ordinance, Duke declared, was to establish "a plain, ordinary
municipal business privilege or license tax similar to those employed in
numerous communities throughout the country." When the U.S. Supreme Court reexamined the case in June 1942, it considered these critical issues.[30]

Covington, seeking the high court's confirmation of his expanded
interpretation of the First Amendment, skillfully argued that Jones and

other Witnesses expected nothing more than the liberty granted by the nation's founders. Taking the offensive as the protector of the Bill of Rights, the Witness attorney charged that the Alabama Supreme Court had in effect placed an alien amendment upon the nation's constitution. It had grossly misconstrued and warped the U.S. Supreme Court's opinions, he asserted. *Cox v. New Hampshire,* relied upon by the Alabama tribunal, had upheld the power of a municipality to license a parade for purpose of regulating the use of the streets, not the licensing or taxing of the distribution of literature. Similarly, Alabama's high court had misread the action of the U.S. Supreme Court in denying the Witness petition for certiorari in *Manchester v. Leiby,* in which Manchester had required a badge of identification for Witnesses.[31] Such a denial allowed the decision of the U.S. First Circuit Court of Appeals to stand but did not amount to an endorsement, Covington observed. Thus the Alabama court had assumed a pattern of restricting the Witnesses that the U.S. Supreme Court had not intended. The "pernicious doctrine" of the Alabama Supreme Court held, he argued, "that constitutionally secured 'free press' extends only to 'free distribution' (or 'gift') of literature." Such an interpretation would sound the "death toll" to freedom of press, rendering it a privilege only of the wealthy.[32]

The ordinance was not, he insisted, a general law for revenue, but a means of controlling ideas under the *guise of a tax.* Furthermore, the arbitrary power to revoke a license without notice was tantamount to *prior censorship.* "No doubt the complaint of some residents annoyed" by Jones's pamphlets "would be considered by the commissioners as ample reason for denial of license." The state was attempting "under the guise of 'reasonable police protection' [to] chisel off" the precious First Amendment liberties by subjecting them to license. Streets were a "natural place" for the dissemination of ideas. Yet, under the Opelika ordinance a "modern-day Tom Paine or John Milton could not safely function."[33]

The pamphlets offered by Rosco Jones, *Face the Facts* and *Fascism or Freedom,* contained speeches delivered by Judge Rutherford in 1938 in London and New York, the fiery counselor explained. They dealt with the "monstrosity of dictatorial, totalitarian rule," criticized the pope's dealings with the Fascist-Nazi "monstrosity," and observed that

Jehovah's Witnesses continued to suffer "great persecutions in all nations, especially where that religious system which has lined up with Fascists, Nazis and other totalitarians [including Communists] exercises control." The nonpolitical Witnesses preached against all such tyrants, exposing the religious hierarchy as part of the unholy combination. In response, the religious authorities persecuted them in all lands, including the United States. But the Witnesses were not alone in being threatened, for their persecution was but a first step toward taking away the rights and liberties from all the rest of the American people," Covington declared.[34]

Rosco Jones, the Witness attorney explained, was an ordained minister distributing literature "as a substitute for talking, or sermons." He was following the example of Jesus, who told his disciples, "Go ye into all the world, and preach the gospel to every creature [Mark 16:15]." For, Covington elaborated, "He went throughout every city and village teaching and preaching the Kingdom of God (Mark 6:6; Luke 8:1)." The worship of Almighty God was a *right, not a privilege* to be licensed by the city, the attorney emphasized. It was noteworthy that the ordinance did not list the occupation of minister and expressly exempted "agents selling Bibles." The city of Opelika had no more power to require Jones to register for a permit than it would have to compel the accepted clergy of the municipality to register before delivering their sermons. Other religious organizations had never been forced to obtain licenses; Jones, Covington asserted, was singled out *because of the manner of his worship*. But, as the Court had rightly stated in 1871, "The law knows no heresy, and is committed to the support of no dogma, the establishment of no sect." Opelika had conceded that Jones's behavior did not threaten morals, personal rights, or the safety of the state, Covington reminded the Court. To construe the ordinance, then, as aimed at one *certain* minister—that is, a Jehovah's Witness—was to authorize "an unlawful joinder of 'state and church.' "[35]

The powerful Texan, remembering the persecution of Rosco and Thelma Jones and other "plain people," made an appeal to the better instincts of the justices, concluding with the plea that the Court rise above "public clamor . . . or personal popularity and interpret the law fearlessly and impartially so as to promote justice." The foundation of democracy was "an informed, educated, and intelligent citizenry," he stressed, and "an unsubsidized press" was essential. Recent persecutions and prosecutions of the Witnesses threatened the essence of the nation as the "land of the free and the home of the brave." Many lower courts had succumbed to "sophistry and fine reasoning," condoning judgments that denied freedom of conscience, of press, and of speech, "under the pretext" of "safeguarding the national defense." Oblivious to the final outcome, anxious members of the judicial structure had "unwittingly dragged . . . this nation closer to totalitarianism." He ended with the entreaty, "In this hour of emergency . . . [let the courts recognize] a *higher* duty to scrutinize . . . reasons adroitly advanced in support of *regulation.* . . . Here, then, let deepest consideration be given to the *effect* of the challenged ordinance rather than merely to the cold black and white text of its provisions."[36]

The amicus brief filed by the ACLU echoed Covington's charge that the license ordinance posed a threat to the dissemination of ideas. As the Court had previously held that restrictions might "not be imposed upon the free distribution of expression of opinion on the public streets," the ACLU stated, "the question to be decided here is whether such restrictions can be imposed because a price is demanded." The decisive factor formerly guiding the Court, the ACLU reasoned, had been the significance of an open market for opinion and information, for it had long recognized the historical importance of pamphlets. Yet the need for such brochures was even greater in modern society because technology had made the conventional media—newspapers and radio—more expensive. Enforcement of the Opelika ordinance would seriously hinder the circulation of ideas, both because the licenses were costly and because it left unanswered the question of whether Witnesses would have been expected to pay as a book agent or as a transient agent. Little doubt existed that if many communities imposed fees similar to those of Opelika the work of itinerant evangelists "would become impossible." Furthermore, communities that disapproved of the activities could "prevent them altogether, either by delaying granting licenses . . . or by revoking them without notice."[37]

The ACLU brief also maintained that the Alabama Supreme Court's reliance upon *Manchester v. Leiby* was invalid, pointing to distinctions between the requirements upheld in *Manchester* and those imposed by the Opelika ordinance. In Manchester an identification badge only was required for fifty cents, refundable when the identifying symbol was relinquished. Furthermore, the Opelika requirement as applied to Jones in actuality did not deal with regulating the use of the streets, for Jones was not positioned in one place for the purpose of establishing a business; thus the edict served no legitimate purpose and should be voided.[38]

Covington and the ACLU were creating a monster out of thin air, the city of Opelika argued. The heart of the matter was really quite simple— the ordinance was a valid exercise of the municipality's taxing and police powers. The law did not violate the First Amendment protections, for neither in intent nor in reality did it prohibit Jones "from distributing literature pertaining to religious or any other subject." It was, Duke reiterated, "a plain, ordinary municipal business privilege or license tax . . . free of any of the pernicious characteristics attributed to it" by the Witnesses. Certainly, the regulation in no way established prior censorship, for the only requirement for issuing a license was payment of the stipulated fee. *Had Jones paid the book agent's fee, "he would unquestionably have received an annual license," for the "plain language" of the statute left the city no "authority to refuse . . . upon tender of the specified fee."* The Opelika ordinance should be clearly distinguished from that overturned in *Lovell v. Griffin,* Duke insisted. The latter statute had affirmatively prohibited the distributing of literature unless the city manager granted specific permission. As used in *Griffin,* the "term ["license"] connoted prior censorship, examination of material and ultimate permission to distribute based thereon," while as used in *Opelika,* its primary purpose was to designate an occupational license tax, Duke declared.[39]

The city of Opelika also challenged Jones's assertion that he had sought only "contributions," stressing that Jones's conviction had been based upon the arresting officer's testimony that he had offered the literature for sale. The pamphlets, Duke averred, presented the religious interpretation of the Jehovah's Witnesses but "could not be considered as a Bible and thus within the exception stated in the ordinance." While the city was in accord with the principles of the First Amendment, Duke called attention to another principle that the Court had historically upheld: "In our peculiar dual form of government nothing is more fundamental than the full power of the State to order its own affairs and govern its own people."[40]

Quoting Justice Benjamin Cardozo, Duke declared that "the right of private judgment has never yet been so exalted above the powers . . . of government" that the citizen for reasons of conscience may refuse to pay taxes toward a cause of which he disapproves. "One who is a martyr to a principle" may act in error and "does not prove by his martyrdom that he has kept within the law," he stated. The all-inclusive nature of the ordinance, Duke emphasized, confirmed the intent of the law to levy a privilege tax on all who engaged in commerce, not to restrain the First Amendment freedoms. Jones was convicted not for religious practices, Duke asserted, but because he sold literature "without first having paid the tax." The intemperate language of the Witnesses' counsel should not be allowed to serve as a smokescreen to the only legitimate question, "the right of any community to assess and collect . . . revenue needed to carry on the functions and duties of government."[41]

Persons engaged in religious or press activities were not exempted per se by the First Amendment from the "normal tax and regulatory burdens incident to orderly and successful government." The Witnesses' reliance on *Grosjean v. American Press Company*[42] failed, Duke stated. In that case the Court overruled a device, in the guise of a tax, aimed solely at large newspapers and deliberately calculated to limit the circulation of public information, but in *Jones* the issue was an ordinary business tax. Why, Duke asked in effect, should Rosco Jones receive privileged treatment? Finally, the city linked *Jones* with a recent case from Arkansas in which the U.S. Supreme Court had denied certiorari, *Coyle v. City of Fort Smith*. In both cases city commercial ordinances had been applied to Jehovah's Witnesses engaged in distributing religious literature.[43]

The argument of Duke for the city of Opelika, Covington retorted, was fatally flawed. Duke had, he asserted, "fallen into the same pit of error as did the trial court and the Alabama Supreme Court." The mistake, he explained, stemmed from "an unsuccessful attempt to jump the broad gap" between legitimate police power to tax and to regulate commerce and the First Amendment's clear prohibition against abridging the "activity of distributing . . . literature containing information or opinion." The inviting and accepting of money donations *to assist the work* did not change the nature of the case. Although at the trial in the Alabama Fifth Circuit Court Opelika had admitted that Jones was a minister, the city had now shifted its position, adopting a "narrow-gauge, restricted view of what constitutes an 'ordained minister' and 'preaching the gospel.'" In insisting that Jones was engaging in "commercial" activity, the city resisted the plain fact that Jones's taking of contributions was "wholly *incidental*" to his primary purpose of preaching the gospel.[44]

On June 8, 1942, the U.S. Supreme Court rendered its decision. Linking *Jones v. Opelika* with two similar cases, the Court ruled against Rosco Jones and the other Witnesses in a closely divided judgment. Justices Byrnes, Frankfurter, Jackson, Reed, and Roberts constituted the majority; the chief justice, Stone—now joined by Justices Black, Douglas, and Murphy—stood in opposition. Justice Reed wrote for the Court. Maintaining that the petitioning Witnesses had not challenged the amount of the fees or advanced a claim that the sums required served as a "substantial clog" upon their activities, the Court would not consider that issue. At any rate, "the same sources" that then supplied funds "to meet whatever deficit" individual Witnesses experienced could presumably also pay any license fee. "The sole constitutional question considered is whether a nondiscriminatory license fee, presumably appropriate in amount, may be imposed upon these activities," Reed declared.[45]

Although personal liberties beyond the reach of the government did exist, those rights covered by the First Amendment to the U.S. Constitution had "a more earthy quality" and were "not absolutes to be exercised independently of other" constitutional provisions. The Court could properly adjudge the action done "under color of a constitutional right . . . to determine whether the claimed right" was limited by other considerations "equally precious," such as the state's right under its reserved powers to "ensure orderly living." "The task of reconcilement" was made more difficult by "the tendency to accept as dominant any . . . claim of interference with the practice of religion or the spread of ideas." But although mankind's "mind and spirit" could "remain forever free," the expressions of that freedom could be regulated as to "times, places, and methods." Unlike the ordinances overruled in *Lovell, Schneider,* and *Cantwell* that absolutely limited free expression, those in question in

Jones regulated operations that were "incidental to the exercise of religion" in a nondiscriminatory manner. The Court had interdicted "prohibition and abridgement" of First Amendment liberty, "not taxation," Reed asserted.[46]

Although the Witnesses might need financial support, if they chose to use commercial methods, vending their "tracts as a source of funds, the financial aspects of their transactions need not be wholly disregarded." The state was entitled to "charge reasonable fees for the privilege of canvassing," Reed stated. The activities involved were not "religious rites," and the funds involved were not "free will offerings." A local community might voluntarily allow "the poor and weak to draw support from the petty sales of religious books" without a charge for the use of the municipality's services, but the First Amendment did not demand such an exemption. The provision of the Opelika ordinance that allowed revocation need not be considered, the justice observed, for Jones had no standing to raise that point, since there had "been neither application for nor revocation of a license. The complaint was bottomed on sales without a license."[47]

Stone's dissent strongly attacked Reed's reasoning. The Opelika ordinance, he declared, was an even "more callous disregard" of the First Amendment right of free speech and press than that in *Lovell*. He elaborated: "There at least the defendant might have been given a license if he had applied for it [and] . . . not been compelled to pay . . . for a license to exercise the privilege of free speech. . . . Jones was prohibited from distributing his pamphlets at all unless he paid in advance a year's tax . . . and subjected himself to termination of the license without cause, notice or hearing, at the will of city officials." History showed that the First Amendment had been aimed at such unrestricted power. It did not matter that Jones had not applied for a license, for the ordinance was "void on its face." Furthermore, the ordinance could not be saved by the separability clause when the state court had not distinguished the constitutional parts from those that were invalid.[48]

Stone also addressed questions that had "been studiously left unanswered by the opinion of the Court," notably that the cumulative effect of such fees throughout the land would prove a substantial clog to the dissemination of ideas. Referring to the taxes as "fees" did not disguise the essential issue, for the ordinances intended the sums as taxes, not nominal fees for a regulatory license aimed at protecting "the good order of the community." The only regulatory effect was to limit or deny publication. To justify the taxes on the grounds that they were "nondiscriminatory" was to ignore the preferred position of the First Amendment and its prohibition of *all* laws abridging freedom of press or religion. "In its potency as a prior restraint on publication, the flat license tax falls short only of outright censorship or suppression. The more humble and needy the cause, the more effective is the suppression." Justices Black, Douglas, and Murphy joined Stone's opinion.[49]

Justice Murphy also dissented, with Black, Douglas, and Stone concurring in that opinion. His argument focused on the fact that the Witnesses were motivated by religious, not commercial, purposes and that the First Amendment thus shielded them. Unfairly, they had been singled out from more orthodox ministers. Their behavior posed no threat to society; but like dissentient groups in the American colonies, their ideas were unpopular because they "ran counter to the established notions of the community." Like Stone, Murphy found the amount of the taxes oppressive, but he objected more strenuously to the very concept of taxing the expression of ideas. The attempt of the majority to isolate freedom of thought rang false, he argued, for "even an aggressive mind is of no missionary value unless there is . . . freedom to communicate its message to others." And freedom must not be limited to those "who can distribute their broadsides without charge." If the Court should err in evaluating claims of freedom of expression, he declared, it was "far better that it err in being overprotective of these precious rights."[50]

Even more powerful than the dissents of Stone or Murphy, however, was the one-paragraph joint dissent of Black, Douglas, and Murphy. In a startling departure from customary procedures, the three went beyond disagreeing with the majority in *Jones* to recant their earlier positions in *Gobitis*. It read:

> The opinion of this Court sanctions a device which . . . tends to suppress the free exercise of a religion practiced by a minority group. This is but another step in the direction . . . *Gobitis* . . . took against the same religious minority and is a logical extension of the principles upon which that

decision rested. Since we joined in . . . [that opinion], we think it is an appropriate occasion to state that we now believe that it was also wrongly decided. Certainly our . . . government . . . has a high responsibility to accommodate itself to the religious views of minorities, however unpopular and unorthodox. . . . The First Amendment does not put the right freely to exercise religion in a subordinate position. We fear, however, that the opinion in this and in the *Gobitis* case do exactly that.[51]

The dramatic statement by the three justices reflected much about the dynamics of the Court in 1942. Reed's opinion clearly showed the Frankfurter influence. The former Harvard professor had tended to consider the younger justices his pupils and to cultivate them. His brilliance and his energetic personality had by 1940 vaulted him into a leadership role with a largely new Court; he had seen the *Gobitis* case as an opportunity to influence the Court, molding it to his concept of legislative supremacy and judicial restraint. His concept of personal liberties rested in English common law; the key to these rights in state and local communities was the due process clause of the Fourteenth Amendment, and such rights were not absolute. Hugo Black, who seemed to Frankfurter rash and less than scholarly at times, resisted the professor's interpretation, however, maintaining that the First Amendment meant to carry individual liberty farther than English common law, that freedom of expression was the essential matrix of American democracy. Because Black argued that the Fourteenth Amendment incorporated the First Amendment, its full guarantees should apply at the state as well as the national level.[52]

In 1940–1941 Black became a counterforce to Frankfurter in First Amendment interpretation, and Douglas and Murphy moved toward Black's pole. The U.S. entry into World War II heightened awareness of the relationship of Nazi-Fascist doctrines and the threats to individual expression. Many liberals, particularly in the press, were highly critical of *Gobitis* as tending toward Hitler-like tactics, and the overwhelming sentiment in the law journals was unfavorable.[53]

By June 8, 1942, when *Jones v. Opelika* was decided, Frankfurter faced a rebellion. He was furious and felt betrayed. Among his papers is the draft opinion of the three mutineers' dissenting opinion. Across it Frankfurter had written, "This was circulated on Saturday, May 30,

1942. It was the first information that I had . . . that the *Gobitis* case would be raised. That case was *not* challenged in the argument and its relevance to these cases . . . never discussed or alluded to in conference." He nursed his wounds not very quietly and continued to house varying degrees of anger toward the rebels for years.[54]

The other judicial response of interest, particularly in light of the justice's later role in reversing *Gobitis,* was that of Robert Jackson. In a concurring opinion that he wrote but did not deliver, he elaborated on his problems with the Witnesses. He declined to take a stand for or against *Gobitis,* since he had not been on the Court at the time of the decision. In the licensing case of Rosco Jones, however, he found the fundamental issue to be not whether one might believe, print, or say what he wished, but "whether there [were] premises . . . in which it [was] inappropriate for the exercise of such a right." In modern society persons do not live in isolation, he emphasized, and as a result, "rights meet each other and conflict." The First Amendment rights had to be balanced against the right to be let alone. If one entered the open door of a church and then attempted to disrupt the service, he would assuredly abuse the rights of those assembled. Logically, then, did the evangelist who intruded into the sanctuary of one's doorstep not offend the right of the householder to privacy? Might not one "withdraw from the . . . public to his own home?" he asked. There one's seclusion should not be hostage to uninvited summons to his door that place upon him "the burden of granting or refusing permission to play phonograph records" or to solicit or to give arguments.[55]

If an individual may oust an intruder from his premises, Jackson reasoned, why can he not speak through his elected officials to limit or to "withdraw altogether the privilege of soliciting?" Even in ordinances limiting the use of the public streets Jackson saw no immediate threat to civil liberties. But, he added, if time should prove that he had been wrong in accepting the ordinances, he would change his views unhesitatingly. In that circumstance, he satirically stated, "I shall prove that I am right by declaring that I have theretofore been wrong. I would not be without precedent."[56]

The press did not share Jackson's private joke. Almost unanimously journalists condemned the decision and praised the three new dissenters as well as Stone. *Time* referred to *Jones* as an "ominous decision," noting that its ramifications for First Amendment freedoms reached far beyond the "small, freakish religious sect." *Collier's* saw the threat to freedom of religion and press as "real and urgent." The *Philadelphia Presbyterian Guardian* observed, "Our lot will not be a happy one if our freedom to propagate our faith can be limited by city councils." The *Watchman Examiner,* a New York Baptist journal, declared that "the sincerity with which we uphold the Bill of Rights is tested by the treatment" accorded the Witnesses. The *Chicago Daily News* noted the parallel of the license fee to the colonial stamp tax, and columnist Samuel Grafton declared, "Under this doctrine, only the unused mind is free. . . . no one may abridge the right of free press, except against persons trying to use it." The dissenters had read history, according to the *Chicago Daily Tribune,* and understood that licensing was "the classic method of repression." In Indiana the *South Bend Tribune* wrote that "power to license is power to destroy," and the *New York Daily News* criticized the "vague, finespun, and hairsplitting" majority opinion.[57]

The chorus swelled—from Boston, Richmond, Hartford, Atlanta, even Montgomery, Alabama—as the media echoed the same theme. "Would the twelve fishermen of Galilee" have had the money required for a license? How could the nation justify fighting for the "four freedoms" while denying at least two of them? Had the First Amendment become a hollow shell? "The really shocking news" came not from Opelika but from Washington, D.C. In Opelika, Alabama, the *Daily News* reported the decision with an Associated Press account but no editorial, as did the *Birmingham Age-Herald.* The *Birmingham News* carried an editorial to the effect that the Court was walking a "thin line." Occasionally, an editorial gave faint praise, as did Florida's *Jacksonville Journal* in commenting that split decisions continued whether liberals or conservatives were on the Court and that that fact reinforced the soundness of the theory that the body should not be a superlegislature.[58]

Reaction from the average citizen is harder to gauge; no evidence of scientific polling on the issue exists, and those persons who wrote to the justices were few in number and probably not "average." Large-scale canvassing by the Witnesses in certain communities increased public awareness, but reactions varied, as the Joneses' and Marsh's divergent experiences indicated. Witness literature and statements made by Witnesses in interviews with me indicate a widespread belief among Witnesses that the clergy, particularly Roman Catholic and Baptist, initiated unfavorable community reaction, but hard proof is lacking. The violence following *Gobitis,* documented by independent sources, clearly revealed an intense hostility toward the sect, but savage behavior occurred primarily in scattered rural areas and resulted more from jingoism than from religious bigotry. By June 1942 the media response heightened public consciousness of the Witnesses' presence and the relationship of their activities to the First Amendment guarantees. The press also pricked the nation's conscience regarding the abuse of Witnesses, particularly as the official organs of all major denominations began to speak out against the most extreme expressions of intolerance.[59]

The impact of the media campaign is evident in mail received by members of the U.S. Supreme Court. Letters to the justices, directed primarily to the dissenters, were predictably varied—full of earnest praise or venomous invective. "Just another boy who is glad to be in camp to fight for his country" wrote to Justice Douglas to "wisen up." The serviceman suggested in an unsigned typewritten letter that the four dissenters resign to allow "four true americans [*sic*]" to replace them, that the "fifth column" Witnesses were "taking the United States Government for a sucker" and that the Bill of Rights was "outmoded."[60] A woman from Orange, California, on the other hand, declared in a handwritten signed note, "I am glad a few men have the courage to uphold our Bill of Rights. . . . What's the good of fighting over the . . . world to establish the freedoms to lose them here. I often shut the door on a . . . Witness but don't think it just to lose our liberties because of them. What's the trouble with the *five license judges?*"[61]

While Rosco and Thelma Jones stood their ground in LaGrange, Georgia, and Grace and Herbert Marsh and their son, Harold, shared the hazards of Witnessing in Mississippi, Hayden Covington and the ACLU leadership laid the foundations for still another hearing on the First Amendment Witness case before the U.S. Supreme Court. Covington filed a supplemental brief by late summer in 1942 and "additional suggestions and authorities" to support the petition, as well as the appendix summarizing the media reaction, in September. The ACLU concurrently prepared another amicus curiae brief, corresponding again with James A. Simpson of Alabama; sent letters seeking broader support to a number of religious groups, including the Salvation Army, the Seventh-Day Adventists, and the National Council of Churches; contacted Douglas Arant again regarding possible American Bar Association support; and communicated with the American Newspaper Publishers Association about possibly filing a brief. The attempts bore limited fruit. Although several groups expressed sympathy, only the Seventh-Day Adventists and the Newspaper Publishers Association agreed to file amici briefs.[62]

The Witnesses' supplemental brief began on a conciliatory note but then argued unyieldingly and bluntly the righteousness of their cause. Covington opened with a statement that "the disagreement between us is not as to fundamentals . . . but . . . [in] the application of the fundamental principles." By returning to fundamentals, they could, he reasoned, find the basis for unity. The Constitution rested in the sovereignty of the people, who, even as they created government, also restrained it. The power to tax, necessary to government, had been balanced with the limits of the First Amendment. For the power of government could, if unchecked, subvert the rights of the people. In 1819, he reminded the Court, Chief Justice John Marshall had spoken for a unanimous Court proclaiming, "the power to tax involves the power to destroy."[63]

The fiery attorney minced no words in attacking the Court's treatment of Witnesses as pariahs. The fallacious branding of Witnesses as "peddlers" or "hawkers" obscured the critical reality—that petitioners were "American citizens exercising the fundamental inherent rights" that could not be abridged under the First Amendment "regardless of what color of glasses any member of the court" used to view their activity. The justices could not "properly say" there was "no 'religious' question involved simply because the majority-opinion judges lacked judicial breadth of vision to discern it," Covington bitingly asserted. The attempt to distinguish the Witnesses from "recognized" clergy by designating their activities "commercial" failed, he charged, for the endeavors clearly paralleled the "free will offering" in a traditional church or Salvation

Army kettle. Jesus and his disciples had sought no license, nor could those modern followers do so without burdening the act of worship, he explained.[64]

The Court erred in attempting to distinguish freedom of mind and spirit from expression, for *"freedom of thought only* [was] a favorite Nazi tenet," not within the meaning of the First Amendment, Covington warned. He reiterated that free expression should not be proscribed because literature was not free, that taxation could substantially clog the flow of information, as historically England had used licensing and taxing to throttle the press. Nor could the Court justify its position by contending that the tax was acceptable because the amount had not been contested.[65]

Finally, the fervent counselor traced the problems that had followed the "stumbling stone" of *Gobitis,* "an instrument for evil in the hands of superpatriots or pseudo-patriots." Mississippi and Louisiana, he recounted, had recently passed laws forbidding the "possession and distribution of literature" explaining the Witnesses' reasons for not saluting the flag. The June 8 decision would, he feared, bring an even greater rash of persecutions, comparable to the oppression of the Witnesses in Germany. The Court had for 150 years "played a vital part in erecting the superstructure of the government and shielding constitutional liberties." In the desperate times of World War II, when the four freedoms were threatened from both within and outside, the Witnesses asked the Court only to grant the Witnesses the same right to First Amendment protections as other Americans. Rosco Jones and other Witnesses were loyal citizens who obeyed all laws that did not violate God's laws. "If the Court rules that any law of the legislature is supreme, over the Constitution and God's law, then we are without argument before this Court," he dramatically concluded, "and rest our case entirely with Almighty God, Jehovah, the Supreme and Final Judge."[66]

The new briefs by the ACLU addressed particularly Reed's statement to the effect that the Witnesses had not shown the *amount* of the tax to be burdensome. In a number of cases, business interests had not been required to prove that amounts exacted on commerce were unreasonable. Why, then, was that position not considered in this more important matter of the First Amendment freedoms? The ACLU suggested that the

Court had operated under misconceptions that the state was merely regulating the time and place and manner of distribution and that the operations were fund-raising activities "incidental" to Witness acts of worship. The Witnesses did not claim immunity from all taxation because of their activities, although universally legislatures had exempted their religious property; they did not contend that they should not pay those taxes, such as income tax, that fell but incidentally upon their functions. But a flat license tax, unlike ad valorem or income taxes, fell *directly* upon the religious functions. The Court's statement that the Constitution does not distinguish between various kinds of taxes was irrelevant, the argument stated, for the real issue was not the form of the tax, but its *effect*. Furthermore, ordinances such as those in question lent themselves to discriminatory enforcement and could become instruments for harassing unpopular political or religious minorities. The Court should be realistic and recognize that the *intent* of such ordinances was not regulation of time and place or to exact payment for services rendered but to interfere with the expression of ideas.[67]

The American Newspaper Publishers Association filed amici curiae briefs expressing concern for the precedent established by the June 1942 *Jones* decision. The fundamental question, whether the "legislature could require a license precedent to the exercise of the rights" of speech, press, and religion, had already been answered by the history underlying the First Amendment. The form or amount of the tax or the procedure under which a license was issued was immaterial; if the power existed "at all, the oppressiveness of the burden" could not "interdict the regulation." Therefore, the First Amendment placed freedom of press in a preferred position in order to assure its independence. "Any tax which fetters the press is unconstitutional," the association brief concluded. The publishers, in resisting impairment of the press, sought no special privilege for themselves, the briefs explained. Their motive, to the contrary, stemmed from their "solemn responsibility as trustees of the right of all . . . to open channels of inquiry and discussion on matters of public importance."[68]

The Seventh-Day Adventist argument hinged on the assertion that there was "no alternative" to the colporteur evangelical system "by which such large quantities of literature" could be "distributed at so low a cost." The trained itinerant supplied a "personal touch necessary to save souls." Providing a summary of the group's history, which called attention to the Adventist educational and medical contributions, the abstract emphasized the status of the denomination as "legitimate and orthodox." The upholding of the ordinance in question would result, nonetheless, in dire consequences for the faith, for "the principal field of colporteur activity" lay in small towns and rural areas, where the taxes in many instances would actually exceed the gross sales of religious literature. Enumerating the fees required in a large number of Arizona towns and relating the charge to the population of each municipality, the Adventist brief made plain "the crushing individual and aggregate effect" of the fees on colporteurs, who normally remained in one vicinity for a short time. "The denial of the only practical method to carry on this religious work is a denial of the right itself," the Adventist counsel concluded.[69]

After the Court granted rehearing in March 1943, the Adventists filed a modified brief emphasizing that until the *Jones* decision in 1942 "the heavy hand of government" had never fallen upon their denomination. They had flourished and gained the "'respect' of all right thinking people." But since the U.S. Supreme Court decision upholding restrictive ordinances, a rash of intolerant local regulations, aimed apparently at the Witnesses, had brought suffering to the Seventh-Day sect as well, "threatening to overwhelm this old and honorable religious faith."[70]

By the time the Court heard the rearguing of Rosco Jones's case in March 1943, James Byrnes's short tenure as a justice had ended with his resignation late in 1942 to head the Office of War Mobilization. In January 1943, Roosevelt nominated Wiley Rutledge, whom he had appointed four years earlier to the U.S. Court of Appeals for the District of Columbia, to fill the vacancy. After Senate confirmation Rutledge was sworn in on February 15, 1943, the same day that the Court agreed to hear Jones's case again. Rutledge, forty-nine, had taught law for fifteen years before Roosevelt named him to the appellate bench. The president had considered him for the U.S. Supreme Court as early as 1938 and had, in fact, asked Frankfurter to make inquiries as to his qualifications. After checking with lawyers whose opinions he respected, Frankfurter had reported that Rutledge would be a "proper" appointment. By the time

Rutledge joined the Court in 1943, however, Frankfurter might well have had reservations. Rutledge had taken a "preferred position" stance on the First Amendment and had dissented in April 1942 from the appeals court majority opinion against the Witnesses in a license ordinance case. His dissent, in fact, had significantly influenced Frank Murphy's dissent in *Jones* two months later.[71]

Not surprisingly, Rutledge provided the crucial fifth vote needed to overturn *Jones v. Opelika*. The trio of cases that had been linked in *Jones* were reconsidered in conjunction with a series of Witness cases coming from Jeanette, Pennsylvania. William O. Douglas wrote for the new majority in *Murdock v. Pennsylvania*, May 3, 1943, with Frankfurter, Jackson, Reed, and Roberts dissenting. Douglas conferred at length with Rutledge, as well as with his more familiar colleagues—Black, Murphy, and Stone—on the wording of the opinion. They wanted to make plain their support of the First Amendment freedoms without implying endorsement of the substance of Witness propaganda and without overruling reasonable community regulations of behavior. The majority was particularly concerned over a concurring opinion Robert Jackson had written in a related case, *Douglas v. Jeanette*, in which he stressed the invasive nature of Witness operations. The new majority still hoped to gain Jackson's vote in a reconsideration of the flag salute issue, *West Virginia v. Barnette*.[72]

The canvassing of homes and the distribution of religious tracts were old and constitutionally protected forms of missionary work, Douglas reasoned in *Murdock*, forms employed with undisputed sincerity by petitioners. The license tax requirement abridged Witnesses' rights because it taxed a religious rite and could not be justified by alleging that Witness activity was commercial in nature, when in fact the soliciting of funds was incidental to their primary religious purpose. Nor could it be justified as regulatory, for it was a flat tax that mandated purchase of a privilege that was, in reality, a right freely granted by the U.S. Constitution. The claim that the tax was nondiscriminatory was immaterial, Douglas emphasized, because First Amendment rights held a preferred position. The provocative nature of the literature was also irrelevant, for petitioners were not charged with breach of the peace or use of retaliatory language; the state might not restrict the dissemination of ideas merely because they were unpopular. A one-paragraph per curiam statement issued with the *Murdock* opinion declared that the judgment in *Jones* had been vacated.[73]

Reed dissented, reaffirming his earlier decision and challenging the majority's interpretation of the First Amendment. The intent of the framers, he asserted, had nothing to do with taxation. They wished to assure "the practice of religion and the right to be heard," not the interdiction of taxation on either, he averred. The protected rites, he declared, were those that were "in essence spiritual," including such things as prayer, mass, or sermon but not distribution of literature. The attempt to draw an analogy between forbidding taxation on interstate commerce was also immaterial, he maintained, for it was "not the power to tax . . . which is interdicted, but the exercise of that power by an unauthorized sovereign, the individual state."[74]

Frankfurter also filed a separate dissent, which Jackson joined. Essentially, he presented the issue in terms of a challenge to a legitimate occupation tax. It could not be invalidated merely because "the exercise of a constitutional privilege is conditioned upon its payment," he declared. The nature of the condition was the critical point to be examined. The power to tax became the power to destroy only when it was misused; not all taxation was misuse. Although in the abstract one might concede that a tax could become oppressive, the facts in the instant case did not prove such despotism. To render government impotent lest it become tyrannical was illogical. Frankfurter then stated that all of the justices were "equally zealous" to protect the freedom of the human spirit, but freedom was not the question at bar. The real issue was "whether the states have power to require those who need additional facilities to help bear the cost," he stated. Otherwise, a religious sect was in effect being "subsidized by the state," offending the most crucial aspect of freedom of religion, the separation of church and state.[75]

Reaction to the overturning of *Jones v. Opelika* was predictably favorable in the national press. In Alabama, the Montgomery *Alabama Journal,* the *Montgomery Advertiser,* and the *Birmingham News* reported the ruling without editorial comment, as did the *Opelika Daily News.* The *Birmingham Post* declared the decision "a welcome reversal," and the *Birmingham Age-Herald* stated that the right to "honest expression of religious views . . . should be clearly and firmly protected." The Methodist *Alabama Christian Advocate,* which in February 1943 had deplored the mistreatment of the Witnesses, wrote an editorial in June supporting the Court's decision respecting the rights of the Witnesses to propagate their faith. The *Alabama Baptist* on May 4 reported, however, that "Nine Old Men [Had] Become Nine Young Women" in changing their collective mind about the distribution of literature by "the so-called Jehovah's Witnesses."[76]

The accounts of Rosco and Thelma Jones do not reveal how they reacted when they first learned of the reversal, but, doubtless, they rejoiced that Jehovah had been vindicated. It is unlikely, nonetheless, that they took time out to celebrate. They were too busy continuing His work in Pensacola, Florida.

5

Marsh v. Alabama

Grace Marsh's roots reached deep into Alabama soil, nurtured by the close ties of friends and family. Born in rural Randolph, near Montevallo in central Alabama, she had been reared in a tightly knit family. In 1920 the family moved to Robertsdale, a small community about twenty-five miles east of Mobile, across the bay, and five years later she married Herbert Marsh, a local farm boy. For a few years the young couple ventured into the metropolitan world of Chicago, where their son, Joseph Harold, was born in 1927. But even then Grace's familial loyalty remained strong, and she honored her father by naming her son for him. After the shock of observing her landlord mistreating an itinerant Witness in 1930, she returned not only to the faith of her father but also to her native soil. Auctioning off their possessions, Herbert and Grace Marsh purchased a trailer and moved it to her parents' yard in Robertsdale. There little Harold was nurtured as a fourth-generation follower of the teachings of the Watch Tower Bible and Tract Society, often accompanying his mother in her house-to-house ministry. Herbert Marsh supported the family by working as an automobile mechanic at Klumpp Motor Company in Fairhope, another small Alabama town not far from the Gulf Coast. He, too, became an active Witness and was named company servant at Robertsdale in 1940.[1]

In the summer of 1941 Grace Marsh once more left the old homeplace, but this time she carried with her the faith of her childhood. Answering an invitation from the Watch Tower Society, she went to serve as a special pioneer in Brookhaven, Mississippi, hostile virgin territory for the Jehovah's Witnesses. Mississippi had been the scene of some of the most severe harassment of Witnesses in 1939 and 1940, with unruly mobs almost commonplace. The society had determined that routine Witnessing would not prevail in such a malevolent environment; the work there would demand the perseverance of the most dedicated—hence the call for numbers of special pioneers. The association paired Marsh with Violet Babin, a sister in the faith from New Orleans. The two women, each with one child, accepted the challenge, taking their children and the Marshes' trailer to Brookhaven. They planned to establish a foothold, and then their husbands would follow.[2]

The special pioneers were aware that their task would not be easy. "We knew when we went that we would probably be persecuted, probably put in prison, but the work had to be done," Grace Marsh recalled many years later. "We had to let this happen to test the constitutionality of the laws." They reasoned that if Jehovah had chosen them, then going to Mississippi was their destiny. The first few months, however, were comparatively easy. Thirteen-year-old Harold Marsh and Violet Babin's ten-year-old daughter entered school, and their mothers placed literature and began Bible studies. Then war came. The bombing of Pearl Harbor in December 1941 roused a spirit of superpatriotism and a fear of conspiracy throughout the land; an uneasy populace demanded that all "true Americans" stand up and be counted. On the homefront in Brookhaven, Mississippi, World War II brought with it combat against the Witnesses, objects of suspicion because of their political neutrality and their refusal to salute the flag. "Everybody was hysterical," Grace Marsh explained, thinking the Witnesses opposed the government, although "Hitler had lined Witnesses up and shot them by the hundreds. Baptists went over there and killed Baptists, Methodists went over there and killed Methodists, and Catholics killed Catholics. . . . No Jehovah's Witnesses . . . kill[ed] their brothers or anybody else's brother. And so that's where so much prejudice came up."[3]

One of the first indications of the gathering storm was Harold's expulsion from school because he refused to salute the flag. His teacher told

Sister Marsh that the boy was "exceptionally smart in his books" and well mannered but that the school principal thought him a bad example because of the flag issue. Mother and son then went to explain their reasons to the principal, playing him a recording of Rutherford's speech "God and State." The official did not yield, nor would the school board. The superintendent of schools, however, resigned to protest Harold's expulsion and on a visit to the trailer offered to finance the child's education in a private school. Marsh thanked the former administrator for his graciousness and assured him that an education would be provided, although formal schooling was not their highest priority.[4]

By late 1941 the Witnesses were under siege in Brookhaven, with warnings to leave town followed by specifically threatening behavior. Late one afternoon several men began to follow the two women as they went door to door. At one home where the Witnesses called, the lady of the house invited them inside. As they began playing one of the judge's talks on the phonograph, several policemen entered the home and informed the listener that the visitors were German spies whom she should order to leave. When the homeowner refused, Marsh recalled, the officers forced the Witnesses out of the house, broke the phonograph against a tree, shredded and burned the Watchtower literature, and advised the evangelists to be out of town by dark. Foreseeing the possibility of such a situation, the society had provided its pioneers with guidelines on how to proceed under such circumstances. The two women reviewed their instructions. Quickly writing letters to the mayor, the chief of police, and the sheriff, they stated that they had been threatened and asked for protection. They delivered the letters personally to each of the officials. By the time the Witnesses returned to their trailer, however, an angry crowd had begun to form, and no defender arrived. By nightfall approximately one hundred men surrounded the trailer, where the two women were alone with their children. "All we could do," Grace Marsh remembered, "was to lock our doors, turn out the lights, and kneel in prayer to Jehovah for his protection over us. After milling around for some time, the mob began to disperse into the dark."[5]

The Witnesses modified their strategy. At daylight of the morning following the encirclement, a couple with whom Marsh and Babin had conducted Bible studies assisted the women in moving the mobile home to their yard, just outside the city limits. Herbert Marsh joined his wife for the Mississippi campaign. The couple decided to take Harold back to Robertsdale, where, the local school principal assured them, he would not be molested. Leaving the child with his grandparents, the Marshes went back to the front lines near Brookhaven. They found that their trailer had been vandalized, with doors torn away, home-canned goods smashed, and bed and clothing strewn on the ground. Their only possession remaining in the trailer was the Watchtower calendar. Adjacent to it, nailed into the trailer wall, was a warrant for the Marshes' arrest. Despite such a welcome, the Witnesses decided to stay. They gathered their possessions and began to renew Bible studies, and for several weeks no official bothered them.[6]

One night in February 1942, however, officials arrested Grace and Herbert Marsh, charged them with trespassing, and placed them together in a small filthy cell. Tried and found guilty in county court on the following day, the Witnesses were assessed fines of $500 each and were sentenced to six months on the "pea farm." Through a regional Watch Tower attorney, G. C. Clark of Waynesboro, Mississippi, they asked for an appeal. The bond was first set at $1,000 but was twice increased until $10,000 was demanded for the two of them. Raising such a sum proved difficult. The society had learned from experience to insist on property bonds, but persons with property in Mississippi who would assist the Witnesses were rare. Clark had wealth, but he had already signed a number of Witness bonds in the state. Eventually, the attorney had his property reassessed for higher taxes in order to have a larger valuation for bond purposes, but he was unable to meet the Marshes' bail in 1942.[7]

Grace and Herbert Marsh were confined for eleven days in a bitterly cold cell with iron slabs fastened to the walls as their only beds. They were given no covering, were served in dirty tin pans, and were at first obliged to use one corner of the cell as a toilet, Grace Marsh recalled. Insects made sleep difficult at best, although the couple learned to sleep in separate shifts so that one could keep the bugs away while the other rested. After three days the jailer, a Mr. Jackson, decided that the Witnesses were not fiends and began to befriend them as much as he could under the circumstances, allowing them to leave the cell at times, bringing them the books and Bible that they had carried at the time of their arrests, and providing a shovel and hamper in order that they might remove the accumulated waste from their quarters. The Marshes took joy in reading the biblical account of St. Paul's prison experiences. When a minister from the Brookhaven First Baptist Church came to assure the Witnesses that if they would agree to leave town, he would use his leverage to see that they were set free, Herbert Marsh refused, telling the clergyman that he felt sure that his influence had put them in jail in the first place![8]

While they were incarcerated, Grace became very ill and lost weight rapidly. Finally, the authorities called in a doctor, who diagnosed her illness as pneumonia. Shortly thereafter, the Marshes were granted a habeas corpus hearing and were released pending another trial. Returning to their trailer, they were again surrounded by a midnight mob. They then decided to move back to Robertsdale but periodically reported to Brookhaven for trial, each time to be told that the trial had been postponed. After a number of delays, the officials dropped the charges.[9]

In so hostile an environment even the special pioneers withdrew for a time. Violet Babin and daughter returned to Louisiana. The Witness movement in that area lay dormant for almost thirty years, Grace Marsh explained, but in the 1970s she was a guest of honor at the ceremonies dedicating the first Kingdom Hall built in Brookhaven.[10]

After a brief rest the reunited Marsh family renewed proselytizing. Grace's health had recovered by the fall of 1943, and Herbert had taken a full-time job as salesman for Malbis Bakery to support his wife and child, although he still contributed several hours each week to Witnessing. During 1943 Grace had resumed full-time ministerial work, and young Harold, turning sixteen, had also begun pioneering. Grace's new assignment was closer to home, the territories of Whistler and Chickasaw, small suburban communities near Mobile. With the favorable rulings for the Witnesses by the U.S. Supreme Court in the summer of 1943—overturning *Jones* and *Gobitis*—and with public attitudes beginning to shift at least in the metropolitan areas, the experienced pioneer had reason to hope that the new territories would be less hazardous than Brookhaven had been and that her health could bear the pressure. Although the dedicated Witness would probably not have allowed personal considerations to decide her course of action, she might have tried to guard her son.[11]

The Marshes moved their trailer to the yard of Aileen Stephens, a Witness friend in Whistler. Aileen's husband was not a member of the Jehovah's Witnesses, and her activities had been limited, but as she observed Grace's ministry she, too, became a pioneer. They found Whistler a responsive community and quickly expanded their operations. They had initially conducted Bible studies on the front porch of the home of Victoria Williams, who was particularly grateful because Grace Marsh had also taught her to read. When the study group grew to sixteen, Williams contributed the lot next door, a brother in the faith loaned the group $1,000, and "everyone who could drive a nail" assisted in building their own "humble Kingdom Hall." By the end of 1943 the society had recognized them as a congregation.[12]

The second territory in Grace Marsh's assignment, Chickasaw, was a company town lying approximately three miles northwest of Mobile's industrial center. Built by Tennessee Coal and Iron in 1918 to accommodate workers at the shipyards, the community included residential areas and a business block. After World War I, when the shipyards became idle, the company had advertised its residential facilities in the larger Mobile area and attracted a number of persons employed outside Chickasaw. By 1941, as the demand for shipbuilding revived, Gulf Shipbuilding Corporation, a subsidiary of the Waterman Steamship Company, acquired the property. Booming during World War II, the shipyards employed three shifts of workers, totaling approximately fifteen thousand people. The residential needs similarly expanded far beyond the housing that the corporation provided.[13]

Except for the fact that Gulf Shipbuilding Corporation held the title to the property, however, nothing distinguished Chickasaw from other Mobile suburbs. It had, in fact, "all the characteristics of any other American town." Not restricted to company employees, the business block became a well-visited shopping center. The business section consisted of a number of buildings connected to a covered concrete sidewalk, approximately 8 feet wide, which ran the length of the block, some 250 feet. Individual businesses rented the buildings from the corporate proprietor. Since its original construction, the area had included a drugstore, grocery, restaurant, and U.S. post office, and by 1943 Gulf Shipbuilding leased the remaining space to several other enterprises. The block's location drew shoppers from outside the company town. The line of buildings paralleled Craft Highway, a four-lane federal road, at a distance of only 30 feet, providing public access. Intersecting roads at each end of the block allowed traffic to move from the highway in a somewhat circular path through the company territory, with unrestricted parking spaces available for persons who wished to stop to trade. Such travelers encountered no discernible boundary separating private from public property as they moved from public highway to private road and into the separate shops, crossing portions of the company-owned sidewalk. Furthermore, not all the corporation's employees resided in the company-owned village. Many left the shipyards at the end of their shifts to cross the town's limits, going to living quarters in other bedroom communities in the thickly settled residential sections. In fact nothing visibly identified the village as a company town in either the residential or the marketing area.[14]

Grace Marsh and Aileen Stephens began to work Chickasaw regularly in November 1943. They usually went door to door in the village during the week, distributing literature or holding Bible studies. By that time the society, under the leadership of Rutherford's successor, Nathan Knorr, had discontinued using the phonograph and asked the Witnesses to know their scripture, to dress modestly, and to remain courteous even in the face of rudeness. On Saturdays, and occasionally on other days, Marsh, Stephens, and a third woman Witness would station themselves at intervals on the outside edge of the sidewalk that ran along the business block. In that manner they could contact the shoppers at the peak point of the marketing week. The usual procedure was to display the society's regular journals, the *Watchtower* and *Consolation,* and to call out in a moderate tone of voice, "Read the latest" or something similar. They did not specifically ask for contributions, but they accepted any donations that were offered. By early December 1943 they had experienced some success in door-to-door forays and appeared to be establishing a pattern for reaching large numbers on Saturdays.[15]

But trouble began on December 11. On that Saturday Grace and Aileen were at their posts on the edge of the business block sidewalk when a Mobile County deputy sheriff accosted them. Gulf Shipbuilding Corporation employed the deputy, A. I. Chatham, to keep order in the village. Chatham told the Witnesses that they were on the private property of Gulf Shipbuilding and that they must leave. The Witnesses told him that they were not soliciting and that their activities were religious in nature and hence were protected by the First Amendment to the U.S. Constitution; still, the deputy maintained that they must leave. When the women refused to move, he took them to the office of Gulf Shipbuilding, where he held them for one or more hours without making charges.[16]

During the following week the two women made an appointment with E. B. Peebles, the vice president and director of housing for Gulf Shipbuilding Corporation. After a lengthy conversation in which the Witnesses explained their religious affiliation and beliefs, Peebles told them that they could not distribute literature without a permit, that he was "not willing to give them a permit under the conditions they wanted," and that they should not come onto the property again. On Saturday, December 18, the women returned to the business block with Watchtower literature, and again Chatham ordered them to leave. When they refused, he instructed them to get into his car and then drove them to the Mobile County Jail. Again the women were not charged and, after Chatham left, were released.[17]

On the following Friday—Christmas Eve—Marsh, Stephens, and Mittie Williamson returned to the business block with the current editions of the *Watchtower* and *Consolation*. The weather had turned quite cold, the temperature hovering near freezing. At approximately three o'clock in the afternoon Deputy Chatham approached. He then repeated to the Witnesses the warning that he had given on the two previous Saturdays but also called their attention to a notice posted in the windows of several of the Chickasaw businesses, a notice visible from the sidewalk. It read, "This is Private Property, and Without Written Permission, No Street, or House Vendor, Agent or Solicitation of Any Kind Will Be Permitted. Gulf Shipbuilding Corporation, Housing Division." He told the three Witnesses that he would have to arrest them if they remained; the Witnesses replied "that their Jehovah God gave them permission to do what they were doing." Chatham further testified, "We taken these three in the car, and was fixing to go to the office with them, to the police station, and we decided to make the block, and I drove around the business block, and then the other three had taken their places." The other three were Alberta Rouse, Cora Smith, and Joseph Harold Marsh. Chatham engaged in similar conversation with the second shift of Witnesses, and they, too, were taken to the jail. The Witnesses were held until the following Monday, December 27, without formal sworn complaint. When cross-examined later as to the reason for the extensive delay, the deputy explained, "Well, it was a holiday. . . . that was the only reason . . . I know."[18]

Grace Marsh was not easily intimidated. After a warrant for her arrest had been issued on December 27 in response to Chatham's complaint that she had trespassed after having been warned, she was released pending trial in the inferior criminal court on January 6, 1944. On December 31 she once more took her magazine bag and stationed herself on the curb edge of the sidewalk of the business block of Chickasaw. Again, she was arrested and by Marsh's account again held over the holidays. On January 6 she was tried before Judge Tisdale J. Touart of the Inferior Court of Mobile County on the December 24 trespass charge and was found guilty. She was sentenced to pay $50 and costs or to spend twenty days in the Mobile County Jail. She was released on $100 bond. Two days later, on Saturday, January 8, Grace Marsh returned to Chickasaw, as she did again on Saturday, January 15, and on Wednesday, January 19. She was arrested each time.[19]

A local attorney, David R. Coley, Jr., represented the Witnesses in inferior court and filed notice of appeal to the circuit court of Mobile, Alabama. Coley had been born and educated in Florida but had lived in Mobile for twenty years, where he had served as an assistant district attorney and as president of the local bar association. A Baptist, a veteran of World War I, and a member of the American Legion, he seemed an unlikely champion of the Witnesses, but defend them he did. In 1941 at the annual meeting of the Alabama Bar Association he had included in his welcoming remarks the statement that lawyers should honor the trust of liberty, but that comment alone does not explain his activity. Marsh states that he admired their work, that he "was a real friend to the Witnesses," and that Coley's mother was a Witness.[20]

With each arrest Marsh had more difficulty in raising bond. Not only did the number of bonds increase, but the amount of each grew successively larger. Sister Peterson, a Witness who owned a number of apartment houses, had sufficient property to cover many bonds, but as the

Witness-Gulf Shipbuilding struggle continued, she finally told Marsh, "Honey, I'm loaded. I can't go any further." Grace Marsh was resourceful, however, and one who had many friends outside the Witness community. When her Mobile assets were exhausted, she had to take other steps. Her husband had come from Fairhope, sixteen miles away. Not timid, she decided to seek help there. Feminine but firm, she approached the problem in a businesslike manner. Thus, she explained,

> I got in my car and came to Fairhope to Klumpp Motor Company [owned and operated by T. J. Klumpp]. He's a Catholic, but my husband had worked for him and he knew me. So I . . . said, "Mr. Klumpp, I want to ask a real favor of you. I have to know pretty quick, so don't take too long to think about it. I want you to go my bond." He said, "What for?" So I told him, he's the sweetest old thing in the world, . . . and he said, "I don't know what you want to get mixed up in all this for! But anyway I'll go on it." . . . [When I told him I needed another] he called his head mechanic over and said, "Now you sign this bond for her. We've got to keep her out of jail." . . . They were wonderful. . . . There's always somebody there. Jehovah finds a way.[21]

It was fortunate for Grace Marsh that Mr. Klumpp agreed, for her repeated imprisonments in 1943–1944 contributed to renewed health problems. When she returned to the physician whose treatment had restored her health following her Mississippi ordeal, he was distressed to find her "breaking down again, . . . extremely nervous and underweight . . . , and a recrudescence of her pulmonary condition." Although he did not discuss Marsh's Mobile County incarceration in detail with her, he attributed her decline to that experience and to the associated mental anguish, and he "told her it would kill her," he testified.[22]

Grace Marsh and Aileen Stephens maintained that they were locked into a small cell within the larger women's quarters for as long as forty-eight hours with no toilet facilities except a five-gallon uncovered bucket; no paper, soap, or towels were provided. They had to sleep on filthy uncovered mattresses with only one dirty blanket for cover. The cells were cleaned and sheets provided only when the grand jury conducted a scheduled inspection trip, the Witnesses declared. The matron, Mrs.

Nellie Cammack, disagreed. She had to lock them in the small cell, she stated, because they pestered other prisoners with their proselytizing and tried to throw things out the window. She maintained that they were allowed to leave the cell every morning, that they always had clean sheets, and that she regularly carried to them fruit and clothing brought by friends. A third party who assisted at the jail, Howard W. Weston, stated that he had heard Mrs. Cammack make prejudicial remarks about the Witnesses, but the sheriff and the matron asserted that Weston was motivated by revenge because he had not received the position to which he felt he was entitled.[23]

On January 27, 1944, the cases of the six Witnesses arrested on December 24, 1943, were tried together before Judge David Henry Edington without a jury in the Alabama Thirteenth Judicial Circuit. Grace Marsh's testimony was considered by the court as representative of the other defendants, who had filed affidavits. Edington had practiced in Mobile for over thirty years, participated in community civic and political affairs, and was active in the Presbyterian faith. A direct heir of a Confederate veteran, Edington held very conservative opinions on blacks, women, and defendants generally. Coley continued to defend the Witnesses, now joined by Grover Powell, the regional Witness attorney from Atlanta, who had earlier carried Rosco Jones's case through the Alabama courts. Carl M. Booth, solicitor from Mobile County, was assisted by the newly appointed deputy solicitor, T. O. Howell, in representing the state. Booth, a Mobile native and an Episcopalian, had received his LL.B. from the University of Alabama, and had been active in community social affairs and in the executive committee of the Mobile Democratic party. Francis Inge, prominent in Mobile society and legal counsel for Waterman Steamship, with which Gulf Shipbuilding was affiliated, served as special counsel for the prosecution.[24]

On January 22 Coley had entered Grace Marsh's plea and filed a demurrer, maintaining that she was not guilty because the statute under which she was charged was void and unconstitutional in that it violated her rights under the First and Fourteenth amendments to the U.S. Constitution and that the charges against her should be dismissed because her activities were purely religious and not for gain. Furthermore, the land owned by Gulf Shipbuilding had been open to "the general public indiscriminately and without restriction for much more than twenty years," her ministerial acts had not created any disturbance or interfered with the rights of others, and the statute under which she was charged had been discriminately applied to her. The state had responded on January 26, moving that all of the petition except the first plea be stricken as frivolous, not containing grounds for defense, and irrelevant or immaterial. On January 27 the court agreed with the state's motion, denying all the defense motions but the plea of "Not Guilty." Coley reacted to the ruling, stating that because the pretrial motions had not been granted, he would not consent to go to trial on the original affidavits, but the court ruled that Coley had no choice, since the pleas had already been filed.[25]

The state opened with the testimony of A. I. Chatham, the deputy sheriff who had been employed by Gulf Shipbuilding to police Chickasaw. He identified the notice that had been posted in the storefront windows and stated that it had been posted for approximately a month before Marsh's arrest. He described the encounters with Marsh and other Witnesses. In cross-examination, Grover Powell asked Chatham why he had not sworn out a warrant until three days after the arrest and why on prior occasions he had held the women for a period of time without charges. Referring to December 18, when the Witnesses had been taken to the Mobile County Jail but then released, Powell pressed, "Why did you bring them down, Mr. Chatham?" Chatham replied, "I can't answer that, because I just brought them down; I was told to bring them down there, and left them in charge of Miss Farmer. Mr. Peebles [said] . . . she would know what to do with them." He further testified that he had been instructed to take them off the block any time that they appeared there. He admitted under questioning that he did not know whether the Witnesses were *selling* the magazines, where the boundaries of Gulf Shipbuilding's property lay, who had put up the notice, or when it had been posted. He conceded that the general public had long used the sidewalk, that the recent notice was the first of which he had knowledge, and that the Witnesses were the first people that he had arrested for offering papers or magazines on the sidewalk. On recross-examination he stated that newsboys and truck farmers obtained permits. He identified the *Watchtower* and *Consolation* as similar to the magazines being offered by the Witnesses on December 24.[26]

E. B. Peebles acknowledged his responsibility for the business block, conveyed when the corporation had purchased the property in 1941; he identified the deed, which was then marked state's exhibit 1. He described the block in its relation to Craft Highway and in terms of the position of the buildings and the sidewalk. He also stated that Gulf Shipbuilding regularly assessed and paid taxes on the sidewalk property and that the corporation had never expressly dedicated the sidewalk to the public. He testified that he had dictated the notice and instructed that it be posted in the latter part of November 1943, and the notice was then identified as state's exhibit 2. He also declared that prior to the posting of the notice, he had required written permits of "peddlers, venders, street sellers, agents, and all solicitors of every kind." Peebles also recounted his conversation with the women that had taken place when they visited his office.[27]

Under cross-examination by Powell, Peebles agreed that much of the business block had been in existence for at least twenty-three years, that the sidewalk was used for ingress and egress to the stores, and that cars could turn into the block from the highway. Then the following exchange took place:

Powell: You never issued any such notice until Jehovah's Witnesses began offering their magazines there?
Peebles: Oh! yes; we have for over a year; we have been issuing permits for over a year.
Powell: I am talking about the notice!
Peebles: On the windows.
Powell: Yes?
Peebles: No sir.[28]

Coley then cross-examined the vice president. He questioned Peebles about the thickly populated nature of the residential areas and about his conversation with Marsh and Stephens. Indeed, the women had told him that they were Jehovah's Witnesses, Peebles said, but he was not certain that they had described their belief that it was their duty to distribute literature. When Coley attempted to develop that point, the state objected. Coley tried again, and the court ruled: "I don't think you have any right to read into the record there." Coley then stated that he took exception not only to that ruling but also to the striking of pleas, concluding, "I cannot try a case without [sic] I can try it." The court again overruled Coley and told him, "Just abide by the rules and we will get along better." The state then rested its case, Coley moved for exclusion of the evidence, and the court denied the motion.[29]

Grace Marsh took the stand. She defined her occupation as that of an ordained minister and began to relate that to her activity at the time of her arrest. "I was calling to the passers by as they came by, 'Watchtower, announcing Jehovah's Kingdom,' and this offers the only hope." The state objected, and the court admonished, "We are not going to have any sermons; you just answer the question." She testified that she had not been selling the magazines, that she had been held against her will at the corporation's office, that she had stated her position when she visited Peebles, telling him of her "sincerity in this work and [that] it meant life and death to us." Again the state attorney and the judge interrupted. She then stated that she had begun working in Chickasaw approximately six months earlier, that the town appeared no different from other towns of its size, and that her first knowledge of the posted notices was on December 24. On Inge's cross-examination she testified that she had been told on December 11 that she was trespassing by soliciting and would have to obtain a permit. She added that she believed that the requirement violated her constitutional rights because she was not soliciting. She agreed that she had never been stopped at Chickasaw when she was only shopping.[30]

The court then inquired of Powell whether the testimony of the other five Witnesses would be substantially the same as that of Grace Marsh, and he said that it would. Inge then declared that the state would be willing to admit that the testimony would be essentially the same. Powell then asked to introduce as defendant's exhibit a Watch Tower Society card identifying Grace Marsh as an ordained minister and describing the nature of her work. He also requested that it be considered as introduced in each of the six cases. The state and the court agreed.[31]

Coley next introduced several witnesses who testified to the effect that the Chickasaw business block, including the sidewalk, had remained largely unchanged for more than twenty years and that throughout its history had been open to the general public. Hugh Calhoun Bedford, a salesman of wholesale groceries, had worked with businesses in the Chickasaw business block as early as 1917. Ethel Smith, a resident of Mobile for twenty-three years, had visited Chickasaw regularly over the years, had observed the public use of the sidewalk, and had never seen a posted notice or been told that the sidewalk was in any way restricted. Under cross-examination Smith testified that she was a member of the Jehovah's Witnesses and that her visits to Chickasaw had been of a casual nature, so that she had no particular reason to pay special attention to the business block. C. C. Peavy, an assistant U.S. postmaster, stated that a post office had been located in the area of the business block for twenty-five years and that no restrictions existed on its use. The original building, replaced in March 1943, had been "set back some little distance" from the sidewalk, but the new one fronted on the sidewalk, he testified.[32]

William C. Myles, the next witness, was the local manager for the Tennessee Land Company. That establishment had owned most of the Chickasaw property before selling it to Chickasaw Development Company, which then sold it to Gulf Shipbuilding, in 1941. He testified that the business block had been constructed in 1921, at that time containing a drug store, grocery store, restaurant, and bakery, with a separate building for the post office approximately one hundred feet south of the block. The concrete sidewalk was in reality part of the building, with the foundation for both laid at the same time. When cross-examined, he confirmed that there were no reservations in the deed by which the property was transferred to Chickasaw Development Company, that while Tennessee Land Company held the land he had assessed the property, including the sidewalk, and paid taxes on it. He further stated that there had been no express dedication of any street or sidewalk to the public and that soliciting, vending, or selling had not been allowed without permits. On recross-examination Coley asked Myles if he had not been aware of the times when Jehovah's Witnesses had "worked all through Chickasaw with . . . sound trucks," and Myles said that he had not. When Coley pressed him, suggesting that he had never arrested anyone for peddling or soliciting without a permit, he replied, "They have stayed away, who were selling something we objected to." The sidewalk was not leased specifically with the building, but certainly the men renting the building had the right to the sidewalk in front, he said. Finally, upon further examination, Coley gained Myles's admission that no one had been prevented from using the streets "so long as they used it in an orderly and proper manner" and were not there "for any gainful purpose." The defense rested.[33]

Powell, for the defense, then moved that all complaints be dismissed because the evidence showed that the defendants were not guilty as charged; the statute properly construed did not apply to the defendants, ordained ministers; the religious literature was sent from the Watchtower Bible and Tract Society in Brooklyn, New York, to be delivered to persons of goodwill. As a result, Powell argued, the statute as applied interfered with interstate commerce, and the statute as construed and applied violated the defendants' right to freedom of conscience, worship, speech, and press, contrary to the First and Fourteenth amendments of the U.S. Constitution and analogous provisions in the Alabama Constitution. The court, however, denied the motion and let the lower court verdict stand. Marsh (as well as each of the codefendants) was again ordered to pay a $50 fine plus court costs or face twenty days in jail. Appeal bond was set at $500 per defendant. Grover Powell as counsel for Grace Marsh then petitioned the Court of Appeals of Alabama for a writ of certiorari. The appellate court granted certiorari.[34]

The two Mobile daily newspapers, while concentrating on war news, rationing, and absentee votes for soldiers, included stories on the Witnesses' trials. The *Mobile Press* on January 28, 1944, reported that Circuit Judge David Edington had upheld the earlier ruling against the Witnesses in inferior court and that Judge Tisdale Touart of the lesser court had passed until June 1 four additional trespass cases against Grace Marsh and Aileen Stephens of Whistler, pending a decision by the Alabama Supreme Court. The *Mobile Register* published a lengthy account of the circuit court trial. It said: "Chickasaw's one block business section held a whole day's spotlight in circuit court Thursday in a criminal case alleging trespass, but which developed into a discussion by attorneys of 'freedom of conscience, of speech, the press and the worship of Almighty God.'" The journal explained that defense counsel David Coley had argued that conviction would in effect allow Gulf Shipbuilding to regulate the thoughts and lives of the persons using the Chickasaw sidewalk.

Despite a hot and stuffy courtroom, *"more than a hundred persons, white and colored, most of them women,* sat throughout the session, listening . . . with rapt attention." The judge, nonetheless, overruled the defense attorneys, the newspaper recounted, finding that trespass was the only question.[35]

Grace Marsh's case was argued before the Alabama Court of Appeals on November 16, 1944. In the interval since the court had heard Rosco Jones's appeal, one change in personnel had occurred. Judge Simpson had been elevated to the state supreme court, and Robert B. Carr, sixty, had filled the vacancy. The grandson of a Confederate veteran, Carr had practiced law in Anniston, Alabama, before his appointment to the appellate court in 1944. A Democrat, Methodist, Mason, Knight of Pythias, and Woodman of the World, Carr was unlikely to threaten the status quo. The court announced its judgment on January 15, 1945.[36]

Rice wrote for the Alabama Court of Appeals. The pertinent Alabama law, he stated, identified one guilty of trespass as "any person who, without legal cause or good excuse, enters . . . on the premises of another, after having been warned, within six months preceding, not to do so; or any person, who, having entered . . . without having been warned . . . and fails or refuses, without legal cause or good excuse, to leave immediately on being ordered [by the owner or his representative] . . . to do so." There was, he observed, no significant dispute as to the facts of the case. Grace Marsh admitted that, after having been warned within the preceding six months, she had entered and remained on the sidewalk of the Chickasaw village business block on December 24, 1943. More than twenty years earlier, the Tennessee Land Company, the owner of the property in question, had erected a shopping center on the premises. This center or business block, which consisted of one building partitioned into several stores, included a concrete sidewalk running the length of the block and a paved road. The shops, sidewalk, and road ran parallel to a public highway but were separated from it by an unpaved strip of land. The Tennessee Land Company had paid the taxes and maintained control of the sidewalk as well as the building until 1941, when Gulf Shipbuilding Corporation purchased the property and assumed payment of taxes.[37]

Grace Marsh would have had the court consider a number of other questions, Rice continued. She emphasized that she was an ordained minister, that in an apostolic manner she carried religious literature to territories assigned to her by the Watch Tower Bible and Tract Society, and that Chickasaw lay in her territory. She ignored the warning by E. B. Peebles that she could not distribute the literature without a permit, asserting that she had a constitutional right to carry on Christian educational work. She also maintained, the opinion stated, that the deed through which Gulf Shipbuilding took possession showed "that there was a recognized dedication of the 'streets, alleys and public roads'" because it provided that the instrument constituted "a quit-claim deed only." Furthermore, she claimed, "the sidewalks have never been restricted for the general, orderly use of the public, peddling excepted." Judge Rice added that Marsh contended that she was not a peddler, that she offered religious magazines freely to interested parties.[38]

The court ruled that Gulf Shipbuilding Corporation's possession and control of the sidewalk was not diminished because the building was partitioned and leased to various businesses and the sidewalk was used for egress and ingress from and to the stores. "Dedication" required public use "without let or hindrance" for a period of twenty years. Testimony indicated clearly that throughout the years permits had been required, Rice observed, confirming Gulf Shipbuilding's assertion that it retained title and control of the walk. Finally, the court stated, Marsh's claim of exemption because of the religious nature of her work was invalid. Citing a Louisiana ruling against a Jehovah's Witness, Judge Rice concluded that First Amendment guarantees did "not sanction trespass in the name of freedom. We must remember," he quoted, "that personal liberty ends where the rights of others begin." To Marsh's argument that she was simply obeying the Master's command to "go ye into all the world, and preach the gospel to every creature (Mark 16:15)," he replied that "this same Master *also cautioned* her, that ' . . . whosoever shall not receive you, nor hear your words, when ye depart out of that house or city, shake off the dust of your feet' (Matthew 10:14); which we take to be an injunction not to go back on private property, after having been duly warned away."[39]

The significance of the trespass issue alerted the upper echelons of the Watch Tower Society. Coley and Powell were now joined by Roy

Swayze, an attorney from Washington, D.C., and by Hayden Covington. On January 22, 1945, they filed an application for a rehearing with the Alabama Court of Appeals, which was denied on February 13. Eleven days later they petitioned the Alabama Supreme Court for a writ of certiorari, which was refused on March 29. Thus, unlike *Jones v. Opelika,* the *Marsh* case was thus heard only at the intermediate appellate level in Alabama. Five weeks later, on May 3, 1945, Covington began to move into familiar territory, petitioning for appeal to the U.S. Supreme Court. The state of Alabama filed a statement opposing jurisdiction and asking the U.S. Supreme Court to dismiss the appeal or affirm the judgment of the Alabama Court of Appeals. In October 1945 the nation's highest court, with Justice Robert Jackson and Justice Harold Burton not participating, indicated probable jurisdiction.[40]

The state of Alabama responded to Covington by bringing in the attorney general, William N. McQueen, and two assistants, John O. Harris and W. W. Callahan. McQueen, an Episcopalian, had been born in 1908 in Eutaw, Alabama, and had received both his B.A. and his LL.B. degrees from the University of Alabama. He had practiced in Tuscaloosa before being appointed acting attorney general while the person elected to that office fulfilled a term of military service. John O. Harris, thirty-four, hailed from Macon County, had attended Troy State Teachers' College (later Troy University) in south-central Alabama, and had then graduated from Jones Law School in Montgomery in 1934. After joining the prestigious Montgomery law firm of Hill, Hill, Whiting, and Harris, the junior partner was selected to head the Criminal Division in the attorney general's office. Harris was a Methodist. Callahan, a native of Lawrence County in north Alabama, had been born in 1863 and was the son of a Confederate veteran. He, too, was Methodist. During his long career, Callahan had read law in Moulton, Alabama, served as a member of the Alabama House of Representatives, and been chosen a judge in the Eighth Judicial Circuit of Alabama. While holding the latter position, Callahan had presided over some of the trials of the "Scottsboro Boys." In 1941, although he was seventy-eight, he had joined the attorney general's staff.[41]

Grace Marsh (photo 3) did not sit idly by waiting for the U.S. Supreme Court to render its decision. She continued proselytizing and, staying out of prison, began to recover her health. She and Aileen Stephens diverted

Gulf Shipbuilding, particularly E. B. Peebles and its allies in the sheriff's department, from their campaign against the Witnesses by filing a civil suit against them in the federal district court in Mobile. The Witnesses alleged conspiracy and malicious prosecution and asked for $5,000 in damages for each of the women. Francis Inge served as counsel for Peebles and associates, and Grover Powell represented the Witnesses. A jury trial in February 1945 ended with a deadlocked jury. In October 1945, just after Grace's father had died, a second trial was held. She did not win the suit, but it accomplished her goal: the interference stopped. In Marsh's words, "I was free to work anywhere. I was Mrs. Marsh no matter where I went."[42]

Eight of the nine justices on the U.S. Supreme Court who had heard *Jones v. Opelika* remained on the high court when it heard *Marsh v. Alabama* late in 1945. Owen Roberts, one of the two Republicans on the Court, retired in 1945, providing a vacancy for an appointment by the new president, Harry Truman. The president recognized that a coalition between Republicans and conservative Democrats in the Senate could derail a nomination; not only did Truman lack the status Franklin D. Roosevelt had enjoyed but also opposition that had been held in abeyance during World War II would now be less restrained. Truman decided to outmaneuver Senate Republicans by appointing one of their own, Harold H. Burton of Ohio, who won unanimous confirmation in twenty-four hours and joined the Court in September. Burton's role would be restricted in *Marsh* but was safely conservative. Robert Jackson, who had voted against the Witnesses' proselytizing efforts as an invasion of privacy but had voted for their right to refuse to salute the flag would not take part; he had gone to Nuremberg, Germany, to preside over the trial of major figures accused of war crimes. Stanley Reed had been outspoken in his opposition to overturning *Jones,* while Black, Douglas, and Murphy had led the charge to rescue the Witnesses in 1942–1943. The other two justices—the aging chief justice, Stone, and the professorial Frankfurter—had split in *Jones, Gobitis,* and *Barnette,* with Stone voting for the Witnesses and Frankfurter, against them. Past voting records provided some insight into the justices' tendencies but were not a certain guide. Trespass on private property introduced a new element as Grace Marsh came to the high court's attention.[43]

The U.S. Supreme Court should hear the case, Covington contended,

Grace Marsh, ca. 1945

because the Alabama trespass statute had "been construed as a means of enforcing with criminal sanctions" the arbitrary whim of the housing director of Chickasaw village. For "all intents and purposes, the Code provision has been construed so as to constitute a peddler's permit law of the type repeatedly struck down" by the U.S. Supreme Court. The director of Gulf Shipbuilding had violated the Witnesses' First Amendment rights, both in requiring a permit and in absolutely prohibiting the Jehovah's Witnesses' preaching through distribution of literature. No evidence suggested that such action was necessary to "prevent clear, present, and substantial danger to the public peace and order, or right of private property." "Constitutional inhibitions applicable to municipal ordinances" should likewise be applied to the Gulf Shipbuilding Corporation because it acted as a de facto municipal corporation in its relationship with the public. The statute and regulation should also fail in that they were vague and indefinite, contrary to the due process and equal protection clauses of the Fourteenth Amendment. Every effort at legal remedy within the Alabama judicial system had been made, Covington explained, for the Court of Appeals was "the court of last resort in criminal cases of the kind here involved." The Alabama Supreme Court had chosen not to use its discretionary power to review through certiorari, neither affirming nor reversing the appellate court decision, thus leaving the intermediate appeals court decision final.[44]

Alabama attorney general William McQueen countered for the state, belittling the questions raised as insubstantial. The sole basis for the charge against Marsh, he emphasized, was violation of the law concerning trespass after warning. No evidence suggested that the area owned by Gulf Shipbuilding, including the walks and streets, had ever been incorporated. The record showed that the corporation had "repeatedly exercised its rights of ownership . . . and treated this area as its private property by requiring permission [of peddlers, vendors, street agents, and solicitors of all kinds] as to its use." The corporation had hired its own agents to police the area and issued its own notices as much as a year before the Witnesses began offering their magazines. Clear evidence showed that the sidewalk was on the property and that Witnesses had been warned not to come. Then McQueen moved to the heart of the matter: Marsh's claims regarding the First and Fourteenth amendments were irrelevant, for they were limited solely to federal and state action; they were limited further in that the police power of the state justified the protection of property or persons of citizens. Finally, the state argued, "At most the sidewalk or road or street constituted no more than a way of necessity." No formal dedication of the sidewalk, roadway, or similar passageway had taken place, and evidence did not support the claim that in reality informal dedication had existed for more than twenty years. In case of doubt, the presumption was that its use was permissive; a way of necessity for egress or ingress did not constitute dedication. The facts showed, Alabama attorney general McQueen concluded in his arguments, that Grace Marsh was guilty of trespassing on private property.[45]

The U.S. Supreme Court heard oral arguments late in 1945. Elaborating on the points made in the petition for appeal, Covington centered his brief on three major themes. First, the law and regulation as applied allowed arbitrary control by the owner of the streets and sidewalk, unreasonably abridging Marsh's First Amendment rights. The use to which the property had been put created "a relationship between the owner and the public similar to that existing between a municipal corporation and its constituents"; thus, Gulf Shipbuilding was effectively a de facto municipal corporation. As such it should recognize that "from time immemorial" the streets, sidewalks, and parks have "been recognized as a place . . . to communicate ideas and discuss problems."[46] Fundamental personal rights to use the streets were no less valid because a private, rather than a municipal, corporation "owns the fee of the street and sidewalk. . . . A private corporation . . . has no higher right than does a municipal corporation. . . . The courts cannot sanction a town or village virtually seceding from the Constitutional Union merely because it is privately owned." The arbitrary power of the manager further invalidated the law. Even if Marsh had applied for a permit, the director of housing claimed the discretion to refuse it, thus exercising "administrative censorship," a form repeatedly overruled by the Court. The purpose of the corporation's restriction was *not* in reality to *regulate* the streets, but to *prohibit* absolutely the dissemination of ideas by Jehovah's Witnesses.[47]

The law and regulation failed other constitutional tests, the dynamic

Texan insisted. They were presumptively unconstitutional and did not fall within the authority of the state's police power. The state had failed to show that Marsh's activity presented any clear, present, and substantial danger or that the regulation was a reasonable exercise of power. "Freedoms of speech, press, and religion are entitled to a preferred constitutional position because they are 'of the very essence of a scheme of ordered liberty,'" Covington emphasized. Such liberties were essential not only to the individuals directly involved but also to the community at large. The people had placed express guarantees in the Constitution to narrow the channel of government activity, to wall in official waters and control the "course of the stream" so that government could not overflow into the "precious fields" of fundamental liberties. Finally, he asserted, the regulations should fall because they were vague and indefinite, failing to define specific conduct. As written, the guilt or innocence of the accused party depended entirely on the interpretation of judge or jury as to whether an offender had "legal cause or good excuse." Such a statute particularly threatened unpopular minorities, such as Grace Marsh and the other Witnesses, because it could easily be enforced in a discriminatory manner. As such the statute was "a dragnet allowing deprivation of liberty in violation of the Fourteenth Amendment to the United States Constitution and the similar provision in the Alabama Constitution."[48]

The state of Alabama filed a brief emphasizing the importance of private property and the aggressive assault upon it by Grace Marsh. Early in the argument, the state introduced a statement by Director of Housing Peebles, "I didn't have much chance to talk; they told me what they were going to do." What right did Marsh have superior to that of the property owner? The controlling question, McQueen argued, was, did Grace Marsh have a right to be where she was, distributing literature? "Was the place a public way" or "a private way"? The trial court found the way to be private, the state explained. There had been neither express nor implied dedication to the public, for the owner had not allowed its unhindered use for a period of twenty years. In case of uncertainty, the burden of proof rested upon the party asserting the claim, and Marsh had failed to establish such proof in the case at bar. While the sidewalk was a way of necessity to the stores, it did "not follow that the general public [might] enter upon the property for any purpose foreign to any of the incident benefits and rights of the tenant." The owner might give consent to one class of persons for use but deny it to another.[49]

As a private way, the sidewalk was not affected by the First and Fourteenth amendments, for they related only to governmental action. The constitutional amendments had further limitations; they should not be construed to restrict the legitimate use by the state of its police power. The law in question regarding trespass was proper. Nothing in its "plain language" sanctioned the deduction that it intended to, or did, interfere with religious freedom. Trespass was the crime, not religious belief. Freedom of speech and religion were not absolute, McQueen emphasized. In *Gobitis*, the Court had held that such freedoms did "not relieve the individual from obedience to a general law not aimed at the prevention and regulation of religious beliefs." Furthermore, the Court had stated in *Murdock*, "Jehovah's Witnesses are not above the law." Clearly, McQueen thought that Grace Marsh should not be.[50]

Hugo Black wrote for the Court, which rendered the decision on January 7, 1946. Unlike *Jones v. Opelika, Marsh* attracted no amici briefs. The journey though the U.S. Supreme Court was direct and rapid, and the media response was muted. The U.S. Supreme Court that heard *Marsh* did not break into the Frankfurter-Black poles of 1943. Perhaps the clearly established recognition of the Witnesses in 1943, the end of World War II, and Jackson's absence combined to ease tensions. Perhaps the issue of the dominance of corporate property edged New Deal Democrats together. For whatever reason, the Court split 5–3, with Frankfurter the deciding vote for Marsh. In an interesting realignment, Stone joined Reed and Burton against the Witnesses, while Frankfurter moved into the camp of Black, Douglas, Murphy, and Rutledge.[51]

The crucial consideration, the justice from Alabama wrote, was that for all practical purposes Chickasaw was just like "any other American town." The business center included a U.S. post office, a deputy sheriff policed the area, traffic moved freely between the business block and a public highway, and only someone familiar with the property lines could distinguish the Gulf Shipbuilding property from the surrounding neighborhood. Had Grace Marsh been arrested for violating a municipal ordinance rather than the ruling of a corporate manager, he stated, no doubt her conviction must be reversed. "Our question then narrows down to this: can those people who live in or come to Chickasaw be denied freedom of press or religion simply because a single company has legal title to all the town?"[52]

The Court could not accept, Black stated, the contention of the state of Alabama that the corporation had the same authority over the inhabitants of Chickasaw that a homeowner would have over the conduct of his guests. An owner who gained advantage by opening his property to the general public correspondingly circumscribed his rights by the rights of those who used it. The people in Chickasaw had a basic "interest in the functioning of the community in such a manner that the channels of communication remain free." The many citizens of the land who lived in company-owned towns were also free; like other citizens, they were entitled to uncensored information. Fundamental liberties such as freedom of speech, press, and religion held a preferred position over property rights. The freedoms protected by the First and Fourteenth amendments did not stop at the gate of a company town.[53]

Frankfurter concurred in *Marsh v. Alabama.* He had not changed his mind about *Jones* or *Murdock,* he stated, but while those views prevailed, he could not "find legal significance in the fact that a town in which the Constitutional freedoms of religion and speech are invoked happens to be company-owned. . . . A company-owned town is a town. In its community aspects it does not differ from other towns."[54]

In the dissent, Stanley Reed continued his opposition to Witness activities and to the constitutional rulings that upheld them. He was particularly disturbed by the "novel Constitutional doctrine" that extended the privilege of religious exercises, and presumably that of press and speech as well, beyond public places. The Court had reached far beyond the First Amendment and its incorporation in the Fourteenth, he stated. As long as federal and state law permitted company towns, the problems of restrictions by owners on licensees should be adjusted by appropriate law or between the parties involved. The Court reached dangerously beyond previous rulings to commandeer private property. "The rights of the owner," Reed stated, "are not outweighed by the interests of the trespasser, even though he trespasses in behalf of religion or free speech."[55]

Press reaction to the *Marsh* decision was relatively quiet, compared with that excited by *Jones* and *Murdock* or *Gobitis* and *Barnette*. The *Mobile Register* gave a factual report, as did the *Mobile Press* on page three. The *Birmingham News* commented in an editorial, "The Court thus shows a very vigilant and broad regard for the protection of religious liberties."[56] The *New York Times* reported the decision objectively without editorial, but the *New Republic* hailed the "little-noticed" opinion, characterizing it as "another long step toward the permanent safeguarding of our democratic rights," applauding it as a "great victory for labor," because property rights in a company town had been held not to be "all-controlling."[57]

Grace, Herbert, and Harold Marsh were glad to be vindicated but saw the U.S. Supreme Court's decision not as their victory but as that of Jehovah. The experience, according to Grace Marsh, taught her to appreciate the freedom to be His minister and "how important it is never to fear what man can do." The Marshes continued to work the Mobile area and helped in the building of the first Kingdom Hall on Emogene Street. Harold studied at Bethel in 1947. Grace and Herbert continued as dedicated Witnesses and finally settled in Fairhope, Alabama, where Herbert worked for his former employer and Grace's bondsman, T. J. Klumpp. Grace surrounded the home with flowers, fountains, and statuary of peaceful animals—her own imperfect reflection of the restored Eden that she expects to come.[58]

6

The Impact of Jones and Marsh

osco Jones and Grace Marsh, with brothers and sisters in their
faith throughout the nation, wrote their "faith into the laws of
the land," winning victories that broadened and reinforced the
meaning of the First Amendment and the concept of equality before the
law. "Through almost constant litigation" between 1938 and 1946, the
Witnesses "made possible an ever-increasing list of precedents"[1] employing the Fourteenth Amendment to enhance freedom of speech and worship, measures with far-reaching impact and benefits that were not confined to Jehovah's Witnesses. *Jones v. Opelika* and *Marsh v. Alabama*
were two key links in that chain of precedents. *Jones* represented a turning point in the U.S. Supreme Court in 1942–1943, and *Marsh* represented the climax of the Witness proselytizing campaign begun in the
1930s. The effects of the cases in Alabama, furthermore, reverberated
through the state and local communities, serving as an entering wedge of
change. The legal challenge to the power structure in Opelika, Chickasaw, and the state at large set an example for later proponents of reform.

Hayden Covington, in directing the Witness campaign to "defend and
establish legally the good news," encouraged fellow Witnesses to put
their faith in the Bill of Rights. He stood firmly on the argument that the
basic personal liberties protected by the first eight amendments to

the U.S. Constitution were guaranteed at all levels of government in the nation through the due process clause of the Fourteenth Amendment. But he concentrated his fire particularly upon violations of the First Amendment guarantees of freedom of religious exercise, speech, and press. As Rosco Jones and Grace Marsh and thousands of other Witnesses suffered arrest and often severe abuse, Covington used their sacrifices in an unrelenting campaign to scrape away the "weight of barnacle-like statutes and ordinances" that were virtually nullifying the Bill of Rights and causing the U.S. Constitution to wallow "in an undemocratic sea." This fight for freedom on the home front was, furthermore, "for everybody alike—whether it was realized or not," he observed.[2]

Covington had come to Bethel in 1939 to direct the Witnesses' legal strategy, convinced that the U.S. Supreme Court could be induced to respond favorably to an expanded view of the Bill of Rights. Since 1925 the Court had been extending the due process clause in increments and since 1937 had begun a thorough discussion "of the theoretical as well as the practical issues involved in 'nationalizing' the Bill of Rights."[3] Covington saw in the discussion of theory the opportunity to persuade the Court that other liberties were also fundamental. The very nature of the Jehovah's Witnesses' religious expression blended speech, press, and religion, for door-to-door calls, preaching, playing the phonograph, and distributing literature had become inherent in Witnessing. But each aspect needed to stand on its own constitutionally.

Covington took steps to lead the Court further down the path of incorporation, to ensure the inclusion of freedom of religious expression. When the arrest of Witnesses playing a phonograph recording of Judge Rutherford's attack on Catholicism offered an ideal test case, the attorney seized the chance. Early in 1940 he secured a unanimous decision for the Witnesses in *Cantwell v. Connecticut*. Within two years, however, the Court established "time, place, and manner" restrictions and reversed the earlier trend in cases involving compulsory flag salutes and "derisive" name calling. Covington, maintaining that state and local officials were laying "every legal snare they could think of to foil" the Witnesses, encouraged the rank and file to continue the pressure. He organized a system of regional attorneys to assist Witnesses who were arrested and to flood the courts with appeals.[4]

In this context Rosco Jones pressed the cause in Alabama. By the time Jones's case had gained the attention of the U.S. Supreme Court in 1942, the Court had split into two major factions on First Amendment questions. Felix Frankfurter and followers advocated judicial restraint, but Hugo Black, under cover of the intent of the framers of the Fourteenth Amendment, led the charge for judicial activism in matters concerning the Bill of Rights.[5]

Jones v. Opelika demarcated the history of the U.S. Supreme Court decisions involving the Witnesses. With Black, Douglas, and Murphy joining Stone in dissenting, the divided Court ruled 5–4 against Rosco Jones in June 1942, setting off a barrage of criticism. Unlike the recent rulings against the Witnesses in *Cox* and *Chaplinsky*, *Jones* was not tied to controlling rude behavior or to regulating the streets reasonably; it involved a broadly drawn license ordinance that could serve as a means of taxing noncommercial distribution of literature out of existence. With very few exceptions the press condemned the decision. "Momentous in its implications," the ruling threatened the very essence of religious freedom, the *Washington Post* charged, in a typical response. The logic of Covington's argument that the Witnesses were resisting a war on the home front against constitutionally guaranteed liberties proved convincing as editorials asked the question: why fight a foreign war for liberty while sacrificing it at home? The closeness of the vote and a public recantation by Black, Douglas, and Murphy of their earlier stand in the *Gobitis* flag salute case also excited attention. Clearly, the retraction by the trio carried the message that *Gobitis* as well as *Jones* could be reversed with the shift of one justice. The *Birmingham News*, for example, noted the "thin, shadowy line" of the vote and stated that it would be hard to be absolute on either *Jones* or *Gobitis*.[6]

Scholarly journals also noted the decision and the general Witness campaign. An unsigned note in the *Indiana Law Journal* in August 1942 saw no clear and present danger in Witness activities and maintained that it was unlikely that "the oppressed minorities of the world" would "accept the value of our vaunted freedoms when we hesitate to protect them ourselves." G. Adler commented in the *Chicago-Kent Law Review*, speculating that "the spirits of departed justices" had been startled to hear that the Court upheld a "tax on the non-commercial distribution" of religious literature. Robert Walsh in the October 1942 issue of the *Michigan Law Review* feared that the decision indicated a trend away from strict scrutiny, a tendency instead to place "civil rights more into line with economic rights by applying a presumption in favor of the legislation in both." The October issue of *Brooklyn Law Review* included Edward E. Haenssler's comment on contemporary judicial decisions, in which he deplored the tendency of the courts to have no sympathy "for any really marked departure from conventional religious practices." In December 1942 a study by Victor Rotman and F. G. Folsom, Jr., in the *American Political Science Review* noted that the small group of Witnesses had "served as a guinea pig" for testing religious liberty, while L. C. E. in the *George Washington Law Review* castigated the license ordinance as unnecessary and undesirable and declared that it should not have been upheld under the Fourteenth Amendment.[7]

Covington and Rosco Jones did not compromise. They persevered, putting their faith in Jehovah and a changing Court. The Witness attorney corresponded with the ACLU in the summer and fall of 1942 regarding the timing of a plea for a rehearing, in view of the departure of Justice Murphy for a stint in the armed services, but held firmly to the position that the Witnesses should not negotiate on the tax issue. To Osmond Fraenkel of the ACLU he wrote, "It is never the duty of a lawyer to follow any court . . . into error." Rather, he "should always warn the court that . . . graver injury will result by further steps in the direction," for "it is never too late to be right." The Court had previously recognized mistakes and corrected them, and he intended to assist the Court in righting the instant wrong. Whether Covington consulted with Rosco Jones at this point is unknown, but certainly Jones would have tended to agree with the counselor's stand. Many years earlier, when Jones had worked as captain of the dining crew at the William Byrd Hotel in Richmond, he had made it clear that he did not compromise on principle. Pressing Jones's cause late in 1942 and early in 1943, Covington obtained the rehearing.[8]

Rosco Jones's case stood on the threshold of a new era for the Witnesses. The popular press, religious periodicals, and legal journals had been joined by a shift in public opinion by late 1942 away from hate for and fear of the Witnesses. The U.S. Congress had enacted a measure that year stating that civilians could show "full respect to the flag . . . by merely standing at attention."[9] The resignation of James Byrnes from the Court late in 1942 and the appointment of Wiley Rutledge early in 1943 then provided the opportunity for the Court to rectify its error.

Jones thus paved the way for the decision in *Murdock v. Pennsylvania* in May 1943, which was accompanied by a twelve-line per curiam decision reversing *Jones.* That same day Justice Black wrote for the five-member majority in upholding the right of Witnesses to go door to door despite a city ordinance in Struthers, Ohio. The press generally welcomed the trend. Irving Dillard in the *New Republic* called the shift the most dramatic reversal since *The Legal Tender Cases* of 1871 and attributed it to the "slight . . . thread" of a new appointment. The brief decision of the Court did not reveal the "pitched battles waged" to achieve that ruling, Dillard observed, but he concluded, "It is better to eat crow than to perpetuate an error." The *Minnesota Law Review* in March 1944 included an article, "The Debt of Constitutional Law to Jehovah's Witnesses," that concluded that personal liberties were "far broader than they were before the spring of 1938," thanks to the "militant persistency" of the Witnesses (photo 4).[10]

Rosco Jones's battle had been a crucial part of that persistency. Stone's dissent in *Jones v. Opelika* in 1942, for example, became the key to much of the reasoning in *Murdock,* stressing not only the right of the individual to distribute literature but also that of the audience to receive information. Douglas's assertion that technological developments increased the cost of the mass media, thus restricting access and favoring those entrenched interests that favored the status quo, echoed Stone. Society as a whole needed the opportunity to hear the ideas of less established groups, he had emphasized, but taxing through licensing could virtually destroy the poorer, weaker minorities. Furthermore, Douglas's observation in *Murdock* that religious belief without the freedom to act in compliance with that faith carried little import was a direct reply to Reed's ruling against Rosco Jones in 1942.[11] Clearly, *Murdock* had its roots in *Jones.*

The circulation and recirculation of draft opinions in the U.S. Supreme Court regarding *Jones* and *Murdock* and other related Witness cases in the spring of 1943 also related to the reversal of *Gobitis* a few months later in *West Virginia v. Barnette.* First, Black, Douglas, and Murphy

Rosco and Thelma Jones with their graduating class from Witness training school, Gilead, in South Lansing, New York, 1955

made plain in 1942 in their short dissent in *Jones* their intentions to reverse the flag salute decision of 1940. Second, the liberal justices hoped to secure another vote. While Black, Douglas, Murphy, and Rutledge appeared a solid bloc for the Witnesses in litigation of similar nature, Justice Stone was getting older and might not be there to vote later. Furthermore, 6–3 would be a firmer vote than 5–4. At least on the issue of the flag salute it was thought that Robert Jackson might go with the Witnesses, although he regularly voted against their missionary activity. Much of the correspondence in 1943 between Douglas and Rutledge was aimed at meeting Jackson's criticisms without totally alienating him. In *Barnette,* delivered two months after the reversal of *Jones,* it was Jackson, breaking with Frankfurter, who wrote the eloquent decision overturning *Gobitis* and the flag salute ordinances.[12]

Grace Marsh's case also left a strong legal mark. *Marsh v. Alabama* was a watershed case, holding the individual's First Amendment rights in a preferred position over the property rights of the owner of a company town. Until *Marsh* it had been assumed that the First Amendment constitutional limits protecting personal liberties applied only to governments, that is, that state action called the free speech–free press guarantees to life. But if a company owned extensive property, even an entire town, to what extent did the private property take on the characteristics of a public forum? "Ownership does not always mean absolute dominion," Justice Black stated. Dedication to the public use was highly relevant. "The more an owner, for his advantage, opens up his property for use by the public in general, the more do his rights become circumscribed by the . . . rights of those who use it." Black's decision did not delve into the question whether the streets should be deemed "public property" but confined the issue to whether a state, in protecting private property rights, could allow "company town owners to invoke trespass laws" that denied "free speech rights which the state could not otherwise deny."[13] *Marsh* thus opened a new area of litigation regarding the limits on power exercised by the property owners in a company town. The *New Republic* on January 21, 1946, had commented on the "little-noticed" decision as a boon for labor, the first court ruling limiting the all-controlling power of the owners in a company town. Exploited workers who had suffered the invasion of their homes and other affronts to personal dignity, the journal editorialized, could take heart. Later studies questioned the concept that *Marsh* proved to be a great gain for labor; earlier prolabor legislation and decisions upholding the rights of unions probably had a more direct impact. Still, *Marsh* was reinforcing.[14]

The decision's potential in litigation expanding the areas of "public forum" to privately owned facilities open to the general public lay largely dormant for more than twenty years.[15] Then in 1968 the U.S. Supreme Court reinvigorated the case by invoking it in *Amalgamated Food Employees Local 590 v. Logan Valley Plaza.* Justice Marshall spoke for the Court, describing the privately owned shopping center as "the functional equivalent" of the *Marsh* business block, freely accessible and open to the public. Interestingly, Justice Black, author of *Marsh*, dissented from the 1968 decision, maintaining that only when property had "taken *all* the attributes of a town" could it be treated as public.[16] In spite of Black's argument, the majority upheld in *Logan Valley* the right to informational picketing by a union that had a grievance against one of the businesses in the center. The decision failed to consider the question of protests not directly related to the locale, however, and in 1972 the Court prohibited the distribution of handbills on the property of a shopping center when the complaint was not directly concerned with the center's operations. Four years later the Court overruled *Logan Valley,* ending the "short-lived era of treating shopping centers like company towns." The narrow interpretation of *Marsh* that Black had set forth in his *Logan Valley* dissent prevailed[17] in spite of Justice Thurgood Marshall's efforts, marking a clear retreat for the Court.

In some sense *Marsh* was revived in 1980 when the Court held in *Pruneyard Shopping Center v. Robins* that state courts had the power to "surpass the protection of the federal Constitution in guaranteeing the freedom of expression on private property." Justice William Rehnquist wrote for the Court, upholding a provision in the California Constitution protecting reasonable expression of free speech and petition on the property of a privately owned shopping center. While the decision produced the effect of defending freedom of expression in privately owned malls, the ruling reflected the Rehnquist Court's emphasis on the autonomy of the state courts, not a return to a "preferred position." Unlike *Marsh,* where the U.S. Supreme Court defended the *individual* in freedom of expression against the state-supported powers of private property, *Pruneyard* defended the *state* in its power to support the individual (within limits) against the power of private property. If the First Amendment does not extend to privately owned malls, then a state's shield is voluntary and may be withdrawn at the pleasure of the state. Since 1980 constitutional scholars have continued to explore the "public function" issue raised by *Marsh*, but the impact on constitutional law remains unclear.[18]

On the religious issue, the one paramount to Grace Marsh, *Marsh* was one in a string of major victories for the Witnesses and other nontraditional sects. *Marsh* was probably the climax to the Witness proselytizing campaign begun during the late 1930s. Although isolated efforts to deny Witnesses the use of public parks remained, most communities ceased their open resistance to Witness evangelical activities, and the Witnesses in turn became less belligerent and more acceptable in the public eye. With the end of World War II and the decrease in the draft, the inflammatory issue of conscientious objection receded but did not disappear.[19] Shortly after *Marsh* was handed down, some opposition from religious groups surfaced, echoing Frankfurter's dissent in *Jones*, declaring that the Witnesses were being given special privileges that could lead to disorder. Such treatment was not recognized in common law, the critics contended; worship of God was *a duty*, not *a right*, and the Founding Fathers had intended only to assure that government did not infringe upon the churches' jurisdiction. A second reproach that drew some support repeated Jackson's angry concurrence in *Douglas v. City of Jeanette* that massive organized campaigns by Witnesses failed to consider the right of the individual to be let alone and violated the old common law adage that a person's home should be a refuge, secure from religious zealots or other uninvited guests. Such activity, the critics argued, in practice granted the aggressive minorities more rights than the majorities.[20] As an overall trend, however, proselytizing by Witnesses became an accepted phenomenon.

The larger constitutional question posed by both *Jones* and *Marsh*—should the Court stand as guardian of First Amendment freedoms, protecting unpopular minorities from the majority—has followed a less certain course. The movement to secure personal liberties, stimulated by the Witnesses, continued for more than two decades following the end of

World War II, peaking under the leadership of Chief Justice Earl Warren in the 1960s, with holdover influence into the 1970s. Community pressures for religious instruction in the public schools, for example, were declared invalid by the U.S. Supreme Court in two landmark cases; the consciences of "sincere" conscientious objectors, whether or not members of an organized faith, were granted protection; and freedom of speech, assembly, and press were expanded. By the late 1970s and the 1980s, however, the influence of conservative appointees to the federal judiciary by Richard M. Nixon, Ronald Reagan, and George Bush began to be felt, with a retreat on some fronts and a tendency to leave much of the decision making to state courts. While most of the victories won by the Witnesses in the 1930s and 1940s appear secure, *Marsh* has been weakened, and the role of the present Court leaves the future uncertain.[21]

The by-products of *Jones* and *Marsh,* the effects beyond the immediate legal issues in Opelika and Chickasaw and Alabama, were significant. In light of the civil rights movement that surfaced in Alabama in the 1950s, the success of Rosco Jones—a black man—in a challenge to the white power structure takes on an added dimension. One must consider whether Jones's suit aroused significant issues in the black community and whether any tie existed between the NAACP and *Jones.* Similarly, the possible impact of *Marsh v. Alabama* on the feminist movement should be appraised. Did Grace Marsh's assertive behavior as a white woman, native to the area, change the attitude of state and local officials toward women or that of other women toward officials? Finally, the effect of the Witness tactics on later reform groups should be evaluated. Did the success of the Witnesses' methods inspire others seeking change?

Rosco Jones's activity was primarily religious, and the support or opposition that he raised centered on that point at the time of his involvement in Opelika. (The post-*Gobitis* chauvinism occurred after he had moved to Georgia.) Clearly, he experienced racism in rural communities in which the elite feared that he was "meddling the niggers," but he also gained a paternalistic form of tolerance or even support from white leaders who discovered that he was not concerned with political power for blacks and who saw his hard work and clean living as exemplary. Jones was willing to work with white brothers and sisters in the faith; his wife, Thelma Jones, was accompanied by a white woman in proselytizing efforts in Seale, Alabama; and the Joneses regularly attended integrated national conventions of Witnesses. But Rosco Jones did not normally initiate contact in the non-Witness white community. Within the small Witness community, however, there was strength and comfort in joining with other Witnesses of whatever race, and this fact was true even in the South, where Witnesses were an extremely small minority. The Witness belief system formally condemned racial prejudice and the injustices of all existing governments, attracting the oppressed to look to the end of the present society and the coming of a new Kingdom in which all problems would be solved.

Although some officials probably saw Jones as "uppity" and therefore threatening, that view does not appear to have been the original reaction in Opelika. Any challenge to the existing power structure was unwelcome, for the leadership in the small mill town did not seek change. It was, an anonymous attorney later recalled, a "sleepy little village, minding its own business." Although many years after *Jones,* the attorney looked back on the Witness experience as the beginning of the black civil rights movement, the evidence suggests that Rosco Jones was not concerned with breaking down racial barriers in the dominant community and the established leaders did not perceive that he was. Jones, one must emphasize, considered his mission to be that of preparing for an impending Armageddon.

The lack of local interest in Jones's case probably stemmed from a combination of circumstances. Originally, the local authorities apparently assumed, first, that a black preacher could be easily controlled and, second, that "nobody" of substance cared and thus that arousing the press was unnecessary. By the time it became clear that Rosco Jones refused to be cowed, a white attorney from Georgia was on hand to observe legalities and raise the hackles of the natives. The judge removed the case from the jury docket and delayed the trial for six months, however, and Jones moved out of state. A flurry of activity occurred when Jones was tried in circuit court, but once the trial ended in November 1939, the case became a battle of attorneys. The first real sign of trouble came with the Alabama Court of Appeals' reversal of Judge Bowling, a move that led to quick action to get the decision into the Alabama

Supreme Court and into more friendly hands. After Judge Thomas's opinion favoring the city, appeals consumed the next two years before the U.S. Supreme Court made its final decision on the matter in 1943. During that interval, war had come, and the case became an abstract problem out of the hands of local folk. The city attorney, William Duke, relied on a Washington firm to help carry the city's cause.

Other indications suggest that Jones did not see his cause as racially oriented. No evidence exists that at any point did he contact the NAACP, the primary organization at that time dedicated to promoting racial justice through the law. The association was not well organized in Alabama; it had no branch in the Tuskegee area until 1944 and 1945, and NAACP national records reveal no concern with the *Jones* case. Rosco Jones's widow, Thelma, insisted years later that the case not be interpreted as part of the civil rights movement. Her paramount concern remained that of preparing for the millennium, in which a just Jehovah would cleanse the earth and resolve its problems. Following the leadership of the Watch Tower Bible and Tract Society, she accepts racial integration but does not make that a first priority.[22]

The fact remains, nonetheless, that Rosco Jones (photo 5), a black man, did challenge the established order in Alabama and win. He won by believing in the righteousness of his cause and standing with the courage of a Daniel. But he won in part because he was supported by a nationally organized, highly motivated group that knew how to publicize the Bill of Rights and how to use the courts of the land to rouse the national conscience. Although no evidence is available to indicate that oppressed blacks observed Jones's example or saluted his stamina or vicariously *enjoyed* his audacity, one may safely speculate that some took note. Clearly, leaders in the ACLU or the NAACP Legal Defense Fund who studied the law became aware of the effectiveness of the Witness legal strategy.

The significance of the precedent established by the Witnesses' crusade has not been adequately recognized. Covington's approach was deliberately to test the laws through a nationally organized monitoring of individual cases. The tactic involved both dedicated litigants and prepared attorneys who refused to settle and preserved error, enabling Covington to argue many particular cases before the nation's highest court. The

Rosco and Thelma Jones in the 1970s

Witnesses' success in dramatizing and highlighting individual actions by making them integral parts of a larger legal strategy set a standard later used by such groups as the NAACP Legal Defense Fund in desegregation suits, opponents of capital punishment, advocates of gay and lesbian rights, and feminists.

Grace Marsh was an independent, self-assured woman with great inner resources; she took the initiative boldly in accosting her landlord, deciding to auction the family goods and return to Alabama, going without her husband to pioneer on the frontier of Mississippi, returning to the Chickasaw business block after three days in jail, and daring to sue the Gulf Shipbuilding Corporation for damages. She would not be intimidated in her effort to "give a good witness" even to the court; when she needed persons to sign her bond, she did not hesitate to ask. Certainly, she was a leader in the Witness community of the greater Mobile area.

But Marsh did not see herself as set apart from other Witnesses. She asserted herself within a certain structure—as her father's daughter, her son's mother, the church member inspired by Pastor Russell or Judge Rutherford, or the spokesperson for the local Witness women. Grace Marsh viewed the world primarily through a traditional woman's perspective, emphasizing family (photo 6), church, female friends, and community (photo 7). The notable exceptions—making the family decisions that her husband apparently accepted or defying the community establishment—were justified in her mind as religious acts, following her father's teachings. Most of the power figures with whom she dealt were men; she opposed those who obstructed her Witnessing and favored those who assisted her cause. Coley, Powell, the school superintendent in Mississippi, Brother Clark, Judge McDuffie, even the Catholic Klumpp were positive counterparts to Deputy Chatham, Peebles, Inge, Judge Touart, and Judge Edington. Grace Marsh saw her crusade as religious— as Rosco Jones also viewed his—and her goal was not a unisex society or one controlled by women. But, again paralleling Jones's behavior, she did not allow a subordinate position to interfere with what she felt she had to do. She would work within or around the system as long as she could still achieve her purposes, but she would not compromise the ultimate end.[23]

What was it about the Witnesses that attracted these strong but generally traditional personalities? What made them willing to endure

Grace Marsh with parents and siblings, 1943. Grace is fourth from the left.

deprivation, threats, imprisonment? Perhaps in identifying with the Witnesses Jones was seeking not only to satisfy an uncertain searching or Marsh to return to the certitude of her childhood; perhaps they also were striving to satisfy a sense of personal worth, of counting as an individual, of making one's mark. As a southern black man without wealth or education, Rosco Jones had very limited options. He was too powerful a personality to settle for mediocrity or to be an "Uncle Tom"; he had too much integrity to turn to a life of crime; he needed a positive conduit for his immense energy. Religion—and not your garden variety religion—may have presented itself as both challenging and rewarding, a means of achieving dignity and a nondestructive way of fighting the system that held blacks in bondage. Grace Marsh as a female in rural Alabama did not have unlimited choices either. Family was a given; higher education was not. Though something of a rebel, she could not go so far as to denounce her father. Personal expression had to come, then, through some channel acceptable to her family. Even the patriarchical Witness worldview had a role for women that demanded fortitude and endurance and personal strength. As a soldier for Jehovah one counted. In standing against a mob, one had dignity.

Whatever their original reasons for becoming dedicated members of Jehovah's Witnesses, once the battle was joined, Jones and Marsh fought the good fight and, in doing so, became aware or more aware of the rigidity of the ruling elite. Once it was clear that the Witnesses would not yield to patronizing settlements, the authorities saw the defendants as less subordinate and more threatening. The gloves came off. The parties in power had a variety of methods from which to choose: arrests without warrants, delayed or hurried trials, and increased bonds, for example, or even looking the other way as nonofficial persons attacked the challengers. As the Witnesses experienced such treatment, their concept of the power structure naturally became more negative. As they publicized the abuses that they suffered, they became agents of changing the government in fact, if not in intention.

Opelika did not change dramatically after the *Jones* decision, and much of the change that did occur was related to the war, the movement of blacks to the North, and industrialization. Still, some changes relevant to the case were perceptible. Witnesses going door to door distributing literature became an accepted and customary sight; listings of the Jehovah's Witnesses' Kingdom Halls in the religion section of the daily paper or the telephone directory gradually became commonplace.[24]

Chickasaw changed rapidly, in part because of the shipyard activity of World War II. In 1945 Gulf Shipbuilding sold the business block to W. B. Leedy Company for $1 million, and by 1949 the village had changed from a company town to an incorporated municipality. Witnesses moved freely, and by 1950 Kingdom Halls were listed regularly in the Mobile area directory and newspapers. Grace Marsh continued to Witness fifty to sixty hours per week even in her eighties; she lived to see a vast expansion of Witnesses in the area and to be treated with courtesy and even respect wherever she moved. Occasionally, she was asked to speak about her case to classes at the local public schools. She has not been to court or had to gain signatures for a bond in many years.[25]

The impact that *Jones* and *Marsh* had on the black civil rights movement of the 1950s and 1960s cannot be measured specifically. The parallel in tactics is clear, however. Day after day, the Witnesses persistently sent person after person to demonstrate peacefully for the constitutional right to freedom of religion, speech, and press. In particularly resistant areas, they organized fleets of Witnesses. As one fell, another took up the banner. The Witnesses generally did not resist but refused to leave and were eventually arrested. They established a network of legal advisers and often a means of meeting Witnesses' bonds. They learned to use martyrdom to gain media attention and public sympathy. Their dedication often shamed their opposition. By nonviolent means, they persuaded the U.S. Supreme Court and the nation to examine the true meaning of the First Amendment.

The impact on women's rights is tenuous at best. Although feminists of the 1960s also used the First and Fourteenth amendments, they were the second or third wave of an earlier movement and were more influenced by their own past and the immediate example of the black movement. Initially led primarily by professional women, the feminists moved in significantly different circles from those of Witnesses Grace Marsh and Rosco and Thelma Jones and were probably unaware of their activities. They would have been offended by Rosco Jones's perspective on women and Thelma Jones's accepting attitude. They would not have shared

Grace Marsh's worldview, but they would have applauded her daring and decisiveness and admired her tenacious endurance.

The worlds of community, state, and nation were permanently affected by the Witnesses' cases in the era of World War II. The Witness victory was a triumph for individual liberty that reached far beyond the ranks of those immediately involved. Under Covington's prodding, the U.S. Supreme Court had reexamined the meaning of the First Amendment both in extending the substantive reach of the religious exercise clause— allowing for religious acts as well as beliefs—and in applying the enhanced protection at state and local levels. The Witness constitutional campaign was national in its scope, with Alabama a critical theater of action.

Rosco Jones and Grace Marsh, on the surface improbable agents of change, believed intensely in the Witness cause and had the courage of their convictions. Their stories record dedication, perseverance, and personal bravery. Although their heroic deeds stemmed from a particular religious faith, they strengthened the broader cause of personal liberties. The ultimate effect of Jones's and Marsh's fearless crusade is a fitting tribute to the instrument that they wielded so effectively—the First Amendment to the U.S. Constitution.

Notes

Acknowledgments

1. At that time I had no real awareness of the thoughts of local blacks on the subject.

2. *Brown v. Board of Education I,* 347 U.S. 483 (1954); *Yates v. United States,* 354 U.S. 298 (1957); *Engel v. Vitale,* 370 U.S. 421 (1963).

3. James MacGregor Burns, J. W. Petalson, and Thomas E. Cronin, *Government by the People,* national, state and local version, 13th alt. ed. (Englewood Cliffs, N.J.: Prentice-Hall, 1989), 67; Philip E. Converse, "The Nature of Mass Belief Systems in Mass Publics," in *Ideology and Dissent,* ed. David Apter (London: Press of Glencoe, 1964); and Howard Schuman et al., *Racial Attitudes in America* (Cambridge, Mass.: Harvard University Press, 1985).

4. *Jones v. Opelika,* 316 U.S. 584 (1943); *Marsh v. Alabama,* 326 U.S. 501 (1946).

Introduction

1. *West Virginia v. Barnette,* 319 U.S. 624, 642 (1943).

2. 316 U.S. 584 (1943) and 326 U.S. 501 (1946).

3. Not everyone agrees that rights are inherent. Ronald Dworkin, "Taking Rights Seriously: Constitutional Cases," and William H. Rehnquist, "The Notion of a Living Constitution," in Walter F. Murphy, James E. Fleming, and Wil-

liam F. Harris II, *American Constitutional Interpretation* (Mineola, N.Y.: Foundation Press, 1986), 163–80.

4. James Madison, "*The Federalist* Number 10," in Burns et al., *Government,* 755–58.

5. Plato, "The Trial of Socrates" from the *Apology,* in *Aspects of Western Civilization: Problems and Sources in History,* ed. Perry M. Rogers, vol. 1 (Englewood Cliffs, N.J.: Prentice-Hall, 1988), 81–82.

6. American Civil Liberties Union, *Annual Reports,* vols. 3 (July 1937–June 1944) and 4 (July 1944–June 1950) (New York: Arno Press & *New York Times,* 1970), especially, in vol. 3, "In the Shadow of War: The Story of Civil Liberty, 1939–1940," 51–52, 67–70, and "The Bill of Rights in War," 78. See also Samuel Walker, *In Defense of American Liberties: A History of the ACLU* (New York: Oxford University Press, 1990), 268, and *Birmingham Post-Herald,* April 13, 1965.

7. 316 U.S. 584 (1943) and 326 U.S. 501 (1946). While an elite governed, the majority of citizens in the state and nation appear to have supported the official actions.

8. Originally incorporated in 1876 as Zion's Watch Tower Tract Society, the organization became what is now the Watch Tower Bible and Tract Society of Pennsylvania. In 1909 the headquarters moved to Brooklyn, New York, and another corporation, the People's Pulpit Association, was formed, now known as the Watchtower Bible and Tract Society of New York, Inc. The latter is currently better known because of its publishing activities and the location of Bethel, which houses the leadership, but both corporations are integral to the association. The Pennsylvania corporation is usually listed as the "author," with the New York center the publisher. Watch Tower Bible and Tract Society of Pennsylvania, *Jehovah's Witnesses in the Twentieth Century* (Brooklyn: Watchtower Bible and Tract Society of New York, 1979), 6. See also Marley Cole, *Jehovah's Witnesses: The New World Society* (New York: Vantage Press, 1955), 50–51, and M. James Penton, *Apocalypse Delayed: The Story of the Jehovah's Witnesses* (Toronto: University of Toronto Press, 1985), 29, 379.

9. Herbert Hewitt Stroup, *The Jehovah's Witnesses* (New York: Columbia University Press, 1945), 72–77, 130; Penton, *Apocalypse,* 255, 261–70; Barbara Harrison, *Visions of Glory: A History and Memory of Jehovah's Witnesses* (New York: Simon & Schuster, 1978), 40–50, 77; Alan T. Rogerson, *Millions Now Living Will Die* (London: Constable, 1969), 174; James A. Beckford, *The Trumpet of Prophecy* (New York: Halsted Press, 1975), 16–17.

For varying views of the roles of the sexes and of children, see Penton, *Apocalypse,* 66, 270–84; Harrison, 40; Ben and Betty Eskridge, interview by author,

August 17, 1990, typewritten transcription of tape recording in possession of the author. For interpretations of racial composition, see Stroup, *Witnesses,* 34; Penton, *Apocalypse,* 358 n. 90; Lee R. Cooper, "'Publish or Perish': Negro Jehovah's Witnesses in the Ghetto," in *Religious Movements in Contemporary America,* ed. Irving I. Zaretsky and Mark P. Leone (Princeton: Princeton University Press, 1975). See also below, chaps. 2, 3, and 6.

10. Penton, *Apocalypse,* 48.

11. For Witness theology, see below, chap. 2.

12. Cole, *Jehovah's Witnesses,* 99–107, and Penton, *Apocalypse,* 65–72, provide an overview of the Witness style. Particular venom was reserved for the Roman Catholic church, which Rutherford dubbed "the Whore of Babylon" in a recording used by Witness Jesse Cantwell. Murphy et al. *Interpretation,* 1014.

13. Henry J. Abraham, *Freedom and the Court: Civil Rights and Liberties in the United States,* 5th ed. (New York: Oxford University Press, 1988), 296–98.

14. 268 U.S. 652, 666 (1925).

15. 293 U.S. 245 (1934).

16. 302 U.S. 319, 325 (1937).

17. 303 U.S. 444 (1938); 308 U.S. 147 (1939).

18. 304 U.S. 144, 152–53 (1938). Although the phrase "discrete and insular minorities" came to be applied most often to racial or ethnic minorities, Stone defended the rights of a "politically helpless minority," the Witnesses, in *Minersville Sch. Dist. v. Gobitis,* 310 U.S. 586, 606 (1940).

19. 310 U.S. 296, 302 (1940).

20. Ibid. at 303–304.

21. The courage of the German *Bibelforscher* is beyond dispute. As late as 1933, however, when Nazis began banning Witnesses and seizing Witness offices, Watch Tower Society leaders Rutherford and Knorr attempted to placate Adolf Hitler by flying to Berlin, issuing a "Declaration of Facts" expressing support for the National Socialist principles, and engaging in anti-Semitic statements. The Watch Tower Bible and Tract Society in 1974 attempted to explain the "Declaration" by blaming the German translator for weakening its message. Penton, *Apocalypse,* 147–48.

22. 310 U.S. 586 (1940).

23. Ibid., with Stone's dissent at 604. For comments on the role of the different justices in *Gobitis* and its aftermath, see Hugo Black, *A Constitutional Faith* (New York: Knopf, 1968), xv; Abraham, *Freedom and the Court,* 296–98; and Murphy et al., *Interpretation,* 1019.

24. Abraham, *Freedom and the Court,* 296–98.

25. The Witnesses were not the only persons to suffer persecution stemming

from chauvinism. Persons of Japanese ancestry were forcibly removed from the West Coast. *Korematsu v. United States,* 323 U.S. 214 (1944).

26. American Civil Liberties Union, *The Persecution of Jehovah's Witnesses: The Record of Violence Against a Religious Organization Unparalleled in America Since the Attack on the Mormons* (New York: ACLU, 1941) (a pamphlet). "Jehovah's Witnesses, Who Refuse to Salute U.S. Flag, Hold Their National Convention," *Life,* August 1940, pp. 20–21. See also Murphy et al. *Interpretation,* 1027.

27. Irving Dillard, "The Flag Salute Cases," in *Quarrels That Have Shaped the Constitution,* ed. John A. Garraty, rev. ed. (New York: Harper & Row, 1987), 285–306.

28. See chap. 4 below.

29. The U.S. Supreme Court upheld the 1942 executive order restricting persons of Japanese ancestry (see chap. 1, n. 25) in a 6–3 decision in 1944. Murphy et al., *Interpretation,* 64–70; Peter Irons, *Justice at War* (New York: Oxford University Press, 1983).

30. See chap. 5 of this book.

Chapter 1. The Setting

1. *Encyclopaedia Britannica,* 1965 ed., s.v. "Alabama," by Charles G. Summersell.

2. U.S. Dept. of Commerce, Jesse H. Jones, Secretary, Bureau of the Census, *Religious Bodies, 1936,* vol. 1 (Washington, D.C.: U.S. Government Printing Office, 1941), 87–97. Adventist bodies total reported ca. 165,000 out of a total national church membership of 55,807,366—0.3 percent—but there is no mention of Jehovah's Witnesses, Bible Students, or Russellites. The Witness records indicate roughly 60,000–70,000 members in 1938. Watch Tower Bible and Tract Society of Pennsylvania, *The Yearbook of the Jehovah's Witnesses, 1975* (Brooklyn: Watchtower Bible and Tract Society of New York, 1976), 192.

3. Jerry Bergman, *Jehovah's Witnesses and Kindred Groups: A Historical Compendium and Bibliography,* Garland Reference Service of Social Science, vol. 180 (New York: Garland Publishing, 1984), xvi; J. Wayne Flynt, "Alabama," in *Encyclopedia of Religion in the South,* ed. Samuel S. Hill (Macon, Ga.: Mercer University Press, 1984), 8–22; Penton, *Apocalypse,* 253–60; Stroup, *Witnesses,* 29, 34, 80–82, and 154. Experts agree that it is difficult to determine the distribution and demographics of the Witnesses, for no membership lists were kept.

4. Victor W. Rotman and F. G. Folsom, Jr., "Recent Restrictions upon Religious Liberty," *American Political Science Review* 36 (December 1942): 53–68.

5. Eskridge interview; Harrison, *Visions*, 40–50; Penton, *Apocalypse*, 255–56. Harrison argues that the oppressed "respond . . . to the assurance that . . . all manner of blessings shall be their reward and the evil oppressors shall be blotted out" (50). Betty Eskridge, a longtime Witness, conjectures that the movement appeals particularly to the dispossessed, since one must be aware of the problems of this life to appreciate fully the hope of a restored Eden.

6. *Marsh v. Gulf Shipbuilding*, records of case with briefs, supporting documents, transcripts, as presented to the U.S. District Court in Mobile, October 18, 1944 (on file in National Archives—Southeast Region, East Point, Ga.); *Marsh v. Alabama*, records of case with briefs, supporting documents, transcripts, as presented to the U.S. Supreme Court, October term, 1945 (on microfiche at University of Alabama Law School); Grace Marsh, interview by the author, July 25, 1990, typewritten transcription of tape recording (in possession of the author). The *Marsh* records clearly give examples of active women. See also Penton, *Apocalypse*, 261–70, and Stroup, *Witnesses*, 32.

7. James McBride Dabbs, *Who Speaks for the South?* (New York: Funk & Wagnalls, 1964), 102–106, 310. Rosco and Thelma Jones found that they could work areas of greatest resistance more effectively if Mrs. Jones went alone in the day, for no one thought much about a black woman walking in the rural areas, but a black man would be suspect. Rosco Jones, "Putting Kingdom Interest First in My Life," 48 (unpublished manuscript in possession of the author [photocopy]).

8. Jody Carlson, *George C. Wallace and the Politics of Powerlessness* (New Brunswick: Transaction Books, 1991), 2; V. O. Key, Jr., *Southern Politics in State and Nation* (New York: Knopf, 1949), 7, 8. For other significant works that portray the mood of the South in the period, see W. J. Cash, *The Mind of the South* (New York: Knopf, 1941); Carl N. Degler, *Place over Time: The Continuity of Southern Distinctiveness* (Baton Rouge: Louisiana State University Press, 1977); and George B. Tindall, *The Emergence of the New South, 1913–1945* (Baton Rouge: Louisiana State University Press, 1967).

9. Ibid., 106. Lee N. Allen, "The Woman Suffrage Movement in Alabama, 1910–1920," in *From Civil War to Civil Rights: Alabama, 1860–1960, An Anthology from the Alabama Review*, ed. Sarah Woolfolk Wiggins (Tuscaloosa: University of Alabama Press, 1987), 279–93. Hallie Farmer, *The Legislative Process in Alabama* (University: Bureau of Public Administration of Alabama, University of Alabama, 1949), 276; David L. Martin, *Alabama's State and Local*

Governments, 2d ed. (Tuscaloosa: University of Alabama Press, 1985), 78; and *Alabama: The News Magazine of the Deep South* 4 (February 20, 1939): 6, and 12 (January 24, 1947): 12. *White v. Crook,* 251 Fed. Supp. 401 (M.D. Ala. 1966); Tinsley Yarbrough, *Judge Frank Johnson and Human Rights in Alabama* (University: University of Alabama Press, 1981), 158. For an interesting view of a somewhat outspoken white Alabama woman, see Virginia Foster Durr, *Outside the Magic Circle: The Autobiography of Virginia Foster Durr,* ed. Hollinger F. Barnard (University: University of Alabama Press, 1986).

10. Dabbs, *Who Speaks,* chap. 21. Officials treated Rosco and Thelma Jones condescendingly; one court official referred to Mrs. Jones as "Thelma," for example, and the arresting officer addressed Mr. Jones as "Rosco" and called to him, "Hey you." *Jones v. City of Opelika,* records of case with briefs, supporting documents, transcripts, as presented to the U.S. Supreme Court, October term, 1941 (on microfiche at University of Alabama Law School), Alabama Proceedings, 42, 47. See also Rosco Jones, "Kingdom," 65–70.

11. Rosco Jones, "Kingdom," 1–4. See also chap. 2 below.

12. Heather Botting and Gary Botting, *The Orwellian World of Jehovah's Witnesses* (Toronto: University of Toronto Press, 1984), 76; Bergman, *Jehovah's Witnesses,* xiii; Stroup, *Witnesses,* 101.

13. Marsh interview, 3; Grace Marsh, "My Biography," 1971 (unpublished manuscript in possession of the author [photocopy]), 1–3; Grace Marsh to Merlin Owen Newton, July 14, 1991 (in possession of the author). See also chap. 2 below.

14. Marsh interview, 5.

15. Pete Daniel, *Standing at the Crossroads: Southern Life Since 1900* (New York: Hill & Wang, 1986), 1–10, 94.

16. Samuel S. Hill, *Religion and the Solid South* (Nashville: Abingdon Press, 1972), 9–54 (quotation on 45). See also Dabbs, *Who Speaks,* 337–40. Bertram Wyatt-Brown, "Ethical Background of Hugo Black's Career: Thoughts Prompted by the Essays of Sheldon Hackney and Paul L. Murphy," in *Justice Hugo Black and Modern America,* ed. Tony Freyer (Tuscaloosa: University of Alabama Press, 1990), 157–68, emphasizes the popularity of the brotherhoods as "bonding" agents, with appeal through "ritual and idolatry." Perhaps such attractions pulled in members who might otherwise have identified with a strictly religious group. David Edwin Harrell, Jr., states that "many evangelical Christians viewed them as rival organizations." Harrell to Merlin Owen Newton, January 28, 1992 (in possession of the author).

17. Dabbs, *Who Speaks,* 108; Daniel, *Crossroads,* 8; Hill, *Solid South,* 35. Alabama State Bar Association *Proceedings,* Sixty-Third Annual Meeting, 1940,

p. 332, quotes from the address by Fitzgerald Hall: "If a man has got anything in him, he will make the grade; and, if he has not, I do not think society need bother or tax itself to save him."

18. Manning J. Dauer, "Recent Political Thought," *Journal of Politics* 10 (May 1948): 327–53 (citing Alan Tate on 333), part of a series, "The Southern Political Scene, 1938–1948"; Ralph McGill, *The South and the Southerner* (Boston: Little, Brown, 1959): 151–71; J. Wayne Flynt, "Religion in the Urban South: The Divided Religious Mind of Birmingham, 1900–1930," in *From Civil War*, ed. Wiggins, 256–78.

19. Hill, *Solid South*, 51.

20. David Edwin Harrell, Jr., "Evolution of Plain-Folk Religion in the South, 1835–1920," in *Varieties of Southern Religious Experience*, ed. Samuel S. Hill (Baton Rouge: Louisiana State University Press, 1988), 24–51, and "The South: Seedbed of Sectarianism," in *Varieties of Southern Evangelicalism*, ed. David Edwin Harrell, Jr. (Macon, Ga.: Mercer University Press, 1981), 50.

21. Harrell, "Seedbed," 50–55.

22. Tony Freyer, *The Little Rock Crisis: A Constitutional Interpretation* (Westport, Conn.: Greenwood Press, 1984), 11–12. Hugo Black, Alabama's great justice, for example, possessed an almost fanatical obedience to the law. Hugo Black, Jr., *My Father: A Remembrance* (New York: Random House, 1975), 152–55. The justice referred to the Constitution as his "legal Bible." Black, *Faith*, 41. William H. Thomas, "College Men and World Currents," An Address to Alumni, Emory University, Ga., 1906, p. 14. Thomas Addresses, Alabama Pamphlets File, Alabama Department of Archives and History, Montgomery, Ala. Dabbs, *Who Speaks*, 67. Wyatt-Brown, "Hugo Black," 162, characterizes the justice as a "Ciceronian" "man of honor."

23. Daniel, *Crossroads*, 63–68. In assessing the reaction of white southerners to the New Deal and World War II, Daniel states, "Southerners had always seen the world as sharply divided between good and evil, us and them, black and white." For Confederate heirs, see Dabbs, *Who Speaks*, 125.

24. Walter B. Jones, "The Alabamian's Creed," *The Alabama Lawyer: Official Organ, State Bar Association* 2 (January 1941): 118. Jones, who had served as a circuit court judge from 1902 to 1914, edited the journal for the Alabama bar association.

25. Jonathan M. Wiener, "Class Structure and Economic Development in the American South," *American Historical Review* 84 (October 1979): 988. Herman Jay Braunhut, "Farm Labor Wage Rates in the South, 1909–1948," *Southern Economic Journal* 16 (October 1949): 189–90, citing U.S. Department of Agriculture Technical Bulletin 895, July 1945. J. Wayne Flynt, "Spindle, Mine, and

Mule: The Poor White Experience in Post–Civil War Alabama," in *From Civil War*, ed. Wiggins, 384. David Eugene Conrad, *The Forgotten Farmers: The Story of Sharecroppers in the New Deal* (Westport, Conn.: Greenwood Press, 1965).

26. Flynt, "Poor White," 387–94; Alexander Kendrick, "Alabama Goes on Strike," *Nation* 139 (August 29, 1934): 233–34; Charles G. Summersell, *Alabama History for Schools* (Birmingham, Ala.: Colonial Press, 1957), 441. TCI sold the property in 1939–1941 to the Chickasaw Development Company, which was soon absorbed into Gulf Shipbuilding Corporation. Records, *Marsh v. Alabama*, Alabama Proceedings, 33–34.

27. C. Vann Woodward, *Origins of the New South, 1877–1913* (Baton Rouge: Louisiana State University Press, 1951); Lawrence Goodwyn, *Democratic Promise: The Populist Moment in America* (New York: Oxford University Press, 1976); Sheldon Hackney, *From Populism to Progressivism in Alabama* (Princeton: Princeton University Press, 1969); J. Morgan Kousser, *The Shaping of Southern Politics: Suffrage Restriction and the Establishment of the One-Party South, 1880–1910* (New Haven: Yale University Press, 1974), 264, 137; Allen W. Jones, "Political Reforms of the Progressive Era," in *From Civil War*, ed. Wiggins, 203–20; Malcolm C. McMillan, *Constitutional Development in Alabama, 1798–1901: Study in Politics, the Negro, and Sectionalism* (Chapel Hill: University of North Carolina Press, 1955); Martin, *Alabama's Governments*, 27–28; Durr, *Outside*, chap. 9; J. Mills Thornton, "Alabama Politics, J. Thomas Heflin, and the Expulsion Movement of 1929," in *From Civil War*, ed. Wiggins, 361.

28. William D. Barnard, *Dixiecrats and Democrats: Alabama Politics, 1942–1950* (University: University of Alabama Press, 1974), 1–10; *Encyclopaedia Britannica*, 1965 ed., s.v. "Alabama."

29. Barnard, *Dixiecrats*, 1–10; Carl Grafton and Anne Permaloff, *Big Mules and Branchheads: James E. Folsom and Political Power in Alabama* (Athens: University of Georgia Press, 1985), 45–50; Key, *Southern Politics*. For a somewhat different view, see Robert Wiebe, *Search for Order, 1877–1920* (New York: Hill & Wang, 1967); Hackney, *Populism to Progressivism;* Richard Hofstadter, *The Age of Reform: From Bryan to FDR* (New York: Vintage Books, 1955). For a nontraditional view of the Ku Klux Klan, Progressives, and Populists in Alabama, see J. Mills Thornton, "Hugo Black and the Golden Age," in *Justice Hugo Black and Modern America* (Tuscaloosa: University of Alabama Press, 1990), ed. Tony Freyer, 139–55, and "Alabama Politics." For another view of Hugo Black, see Virginia van der Veer Hamilton, *Hugo Black: The Alabama Years* (Baton Rouge: Louisiana State University Press, 1972).

A few small breezes of change stirred toward altering the near-total control by whites over the black community even before World War II, but the whirlwinds that would transform the state had not yet developed. See Robert J. Norrell, "Labor at the Ballot Box: Alabama Politics from the New Deal to the Dixiecrat Movement," *Journal of Southern History* 42 (May 1991): 201–34, and *Reaping the Whirlwind: The Civil Rights Movement in Tuskegee* (New York: Knopf, 1985); and J. Mills Thornton, "Challenge and Response in the Montgomery Bus Boycott of 1955–1956," in *From Civil War,* ed. Wiggins, 463–519.

30. H. C. Nixon, "Southern Legislatures and Legislation," *Journal of Southern Politics* 10 (May 1948): 410–17, part of a series, "The Southern Political Scene, 1938–1948." See also Martin, *Alabama's Governments,* 78; William D. Barnard, "The Old Order Changes: Graves, Sparks, Folsom, and the Gubernatorial Election of 1942," in *From Civil War,* ed. Wiggins, 415–18; Durr, *Outside,* 172–73 (on the split among Alabama's congressional delegation); Grafton and Permaloff, *Big Mules,* 51–55; William E. Gilbert, "Bibb Graves as a Progressive, 1927–1930," in *From Civil War,* ed. Wiggins, 336–48; Carl Grafton, "Community Power Methodology and Alabama Politics," *Alabama Historical Quarterly* 38 (Winter 1976): 271–90.

31. Grafton and Permaloff, *Big Mules,* 39–42, 51–53; *Alabama* 8 (January 15, 1943): 5. McCorvey and Dixon clearly belonged to the elite. For specifics as to social and religious ties, see Marie Bankhead Owen, *The Story of Alabama: A History of the State,* 5 vols. (New York: Lewis Historical Publishing, 1949), 4:404–405 and 5:1258.

32. Barnard, "Old Order." See also George E. Sims, *The Little Man's Big Friend: James E. Folsom in Alabama Politics, 1946–1958* (University: University of Alabama Press, 1985), chap. 1. *Alabama* 8 (January 22, 1943): 104. Daniel, *Crossroads,* 147; Committee on History of Alabama Division of the American Association of University Women [Ann Gary (Pannell) Taylor], *A Half Century of AAUW in Alabama, 1927–1977* (Tuscaloosa: Drake Printers, 1975), 12.

33. See Martin, *Alabama's Governments,* 107–13, for a description of the offices, and *Alabama* 5 (1940) as to male dominance and 12 (January 1947). See also above, my introduction, n. 9, and Alabama State Bar Association *Proceedings* of annual meetings, 1938–1948, for attitudes about blacks and "ladies." For congressional delegation, see Key, *Southern Politics,* 362, and *Alabama* 2 (December 6, 1937): 5 and *Alabama* 4 (June 19, 1939): 10–11.

34. Lee S. Greene, "The Southern State Judiciary," *Journal of Politics* 10 (August 1948): 441–64 (part of a series, "The Southern Political Scene, 1938–1948"); Owen, *History,* 2:310–13; Summersell, *History for Schools,* 457–58; Robert J. Frye, *The Alabama Supreme Court: An Institutional View* (University: Bureau of Public Administration, University of Alabama, 1969), 85–87.

35. The religious affiliation of a small percentage was unknown. Ibid., quotation on 88; statistics, 28–34.

36. Compiled by the author from *Alabama Blue Book and Social Register* (Birmingham, Ala.: Blue Book Publishing, 1929), 313, 315, and 324; Alabama Department of Archives and History, *Official and Statistical Register, 1943* (Wetumpka, Ala.: Wetumpka Printing, 1944), 193–99; Frank A. Grove, *Library of Alabama Lives* (Hopkinsville, Ky.: Historical Record Association, 1961), 328; Albert B. Moore, *History of Alabama and Her People* (Chicago: American Historical Society, 1927), 2:4, 35, 281–82, 518, 578; 3:4–5, 535; Owen, *History*, 2:323–24, 339–40, 903; 4:1221; John W. Sayers, comp. *Who's Who in Alabama*, (Birmingham, Ala.: Sayers Enterprises, 1965–1969), 1:207, 212, 323; 2:397; Records on Virgil Bouldin, Joel Brown, Arthur Foster, Lucien Gardner, Thomas Lawson, J. E. Livingston, Robert T. Simpson, Jr., Davis Stakely, and William H. Thomas, Surname Files, miscellaneous clippings and other information on some prominent Alabamians, alphabetically arranged by surname (microfilm), Alabama Department of Archives and History, Montgomery, Ala.

The Thirteen, created in Montgomery in 1902, has as its object "feasts of mind, with stomachs not neglected." The membership was restricted to thirteen; when a vacancy occurred, the existing members had to agree unanimously on the new associate. William H. Thomas of the Alabama Supreme Court was one of the founders; Virgil Bouldin and Lucien Gardner were members by the late 1930s. The men met twice a month except during the summer, and each took a turn in presenting a paper on some learned subject. Boxes 1–7 (unorganized, though essays are roughly chronological, beginning with Box 3), The Thirteen, Manuscript Division, Alabama Department of Archives and History, Montgomery, Ala. Some of Thomas's papers appear in various folders of the boxes, as do some papers by Bouldin and Gardner.

37. *Blue Book*, 313, 429; Moore, *History*, 2:38, 69–70; Owen, *History*, 2:317–18, 334–35; Charles R. Bricken, James Rice, and Robert T. Simpson, Jr., Surname Files; Alabama, *Statistical Register, 1943*, pp. 198–201. Robert Bryan Carr replaced Simpson in 1944, when the latter was elevated to the state supreme court. Alabama, *Statistical Register, 1947*, pp. 142–43.

38. *Blue Book*, 243–44; William H. Bowling, Surname Files; Moore, *History*, 3:560–61.

39. Owen, *History*, 4:238; David Edington, Surname Files: *Alabama Journal*, April 23, 1947, for comment on jurors; *Mobile Press*, March 20, 1946, for comment on blacks; *Mobile Register*, January 18, 1948, for "right road" comment.

40. Martin, *Alabama's Governments,* 67; Owen, *History,* 4:340; Alabama, *Statistical Register,* 1939, p. 394.

41. Church Listings and accounts of activities, *Opelika Daily News,* 1939–1943; Thelma Jones, "Leaving All Things Behind to Follow in the Footsteps of Christ Jesus: True Life Story," 17 (unpublished manuscript in possession of the author [photocopy]).

42. Alexander Nunn, ed., *Lee County and Her Forbears* (Montgomery, Ala.: Herff Jones, 1983), 24–36; Alabama, *Statistical Register,* 1939, p. 452; 1943, p. 474.

43. For a discussion of the national attitude toward foreign policy, see John M. Blum, William S. McFeely, Edmund S. Morgan, Arthur M. Schlesinger, Jr., Kenneth M. Stampp, and C. Vann Woodward, *The National Experience: A History of the United States,* 7th ed. (San Diego: Harcourt Brace Jovanovich, 1988), 649–52.

44. T. D. Samford, Jr., also shared ties with Bill Duke—both had grown up in Opelika and graduated from Alabama Polytechnic Institute, and both served as counselors for the First National Bank of Opelika. *Blue Book,* 372–73; Moore, *History,* 2:681; Owen, *History,* 4:773–74; *The Martindale-Hubbell Law Directory, 1966* (New York: Martindale-Hubbell Publishers, 1966), 1: Biographical Data, 80B–81B.

45. C. E. Matthews and Anderson Brown, *Highlights of 100 Years in Mobile* (Mobile, Ala.: Powers, 1965), 121; L. J. Smith, *A Brief Sketch of the History of Chickasaw* (n.p.: Chickasaw Chamber of Commerce, 1958 [pamphlet]), 3, 6, 11–14, 22, 26. For evidence of Gulf ties to Waterman, see *Alabama* 6 (September 15, 1941).

46. *Blue Book,* 274–75; Francis Inge and Emory B. Peebles, Surname Files; *Martindale-Hubbell,* 1952, 1:44.

47. Marsh interview, 2; Records, *Marsh v. Gulf,* 128–31; Marsh to Newton, July 14, 1991; Thelma Jones, "Follow Christ," 3. Bergman, *Jehovah's Witnesses,* xiii; Penton, *Apocalypse,* 139; Stroup, *Witnesses,* 159, 165. Witnesses were "in this world but not of it" (Eskridge interview, 1). See also Melvin Dotson Curry, "Jehovah's Witnesses: The Effects of Millenarianism on the Maintenance of a Religious Sect" (Ph.D. diss., Florida State University, Tallahassee, 1980). The only Alabama attorney acting directly for the Witnesses in the two cases that I consider here was David R. Coley, Jr., of Mobile, not himself a Witness. *Mobile Register,* May 16, 1974. His motivation is unclear. Records of the Alabama State Bar Association *Proceedings,* Sixty-Fourth Annual Meeting in Mobile in 1941, pp. 13–14; Richard W. Vollmer, Jr., to Merlin Owen Newton, May 14, 1991 (in possession of the author).

James A. Simpson of Birmingham agreed to sign the ACLU brief supporting the *Jones* appeal to the U.S. Supreme Court. ACLU to James A. Simpson, December 8, 9, 11, 1941; June 15, 26, 1942. Simpson to ACLU, June 17, 29, 1942; ACLU wire to Hayden Covington, January 19, 1942; ACLU minutes of national meeting, January 19, 1942; ACLU Correspondence, 1941: *Jones v. Opelika*, vol. 2317; ACLU Correspondence, 1942; *Jones v. Opelika*, vol. 2403; ACLU Files, Seeley G. Mudd Library, Princeton University, Princeton, N.J. Simpson's motive, like that of Coley, is not clear; *Alabama* 1–9 (1936–1944); Leah Rawls Atkins, "Senator James A. Simpson and Birmingham Politics of the 1930s: His Fight Against the Spoilsmen and the Pie-Men," *Alabama Review* 41 (January 1988): 3–29; Barnard, *Dixiecrats*, 3–4, 23, 55–58, 98, and 166; Virginia van der Veer Hamilton, *Lister Hill: Statesman from the South* (Chapel Hill: University of North Carolina Press, 1987), 76, 90, 116–30, 134, 144–46, 165, 170, 194, 203, 248, 322 n. 31; Grove, *Lives*, 387; and Sayers, *Who's Who*, 2:297; James E. Simpson to Merlin Owen Newton, January 8, 1991 (in possession of the author).

Douglas Arant of Birmingham, chairman of the American Bar Association's Committee for the Bill of Rights, corresponded with the ACLU regarding Simpson's involvement in support of *Jones* and the possibility of the committee's support of the ACLU brief. (The committee had earlier supported the ACLU brief in *Gobitis*.) Arant and the committee decided against supporting the brief in *Jones*. Douglas Arant to ACLU, December 20, 1941; June 29, July 7, and August 31, 1942; ACLU to Arant June 26, July 1, July 9, August 13, and September 2, 1942. ACLU Correspondence 1941 and 1942: *Jones v. Opelika*, vols. 2317 and 2403, ACLU Files. Arant had overcome a background of poverty but never forgot his roots. *Birmingham News*, May 2, 1976; *Alabama* 2 (July 19, 1937): 4; Sarah Woolfolk Wiggins to Merlin Newton, summer 1991 (in possession of the author).

In other cases in which Alabama Witnesses appealed to the ACLU for assistance, the Union had no luck in finding local attorneys who would represent them. ACLU Correspondence 1941: Alabama, Jehovah's Witnesses, vol. 2306, ACLU Files, includes J. W. Brashier, Mobile, to ACLU, June 28; ACLU to Brashier, July 12; ACLU to Mobile attorney Norman Rattner (regarding Brashier) July 12; ACLU to Shelley Floyd [or Floz], Route 1, Sampson, and W. McLean Pitts, attorney, Selma, September 6; ACLU to J. Edward Thornton, Montgomery, September 12 and 24, regarding Floyd; Pitts to ACLU, September 9; Floyd to ACLU, September 15; and Thornton to ACLU, October 8; three telegrams, T. A. Hilldring, Selma, to ACLU, December 12; two telegrams, ACLU to Hilldring, December 12; Hilldring to ACLU, December 14; Dewey Fountain to ACLU, December 15; ACLU to Hilldring, December 17. Hilldring stated that local officials and attorneys were prejudiced.

Chapter 2. The World of the Witnesses

1. For the rarity of second- and third-generation Witnesses, see Penton, *Apocalypse*, 254.

2. Marsh, "Biography," 1. The magazine was originally called *Zion's Watch Tower and Herald of Christ's Presence*. The title was amended several times before becoming the *Watchtower Announcing Jehovah's Kingdom* in 1939. The organization was initially incorporated as Zion's Watch Tower Tract Society, later known as Watch Tower Bible and Tract Society of Pennsylvania. In 1909, when the headquarters moved to Brooklyn, another corporation, the People's Pulpit Association, was formed, now known as the Watchtower Bible and Tract Society of New York, Incorporated. Cole, *Jehovah's Witnesses*, 50–51; Penton, *Apocalypse*, 29, 379; and Watch Tower, *Jehovah's Witnesses*, 6. In this study, "Watch Tower" is used when referring to the parent organization, and "Watchtower," when referring to the publications.

3. Marsh, "Biography," 1.

4. Ibid., 2; Marsh to Newton, July 14, 1991; Botting, *Orwellian World*, xix, 29, 118, 120–21; Penton, *Apocalypse*, 66, 280.

5. Marsh, "Biography," 1–2.

6. Russell began publishing by 1874 with *The Object and Manner of Our Lord's Return*, but his most important work was the multivolume *Studies in the Scriptures*. Particularly influenced by George Storrs and Dr. Nelson H. Barbour, once followers of William Miller, Russell constructed a "divine plan" that explained man's history and foresaw Christ's second coming and a millennium in which man could attain perfection through accepting Christ's ransom. Russell "correlated apocalyptic visions of transformation in the Bible with the groundswell of revolution fomenting in the Western world during his lifetime." Botting, *Orwellian World*, 3–16, 36–38; Cole, *Jehovah's Witnesses*, 50–51, 210; Penton, *Apocalypse*, 14–29, 75, 184–208. See also Anthony A. Hoekma, *The Four Major Cults* (Grand Rapids, Mich.: William B. Eerdmans, 1939), 258–308.

7. Penton, *Apocalypse*, 29–32, 44–46; Botting, *Orwellian World*, 36–38; Cole, *Jehovah's Witnesses*, 50–79; Watch Tower, *Jehovah's Witnesses*, 6. For the two young girls' memories of the Photo-Drama, see Marsh, "Biography," 2, and Thelma Jones, "Follow Christ," 1.

8. Russell's ambivalence on doctrine led to the secession of several hundred followers in 1909. Hostile clergymen and elements of the press also questioned his training, character, finances, and use of the Watch Tower corporation for personal publishing. His problems were compounded by an unsteady relationship with Maria Ackley, whom he had married in 1879, and the couple separated in 1897. In a bitter fight to legalize the separation, Maria implied that Charles was a near-adulterer. Cole, *Jehovah's Witnesses*, 62–72 and 209, and Penton, *Apocalypse*, 29–44, agree that Pastor Russell was fundamentally honest, if at times naive, and that Maria did not actually charge adultery. (She stated that the pastor had likened himself to a jellyfish that floated around and embraced anyone who responded to his touch.) Russell had no seminary training, but, Penton states (26), he read well and had a "reasonably good" writing style.

9. Penton, *Apocalypse*, 44–46.

10. As a young attorney Rutherford had substituted briefly as a special judge in Booneville, Missouri, from which he gained the honorary title, "Judge." Bergman, *Jehovah's Witnesses*, xviii; Cole, *Jehovah's Witnesses*, 213–14; Penton, *Apocalypse*, 47–48.

11. Penton, *Apocalypse*, 47–96 (quotation, 51). For varying accounts, see also Bergman, *Jehovah's Witnesses*, xx; Botting, *Orwellian World*, 38–39; Cole, *Jehovah's Witnesses*, 80–108; Curry, "Millenarianism," 185; Stroup, *Witnesses*, 13–15. Rutherford in 1917 had unilaterally commissioned the publishing of *The Finished Mystery*, which he stated was the seventh volume of Russell's series on the scriptures, although the vitriolic tone suggests the judge's hand. Although some "Russellites" left the Rutherford-controlled Witnesses, others stayed, causing tension between former followers of Russell and those who fully accepted Rutherford's new emphasis. The argument concerned whether to accept the "present truth," expressed in the Watchtower publications following Rutherford's ascendancy, or to cling to the pre-Rutherford Watchtower interpretation.

12. Botting, *Orwellian World*, 39–40; Cole, *Jehovah's Witnesses*, 90–94; Penton, *Apocalypse*, 55. The 1917 Espionage Act "punished anyone . . . seeking to cause disobedience in the armed services, or obstructing recruitment or enlistment." Fear of labor unrest and Bolshevism inspired additional restrictive legislation in 1918, the Sedition Act and the Alien Act, and the "Red Scare" of 1919–1920. Melvin I. Urofsky, *A March of Liberty: A Constitutional History of the United States* (New York: Knopf, 1988), 608–14.

13. Bergman, *Jehovah's Witnesses*, xix; Cole, *Jehovah's Witnesses*, 90–95 (quotation, 90–91); Penton, *Apocalypse*, 55–56; Stroup, *Witnesses*, 17. The *Golden Age* was renamed *Consolation* in 1937 and then *Awake!* in 1949. Cole, 95; Penton, 379.

By 1920 challenges to the wartime legislation had reached the U.S. Supreme Court, inspiring strong dissents by Justices Louis Brandeis and Oliver Wendell Holmes, Jr., Urofsky, *March,* 609–14.

14. Cole, *Jehovah's Witnesses,* 83, 96–98. See also Bergman, *Jehovah's Witnesses,* xxvii; Penton, *Apocalypse,* 56–57, 71–73.

15. Rosco Jones, "Kingdom," 1–4.

16. Thelma Jones, "Follow Christ," 4.

17. Rosco Jones, "Kingdom," 4–5; Thelma Jones, "Follow Christ," 2–3.

18. Rosco Jones, "Kingdom," 5–10.

19. Marsh, "Biography," 2.

20. Ibid., 2–3; Marsh to Newton, July 14, 1991.

21. Rosco Jones, "Kingdom," 1, 10–14; Penton, *Apocalypse,* 271.

22. Ibid.

23. Rosco Jones, "Kingdom," 10–22; Thelma Jones, "Follow Christ," 3–4. For the nature of the rift, see above, chap. 2, n. 11.

24. Thelma Jones, "Follow Christ," 4–5; Rosco Jones, "Kingdom," 21–22.

25. Penton, *Apocalypse,* 265–68. For an overview of the Witness world of sexual relationships, see W. Seward Salisbury, *Religion in American Culture* (Homewood, Ill.: Dorsey Press, 1964), 195–205. See also Witness literature, such as Watch Tower Bible and Tract Society of Pennsylvania, *You Can Live Forever in Paradise on Earth* (Brooklyn: Watchtower Bible and Tract Society of New York, 1982). In the mid-1950s, after Hayden Covington and then Nathan Knorr had taken brides, attitudes shifted. Women were always considered subordinate to men, and a good wife was expected to be obedient and modest. Eskridge interview; Harrison, *Visions,* 77; Penton, *Apocalypse,* 261–70. Jones to Newton, March 14, 1991.

26. Penton, *Apocalypse,* 62; Cole, *Jehovah's Witnesses,* 101.

27. Cole, *Jehovah's Witnesses,* 102; Penton, *Apocalypse,* 62–63.

28. Rosco Jones, "Kingdom," 22–24; Thelma Jones, "Follow Christ," 5; Rogerson, *Millions,* 60. See also Witness testimony in Records, *Jones v. Opelika, Marsh v. Alabama,* and *Marsh v. Gulf.*

29. Botting, *Orwellian World,* 3–26; Hoekma, *Cults,* 258–323; Penton, *Apocalypse,* 64–65, 68–70, 184–208; Stroup, *Witnesses,* 134.

30. Ibid., with quotation from Hoekma, *Cults,* 278–79.

31. Salisbury, *Religion,* 195–205, for overview. See also Watch Tower, *Paradise.* Thelma Jones believes that she and her husband are among the "anointed," but Grace Marsh looks forward to living eternally in an earthly Eden. Jones interview, Marsh interview. Murphy et al., *Interpretation,* 1014 ("Whore").

32. Bergman, *Jehovah's Witnesses,* xiii, xxi, xxiii, 20; Cole, *Jehovah's Wit-*

nesses, 24, 106–108; Curry, "Millenarianism," 69; Penton, *Apocalypse,* 70–76 and 151. Grace Marsh has a more tolerant view of non-Witnesses. Marsh interview, 8.

33. Penton, *Apocalypse,* 239; Rosco Jones, "Kingdom," 25, 30; Thelma Jones, "Follow Christ," 5–7.

34. Rosco Jones, "Kingdom," 27–28.

35. Cole, *Jehovah's Witnesses,* 99; Rosco Jones, "Kingdom," 25; Thelma Jones, "Follow Christ," 9; Marsh, "Biography," 6; Penton, *Apocalypse,* 71.

36. Rosco Jones, "Kingdom," 25–27.

37. Rosco Jones, "Kingdom," 30.

38. Brown was the brother of comedian Joe E. Brown. Thelma Jones, "Follow Christ," 10; Rosco Jones, "Kingdom," 31–32.

39. Rosco Jones, "Kingdom," 33–34; Penton, *Apocalypse,* 65.

40. Thelma Jones, "Follow Christ," 10–11.

41. Rosco Jones, "Kingdom," 36–39, 41.

42. Ibid., 41–42; regarding the Pentecostals, see Harrell, "Seedbed," 55.

43. Rosco Jones, "Kingdom," 42–43; Thelma Jones, "Follow Christ," 11–12.

44. Thelma Jones, "Follow Christ," 13–14.

45. Rosco Jones, "Kingdom," 43–45.

46. Ibid., 45–46.

47. Ibid., 45–48.

48. Ibid., 50–53.

49. Ibid., 55–57. It was probably not dangerous for a well-to-do southern white woman to be seen engaging in religious activity with polite, diminutive Thelma Jones, if that activity was confined to women and children and as long as the relationship fell within the prescribed structure. Mistresses of plantation days had befriended servants on occasions, caring for the sick, for example. The Joneses' records do not make clear the exact nature of the two women's joint evangelical activities.

50. Rosco Jones, "Kingdom," 31–32.

51. Rosco Jones, "Kingdom," 53–56; Thelma Jones, "Follow Christ," 15–16. The identity of the lawyer is unknown, but it is highly probable that he was white. Thelma Jones to Merlin Owen Newton, March 1, 1991 (in possession of the author).

52. Marsh, "Biography," 3–4.

53. Beckford, *Trumpet of Prophecy,* 16–17; Botting, *Orwellian World,* 4–6; Cole, *Jehovah's Witnesses,* 103–104. The position of elected elder was restored in 1972. See also Penton, *Apocalypse,* 69. David R. Manwaring, *Render unto*

Caesar: The Flag Salute Controversy (Chicago: University of Chicago Press, 1962).

54. See my introduction for Covington's role. See also Cole, *Jehovah's Witnesses*, 109–14.

Chapter 3. *Jones v. Opelika*

1. Rosco Jones, "Kingdom," 59; Jones to Newton, March 14, 1991; Thelma Jones, "Follow Christ," 16–17.

2. Rosco Jones, "Kingdom," 59.

3. Thelma Jones, "Follow Christ," 17. The zone director was appointed by the society to oversee about twenty congregations, encouraging preaching and "unity of action." Penton, *Apocalypse*, 69.

4. Rosco Jones, "Kingdom," 59–60.

5. Rosco Jones, "Kingdom," 61–65. "The clergymen started fighting against the truth for their lives," Rosco Jones stated, preferring "the good life" of free rent, a new car every two years, etc., to the truth. Thelma Jones, "Follow Christ," 19, refers to a "conspiracy" against their work. It was common for Witnesses to think that the community leaders conspired against them. Richard Hofstadter, *The Paranoid Style in American Politics and Other Essays* (New York: Vintage Books, 1967), 38, refers to Norman Cohn's definition of millenarianism in *The Pursuit of the Millennium* (London, 1957), 309–10. Medieval millennial sects revealed, he noted, "a persistent psychological complex . . . made up of . . . 'the megalomanic view of oneself as the Elect, wholly good, abominably persecuted yet assured of ultimate triumph . . . , the obsession with inerrable prophecies.'" The Witness belief system displays many of these attributes.

6. Thelma Jones, "Follow Christ," 18–19; Jones to Newton, March 14, 1991; Rosco Jones, "Kingdom," 65–66; Records, *Jones v. Opelika*, Alabama Proceedings, 40. The booklets attacked established religions, especially Roman Catholicism, for compromising with Mussolini. The accounts given by Rosco and Thelma Jones ("Kingdom" and "Follow Christ") are similar but were reconstructed many years after the arrest and differ on certain points from the official transcript of the trial in circuit court in November 1939. The major discrepancy involves whether Rosco brought, or assisted Thelma in bringing, the banner within the city limits of Opelika or whether she brought it alone. At the time of the trial Rosco Jones testified that he had confined proselytizing activities to the rural areas, that he had constructed the sign but that he had not brought it into

Opelika, that he and Thelma Jones had parted that day before the sign was brought to Ninth Street. The later accounts of both the Joneses do not mention her bringing the sign and even state that he left her with the banner ("Kingdom," 66; "Follow Christ," 19). There is no available official record of the arrest and trial in inferior court, events of April 1–3, 1939, but references to statements allegedly made during the trial in recorder's court occur in the record of the November circuit court trial. (Records, *Jones v. Opelika*, Alabama Proceedings, 40–49.)

Apparently officials originally charged Jones because they assumed the man of the house was responsible for the stand. According to Rosco Jones ("Kingdom," 69), he had no counsel in the recorder's court and acted to defend himself. Since he had not been with the sign at the time of Thelma's arrest, his original defense apparently centered on that point. (The couple probably assumed that Rosco was the main target and that if he were not convicted, the cases might be dropped, and they could continue their proselytizing.) But after both were charged and the recorder's court found Rosco guilty, they appealed to the circuit court and were represented by Witness attorney Grover Powell of Atlanta, who shifted the defense to the larger issue of First Amendment freedoms.

7. Thelma Jones, "Follow Christ," 19.

8. Records, *Jones v. Opelika*, Alabama Proceedings, 47.

9. Rosco Jones, "Kingdom," 67–68; Thelma Jones, "Follow Christ," 19; Jones to Newton, March 14, 1991. William S. Duke, counsel for the city of Opelika, agreed to an interview by Merlin Owen Newton, July 9, 1990 (tape recording and transcription in possession of author), but failed to respond to repeated requests to validate all or parts of the transcription of the taped interview. Information regarding Duke's role can thus only be surmised from common practices and from what can be gleaned from statements in the court records.

10. Rosco Jones, "Kingdom," 68–70; Thelma Jones to Merlin Owen Newton, March 28, 1991 (in possession of the author); Records, *Jones v. Opelika*, Alabama Proceedings, 11. Thelma Jones was also charged, but apparently her case was considered secondary to that of her husband. Whether she was tried in recorder's court or was simply bound over is unsure. Similarly, it is unclear whether she had to make bond. At the time of the later circuit court trial, her case was postponed, pending the outcome of Rosco Jones's appeal. See below, chap.3, n. 32.

11. *Opelika Daily News*, April 1–30, 1939.

12. Personal observations by the author and by the author's spouse, Wesley P. Newton, both of whom grew up in southern communities in the 1930s and 1940s. Wesley Phillips Newton, memo to Merlin Newton, October 7, 1991 (in

possession of the author). Records, *Jones v. Opelika,* Brief for Respondent in Opposition to Writ of Certiorari to U.S. Supreme Court, 6. W. B. Bowling, the Alabama trial court judge who heard Jones's case at the circuit court level, emphasized in his rulings during the trial that the only question was whether Jones "was violating a simple ordinance here that has been in effect for a long time," that he had no more "right to sell books on the streets than a person . . . not a minister." Records, *Jones v. Opelika,* Alabama Proceedings, 46.

13. Rosco Jones, "Kingdom," 61–65; Thelma Jones, "Follow Christ," 19. See also above, chap. 3, n. 5.

14. 303 U.S. 444 (1938).

15. 310 U.S. 296 (1940).

16. *Martindale-Hubbell, 1966;* 1:913; Records, *Jones v. Opelika,* Alabama Proceedings, 11–12.

17. *Opelika Daily News,* May 19, 1939. For details of a concurrent effort by Jones to ensure a jury trial, see *Jones v. Opelika,* 30 Ala. App. 274 (1939), 4 So.2d 507 (1941).

18. Records, *Jones v. Opelika,* Alabama Proceedings, 44–45; Rosco Jones, "Kingdom," 70–71.

19. Rosco Jones, "Kingdom," 71–72. Possibly Jones exaggerated the amount of the bond, since the bond set at the recorder's court proceeding on April 8 had been only $125, and the bond set after Jones's conviction in the Fifth Circuit Court on November 2 was only $200. (Records, *Jones v. Opelika,* Alabama Proceedings, 17). Perhaps, however, the bonds were raised as the Joneses were repeatedly arrested. Grace Marsh, for example, experienced a dramatic increase in the bond required for similar offenses as those offenses were repeated (Records, *Marsh v. Gulf,* 100–101). Unfortunately, the city of Opelika has no records available on events in municipal court in 1939. The larger question of the judge's putative offer to settle for twenty dollars cannot be verified or disproved by any other known source.

20. *Opelika Daily News,* November 2, 1939.

21. Records, *Jones v. Opelika,* Alabama Proceedings, 12–14, 16.

22. Ibid., 21–39, 60–61.

23. Ibid., 39–41.

24. Ibid., 41–44.

25. Ibid., 14–16.

26. Ibid., 41–42, 45–47.

27. Ibid., 44–50.

28. Ibid., 50–53. The transcript identifies both Baker and McLeod as Methodists but does not list the church that Baker pastored. It misspells McLeod's

name as McCloud. The *Opelika Daily News* of November 3, 1939, stated that Baker was associated with Trinity Methodist.

29. Records, *Jones v. Opelika*, Alabama Proceedings, 50–53. The ministers who were not allowed to testify were A. C. Windham, W. H. Perry, M. C. Schrader, O. M. Mesick, Wilbur Walton, J. B. Seay, W. A. Hamilton, and J. L. Griffin. Perry was white. It is probable that some of the ministers were black (*Opelika Daily News*, May 10, 1939). Powell was apparently wishing to cross-examine the previous city witnesses, but Duke did not want him to have that advantage at that point. The term "rebuttal" was probably used in a general sense rather than in the strictly legal sense.

30. Ibid., 53–54. The character witnesses who were not allowed to take the stand were J. L. Battle, Fred Slaughter, and Albert Trimble. (Thelma Jones, "Follow Christ," 18, refers to a Witness in Opelika named Elbert Trimble, probably the same person called by the defense to testify as to Jones's good reputation. Elbert Trimble was black, but I do not know the race of the others.)

31. Ibid., 15–17.

32. *Opelika Daily News*, November 3, 1939.

33. Rosco Jones, "Kingdom," 74–76. Linch is listed as sheriff in Alabama, *Statistical Register*, 1939, p. 373. The state highway patrol was still very young in the 1930s, and the listing in Alabama, *Statistical Register*, 1935, p. 89, covering the period before Linch became sheriff includes only the highest echelon. The author cannot confirm that Linch was in the patrol before becoming sheriff. It is possible that he may have been a deputy sheriff, rather than a patrolman, when he allegedly stopped Jones.

34. Records, *Jones v. Opelika*, Alabama Proceedings, 17–21, 56–61.

35. *Blue Book*, 313, 429; Alabama, *Statistical Register*, 1943, pp. 198–201; Grove, *Library*, 486; Moore, *History*, 2:38, 69–70; Owen, *History*, 2:317–18, 334–35; Sayers, *Who's Who*, 2:297; Frye, *Alabama Supreme Court*, 55–57, 85; Alabama Legislative Reference, Alabama State Capitol, Montgomery, *Alabama Courts* (December 15, 1954), 7. Typewritten pamphlet.

36. *Blue Book*, 429; Moore, *History*, 2:69–70; James Rice, Surname Files; *Lovell v. Griffin*, 303 U.S. 444 (1938).

37. 3 So.2d 74 (Ala. Ct. App. 1941).

38. Lum Duke had died in December 1940, but William Duke continued to use the firm name for several years. Lum Duke, Surname Files; *Martindale-Hubbell*, 1942, 1:16.

39. 3 So.2d 76 (Ala. 1941). A per curiam decision is an opinion of the whole court as distinct from an opinion written by one judge. A writ of certiorari, when

it is granted, signifies that an appellate court is exercising its discretion to hear an appeal; once granted, the writ orders the lower court to send up the records so that the higher court can review the case.

40. Frye, *Alabama Supreme Court*, 55–57, 85. Also see above, chap. 1.

41. Frye, *Alabama Supreme Court*, 35–42; John L. Goodwyn, "The Supreme Court at Work," *Alabama Lawyer: Official Organ State Bar of Alabama* 21 (January 1960): 6–10.

42. For information that reveals the interlocking relationships, see *Blue Book*, 324 (Gardner) and 360 (W. H. Thomas); Moore, *History*, 2:4 (Gardner) and 3:4–5 (W. H. Thomas); Alabama, *Statistical Register*, 1943, pp. 194–98; and Lucien Gardner and William Holcombe Thomas, Surname Files. See also Boxes 1–7, The Thirteen. For information on The Thirteen, see above, chap. 1, n. 36.

43. Alabama, *Statistical Register*, 1943, p. 224. Georgia Thomas had married William Varner of Tuskegee. For Thomas's Chambers and Lee County ties, see Alabama, *Statistical Register*, 360 (Thomas) and 372–73 (T. D. Samford); Moore, *History*, 2:681 (Duke) and 3:4–5 (Thomas), 560–61 (Bowling); Owen, *History*, 2:339–40 (Thomas); and William B. Bowling, Lum Duke, and William Holcombe Thomas, Surname Files.

44. Thomas, "College Men," 13–14, and "Law and License," 4, in Thomas Addresses.

45. Thomas, "College Men," 13–14; "The New South—An Inside View," 1–10, 18; in Thomas Addresses. William Holcombe Thomas, "The Layman in Religious Life," *Alabama Christian Advocate*, June 10, 1908, pp. 2–4. See also William Holcombe Thomas, Surname Files. Thomas's views by 1940–1941 did not necessarily reflect the official opinion of southern Methodism. The *Christian Advocate* during 1940 and much of 1941 was concerned with opposing liquor, gambling, and war, not with Jehovah's Witnesses. See, for example, April 26, May 14, July 11, September 26, and November 14, 1940; and May 26 and July 3, 1941. By December 11, 1941, however, the journal had taken a stand against forcing flag salutes. On racial questions, the *Advocate* did not promote racial equality, but it did take some positions toward a more just policy. It declared on November 7, 1940, that the courts should not make racial distinctions; observed on January 9, 1941, that Nazi treatment of Jews was wrong and a threat to Christianity as well as Judaism; and on July 10, 1941, spoke out against lynching.

46. 3 So.2d 76 (Ala. 1941). *Cox v. New Hampshire*, 312 U.S. 569 (1941), and *Schneider v. Irvington, New Jersey*, 308 U.S. 147 (1939).

47. See, for example, the two major newspapers of the state capital, the *Montgomery Advertiser* and the *Alabama Journal*, and the two primary papers in

the state's largest city, the *Birmingham Age-Herald* and the *Birmingham News*, May 22 and May 23, 1941. The *Opelika Daily News* report ran on May 22, 1941. *Alabama Baptist,* October 30, 1941, p. 4.

48. 314 U.S. 593 (1941); 3 So.2d 74 (Ala. Ct. App. 1941); Records, *Jones v. Opelika,* Petitioner's Brief to U.S. Supreme Court, 2. 315 U.S. 782 (1941); Records, *Jones v. Opelika,* Respondent's Brief. The firm assisting Duke was Hogan & Hartson, John W. Guideer, Lester Cohen.

49. Records, *Jones v. Opelika,* Petition for Rehearing and Appendixes.

50. Rosco Jones, "Kingdom," 7, 78–83; Cole, *Jehovah's Witnesses,* 106; Thelma Jones, "Follow Christ," 23–25.

Chapter 4. An Uneasy Supreme Court

1. Osmond F. Fraenkel to ACLU, November 26, 1941, ACLU Correspondence, 1941: *Jones v. Opelika,* vol. 2317, ACLU Files.

2. The larger point was, of course, the national constitution, but while the case was being considered at state level, the Witnesses also relied on the Alabama provisions regarding freedom of press and religion.

3. Records, *Jones v. Opelika,* Alabama Proceedings, particularly 56–61 and 62–65.

4. Adolpheus T. Mason, *Harlan Fiske Stone: Pillar of the Law* (New York: Archon Books, 1968), 508–33. For information on *United States v. Carolene Products Co.,* 304 U.S. 144 (1938), see above, my introduction.

5. 310 U.S. 586 (1940).

6. Ibid. For an interview with Lillian Gobitis many years after, see Peter Irons, *The Courage of Their Convictions: Sixteen Americans Who Fought Their Way to the Supreme Court* (New York: Free Press, 1988), 15–35.

7. Michael E. Parrish, *Felix Frankfurter and His Times: The Reform Years* (New York: Free Press, 1982), 1–3. Frankfurter's liberal causes included participation in the founding of the *New Republic* and in the Sacco-Vanzetti defense.

8. *Minersville Sch. Dist. v. Gobitis,* 310 U.S. 586, 598–600 (1944).

9. C. Herman Pritchett, "Stanley Reed," in *The Justices of the United States Supreme Court, 1789–1969: Their Lives and Major Opinions,* ed. Leon Friedman and Fred L. Israel (New York: Chelsea House Publishers and R. R. Bowker, 1969), 2373–99. See also Abraham, *Freedom and the Court,* 296–98, and Murphy et al., *Interpretation,* 163–80.

10. David Bruner, "Owen J. Roberts," in *Justices,* ed. Freidman and Israel, 2253–63.

11. Tony Freyer, *Hugo L. Black and the Dilemma of American Liberalism* (Glenview, Ill.: Scott Foresman/Little, Brown Higher Education, 1990), 78. For Black's pre-Court years, see also Hamilton, *Black: Alabama Years*.

12. Vern Countryman, "Justice Douglas and Freedom of Expression," in *Six Justices on Civil Rights*, David C. Baum Memorial Lectures, ed. and with an introduction by Ronald D. Rotunda (New York: Oceana Publications, 1983), 107–33; J. Woodford Howard, Jr., *Mr. Justice Murphy: A Political Biography* (Princeton: Princeton University Press, 1968), 203.

13. 310 U.S. 586, 604–606 (1940); Mason, *Stone*, 532–33.

14. ACLU, *Persecution; Cox v. New Hampshire*, 312 U.S. 569 (1941); *Chaplinsky v. New Hampshire*, 315 U.S. 568, 569 (1942). Chaplinsky had allegedly called the marshal "a God damned racketeer" and "a damned Fascist." See above, chap. 3, re Jones, and below, chap. 5, re Marsh.

15. Philip B. Kurland, "Justice Robert H. Jackson—Impact on Civil Rights and Civil Liberties," in Rotunda, *Six Justices*, 60. See also Milton R. Konvitz, *Religious Liberty and Conscience: A Constitutional Inquiry* (New York: Viking Press, 1968), 41–43.

16. Craig R. Ducat and Harold W. Chase, *Constitutional Interpretation*, 4th ed. (St. Paul: West Publishing, 1988), 1583–84; Murphy et al., *Interpretation*, 61–70. For the dynamics of the Court, see also Walter F. Murphy, *Elements of Judicial Strategy* (Chicago: University of Chicago Press, 1964), and Mason, *Stone*.

17. Penton, *Apocalypse*, 48, 72–78. See also Bergman, *Jehovah's Witnesses*, xx, xxv; Botting, *Orwellian World*, 40–42; and Cole, *Jehovah's Witnesses*, 106–107. Although Rutherford disciplined and organized a zealous following, with regard to his private life he was widely criticized for heavy drinking, extreme bursts of temper, extravagant living, and secretive behavior with respect to finances. His abusive language is well documented throughout Watchtower publications and other accounts of his speeches. Cole's semiofficial history emphasizes that Rutherford came to power in a time of division and that he came and went fighting. Whatever his flaws, he evoked strong positive emotions in his followers. Hayden Covington, the extremely effective legal counsel for the Witnesses, declared, "God was writing through Rutherford," who was "definitely inspired" (Bergman, 20). There is little question that many others shared the feeling of near-reverence for the judge. Certainly, Ben and Betty Eskridge, Thelma Jones, and Grace Marsh thought him inspired (Eskridge, Jones, and Marsh interviews). Knorr, Franz, and Covington were white. Most of the top positions in the society were filled by white males. For a discussion of the racial composition of the Witnesses, see above, my introduction, n. 9.

18. Ibid., Botting, *Orwellian World,* 41–43; Cole, *Jehovah's Witnesses,* 100–108, 210–13 (quotation). Franz, born in Covington, Kentucky, in 1893, remained a key figure behind the scenes, recognized as a "first-class scholar" and fluent in five languages. He eventually replaced Covington as vice president of the Watch Tower Society and, after Knorr's death in 1977, became president. He died December 22, 1992, with very little known about his private life (Bergman, *Jehovah's Witnesses,* xxxv–xxxvii).

19. Cole, *Jehovah's Witnesses,* 212–13. "Religion," *Newsweek,* March 22, 1943, pp. 68–69. The article ends with a quotation from the court clerk, "He may not have done more talking than anyone I've heard here, but he did more calisthenics."

20. Roger Baldwin to Hayden Covington, September 4, 1942, ACLU Correspondence 1942: *Jones v. Opelika,* vol. 2403, ACLU Files. Covington was not held in contempt, and he won the case.

21. 314 U.S. 593 (1941); 3 So.2d 74 (Ala. Ct. App. 1941), Records, *Jones v. Opelika,* Brief for Respondent in Opposition to Petition for Writ of Certiorari, 5, citing *Haseltine v. Central Bank of Springfield, Mo.,* 183 U.S. 130, 131 (1901); Petition and Petitioner's Brief for a Writ of Certiorari to the U.S. Supreme Court, particularly 17–18; Petitioner's Reply Brief.

22. 314 U.S. 593 (1941); Records, *Jones v. Opelika,* Respondent's Brief, 1–16.

23. Ibid., Petitioner's Reply Brief on Certiorari, 2–4 (italics mine).

24. 315 U.S. 593 (1942); 7 So.2d 503 (Ala. 1942). For a more complete discussion of the technicalities of the appeal process, see above, chap. 3.

25. 316 U.S. 584 (1942); Records, *Jones v. Opelika,* Suggestion That Jurisdictional Defect Has Been Supplied and Petition for Rehearing.

26. Clifford Forster to Osmond K. Fraenkel, November 21 and December 9; Fraenkel to ACLU, November 21; Minutes of ACLU Board of Directors, December 8; ACLU to William S. Duke, December 8, 12, and 17; Lester Cohen of Hogan & Hartson to Arthur Garfield Hays, General Counsel ACLU, December 16; Hays to Cohen, December 17; ACLU Correspondence, 1941: *Jones v. Opelika,* vol. 2317 ACLU Files; Cohen to Fraenkel, January 28, ACLU Correspondence, 1942: *Jones v. Opelika,* vol. 2403, ACLU Files.

27. Arant to ACLU, December 20, ACLU Correspondence, 1941: *Jones v. Opelika,* vol. 2317, ACLU Files; Arant to ACLU, June 19, July 7, August 31; ACLU to Arant, June 26, July 1, July 9, August 13, and September 2, ACLU Correspondence, 1942: *Jones v. Opelika,* vol. 2403, ACLU Files. For more information on Arant, see above, chap. 1, n. 47.

28. Atkins, "Simpson," 3–29. See also Thornton, "Golden Age," for a discussion of the relationship of the Klan and New Deal liberalism.

29. ACLU to Simpson, December 8, 9, 11; Arant to ACLU, December 20; ACLU to Fraenkel regarding Simpson's acceptance, December 22, ACLU Correspondence, 1941: *Jones v. Opelika*, vol. 2317, ACLU Files. Clifford Forster, ACLU Staff Counsel, to Hayden Covington, January 19, ACLU Correspondence, 1942: *Jones v. Opelika*, vol. 2403, ACLU Files. In response to a similar request of March 8, 1943, Covington reportedly stated that Watch Tower President Nathan Knorr had entrusted the full control over the case to him and that under those circumstances he could not share the time. Roger Baldwin to Osmond Fraenkel, March 9, 1943, relaying a telephone conversation with Attorney Roy A. Swayze, Washington, D.C., of the Jehovah's Witnesses. For more information on Swayze, see below, chap. 5, n. 40.

30. 316 U.S. 584 (1942); Records, *Jones v. Opelika*, Petitioner's Brief; Respondent's Brief on Petition of Certiorari, 5–6.

31. 3 U.S. 562 (1941); 117 F.2d 661 (1st Cir. 1941).

32. Records, *Jones v. Opelika*, Brief in Support of Petition for Writ of Certiorari, 17–18.

33. Ibid., 23, 24; Petitioner's Brief, 16, 32.

34. Ibid., Petitioner's Brief, 6–9.

35. *Watson v. Jones*, 80 U.S. 679, 728 (1871). Records, *Jones v. Opelika*, Petition for Certiorari, 5, 19; Petitioner's Brief in Support of Petition for Certiorari, 10, 14, 18, 19–20; Petitioner's Reply Brief on Certiorari, 4.

36. Records, *Jones v. Opelika*, Petitioner's Brief, 38–39.

37. *Schneider v. Irvington, New Jersey*, 308 U.S. 147 (1939). Records, *Jones v. Opelika*, ACLU Amicus Curiae Brief, 1–9.

38. Records, *Jones v. Opelika*, ACLU Amicus Brief.

39. Ibid., Respondent's Brief on Petition for Certiorari, 5–13 (italics mine).

40. Ibid., Respondent's Brief on Certiorari, 4, 16, citing *Twining v. New Jersey*, 211 U.S. 78, 106 (1908).

41. Ibid., 17–18, quoting Mr. Justice Cardozo, *Hamilton v. Regents*, 293 U.S. 245, 268 (1934).

42. 297 U.S. 233 (1936). The Court defeated an attempt by Huey Long to tax papers that criticized him out of business. (See Justice Sandra Day O'Connor's opinion in *Minneapolis Star v. Minnesota Commissioner of Revenue*, 460 U.S. 575 [1983].) Covington likened the Opelika ordinance to Long's "device." Duke was attempting to refute that, maintaining that the case had not overruled *all* taxes on newspapers, only illegitimate ones.

43. Records, *Jones v. Opelika*, Respondent's Brief 19, 29–31, and 33–34. Duke was arguing regarding *Coyle* that the Court's refusal to grant certiorari there should also be applied to *Jones*. When the Court ruled in June 1942, it linked *Jones* to *Coyle*, which it reported as *Bowden and Sanders v. Fort Smith*, as well as to a third case, *Jobin v. Arizona*. All involved Witnesses who were convicted for failure to obtain a license through payment of a fee. The fee in Arkansas was prohibitive for "peddlers," $25 per month, $10 per week, or $2.50 per day. In Arizona, the requirement demanded a quarterly fee of $25, payable in advance. Unlike the Opelika ordinance, neither the Arkansas nor the Arizona regulation carried the provision that the license could be revoked without notice. 316 U.S. 584 (1942).

44. Records, *Jones v. Opelika*, Petitioner's Reply Brief on Certiorari, 1–7.

45. 316 U.S. 584, 592–93 (1942).

46. Ibid. at 593–97.

47. Ibid. at 597–99.

48. A separability clause is intended to protect individual parts of a law; the Alabama ordinance regarding licensing had provided that "should any section, condition, or provision or any rate or amount scheduled . . . be held void or invalid, such invalidity shall not effect any other section, rate or provision of this license schedule." Ibid. at 602–603 (Stone, C. J., dissenting).

49. Ibid. at 604–11.

50. Ibid. at 611–23 (Murphy, J., dissenting). The papers of Chief Justice Stone and those of Justices Black, Murphy, and Douglas reveal comments on the draft opinions and notes of support for each of the dissents from the other three liberal justices. Hugo L. Black Papers; William O. Douglas Papers; Harlan Fiske Stone Papers; all in Manuscript Division, Library of Congress, Washington, D.C. Frank Murphy Papers, Michigan Historical Collection, Bentley Historical Library, University of Michigan, Ann Arbor, Mich.

51. Ibid. at 623–24 (joint dissent of Black, Douglas, and Murphy, J.). Douglas apparently composed the dissent. Some have attributed it to Black, perhaps because Black's name was first or because he elaborated on the reasons for changing his mind in a concurring opinion in *West Virginia v. Barnette*, 319 U.S. 624 (1943). But several versions, from handwritten to typewritten with editing, appear in Douglas's handwriting in Box 72 of the William O. Douglas Papers.

52. Reed inserted the statement distinguishing the case from *Gobitis* as a rider after circulating a draft opinion. Other changes made after circulating his draft included an effort to recast "taxes" as "fees"; the statement that it was prohibition, not taxing, that was interdicted; and the declaration beginning, "The task of

reconcilement." The emphasis on balancing is very Frankfurterian, as is the sentence, "The complaint was bottomed on sales without a license." Records in the Stanley Reed Papers, Special Collections, University of Kentucky Libraries, Lexington, KY, regarding *Jones v. Opelika* include several pieces of correspondence from Frankfurter in 1943 when Jones was reargued, but there are none in the 1942 material.

Reed was in a sense a "swing vote" between the Black-Frankfurter poles, voting in the Witnesses cases with Frankfurter in 1940–1943, for example, but with Black in *Bridges v. California,* 314 U.S. 252 (1941), denying judges the power to punish their press with contempt of court, and in several propicketing decisions. Pritchett, "Stanley Reed," 2373–99.

In *Marsh v. Alabama,* 326 U.S. 501 (1946), Frankfurter joined Black for the Witness in a company town, but Reed continued his opposition. Ironically, Reed had sent a draft of his dissent with an added statement for private property, marked "For F.F. but not for circulation." Frankfurter Papers relevant to *Marsh* are available on microfilm in the Manuscript Division, Library of Congress, Washington, D.C., Reel 13, Part 1, Frame 0654 and following. See also Freyer, *Hugo Black: Dilemma,* 98–102.

53. Dillard, "Flag Salute," 285–306. Manwaring, *Flag Salute,* 207, states that Black, Douglas, and Murphy "began to doubt the good faith of local authorities."

54. Frankfurter's papers relevant to *Jones v. Opelika* are available on microfilm in the Manuscript Division of the Library of Congress, Washington, D.C., Reel 4, Part 1, Frame 0911 and following.

Frankfurter continued to be very unhappy over the Witness cases and over the "politics" of Black and Douglas. In 1943 when *Jones* was reversed, he wrote to Reed several times, encouraging him to write a dissent and then praising it. He also wrote his own dissent, as well as a memorandum to the Court to the effect that he disagreed with the efforts to decide what constituted "religious rites," for they opened Pandora's box. A note to Reed on March 16, 1943, found in Box 76, the Stanley Reed Papers, reveals some of the Frankfurter technique. It read: "Dear Stanley, Talk with you is so beguiling that I did not say what I really came to say. To wit, that I hope you will tell the Chief promptly that that which was a majority opinion does not serve the purposes of dissent, and that at least you will want to say something fresh in *Opelika.* Ever yours, F.F." Excerpts from Frankfurter's diaries also reflect his unhappiness with the "Axis"—Black, Douglas, and Murphy—and with the *Jones* case. Joseph P. Lash, *From the Diaries of Felix Frankfurter* (New York: W. W. Norton, 1975), 154–55, 174–86, 234–35. For an in-depth study of the relationship between Black and Frankfurter, see James E. Simon, *The Antagonists: Hugo Black, Felix Frankfurter, and Civil Liberties in Modern America* (New York: Simon & Schuster, 1989), 70.

55. Robert Jackson Papers, Box 143, Manuscript Division, Library of Congress, Washington, D.C., unpublished concurring decision in *Jones v. Opelika,* 1942 (three pages).

56. Ibid.

57. Records, *Jones v. Opelika,* Petitioner's Appendix on Motion for Rehearing, September 1942, includes quotations from fifty publications. A representative sampling included *Time,* June 22, 1942; *Collier's,* July 18, 1942; *Philadelphia Presbyterian Guardian,* June 25, 1942; *Watchman Examiner* (New York), July 2, 1942; *Chicago Daily News,* June 11, 1942; Samuel Grafton, "I'd Rather Be Right," *New York Post,* June 11, 1942; *Chicago Daily Tribune,* June 10, 1942; *South Bend Tribune,* June 11, 1942; *New York Daily News,* June 12, 1942.

58. *Richmond Times-Dispatch,* June 12, 1942; *Atlanta Constitution,* June 22, 1942; *Lexington Leader,* June 17, 1942; *Boston Traveler,* June 11, 1942; Hugh Russell Fraser, "A Black Day in Court," *Madison Progressive* (Wisconsin), June 21, 1942; Samuel Pettengill, "Religious Freedom," *Hartford Times* (Connecticut), June 20, 1942; Ibid. See also *Alabama Journal,* June 9, 1942; *Birmingham Age-Herald,* June 9, 1942; *Birmingham News,* June 10, 1942; *Montgomery Advertiser,* June 23, 1942; *Opelika Daily News,* June 8, 1942. Clippings related to *Jones v. Opelika* in Frank Murphy Papers, Box 65, include *Jacksonville Journal,* June 16, 1942; *Bay City Times,* June 10, 1942; and many other articles or editorials of similar vein. Further evidence of the overwhelming reaction against the decision appears in the clippings related to the case in Stanley Reed Papers, Boxes 70 and 76.

Contemporary law journals joined in the opposition to the decision in *Jones v. Opelika,* 1942. Edward E. Haenssler deplored the "unwelcome trend" begun by *Gobitis* and the "little sympathy in the courts for any really marked departure from conventional religious principles," "Decisions," *Brooklyn Law Review* 12 (October 1942): 71–74. G. Adler in "Comments: Licensing the Distribution of Religious Pamphlets," *Chicago-Kent Law Review* 20 (September 1942): 349–54, described the decision as turning "the pages of history back more than one hundred years to uphold a tax strongly reminiscent of the Stamp Taxes." Monroe R. Lazare commented in "State Licensing of the Distribution of Literature and Freedom of the Press and of Religion," *Fordham Law Review* 11 (1942): 230–33, that the decision "fails to recognize the need for a refined adjustment between the state's power to tax business and the individual's right to freedom of press and religion."

59. For documentation of violence, see ACLU, *Persecution,* and Rotman and Folsom, "Restrictions." For Witness views of the clergy, see Penton, *Apocalypse,* 129–30; Thelma Jones, "Follow Christ," 19; Rosco Jones, "Kingdom," 64; Marsh, "Biography," 5; Marsh Interview, 3.

60. Two-page single-spaced typewritten letter, unsigned, from Washington, D.C., July 21, 1942, in William O. Douglas Papers, Box 72.

61. Ibid., Mrs. Mueller of Rural Route 2 #191 to Justice Douglas, June 17, 1942.

62. ACLU to Douglas Arant, June 26, July 1, July 9, August 13, September 2, 1942; ACLU to James A. Simpson, June 15, 26, 1942; ACLU to E. D. Dick, Seventh-Day Adventists; Edward J. Parker, Salvation Army; Dr. Samuel McCrea Cavert, Federal Council of Churches; all June 24 and 30, 1942; ACLU to Dr. J. Edgar Washabaugh, Methodist Publishing, June 25 and 30, 1942; ACLU to Cavert, June 30, 1942; ACLU to Parker, July 3, 1942; ACLU to Cranston Williams, American Newspaper Publishers Association, August 4, 1942; W. H. Barrett, Salvation Army, to ACLU, July 10, 1942; E. D. Dick to ACLU, July 13 and August 24, 1942; Samuel McCrea Cavert to ACLU, June 26, 1942; Cranston Williams to ACLU, August 8 and September 3, 1942. ACLU Correspondence, 1942: *Jones v. Opelika,* vol. 2403, ACLU Files.

63. Records, *Jones v. Opelika,* Petitioner's Supplemental Brief, 2–16. The decision referred to was *McCulloch v. Maryland,* 4 Wheat 316, 431 (1819).

64. Ibid.

65. Ibid., 16–28.

66. Ibid., 28–34. (As noted above, introduction, nn. 25 and 29, other basic rights of many American citizens of Japanese ancestry were being violated during 1942–1943, but the Court had not ruled in the matter at the time of Covington's appeal.)

67. Ibid., ACLU Amicus Curiae Briefs on Applications for Rehearing, August 1942, and Reargument, March 1943.

68. Records, *Jones v. Opelika,* American Newspaper Publishers Association Amici Curiae Briefs on Applications for Rehearing, August, 1942, and Reargument, March 1943.

69. Ibid., Brief on Behalf of the General Conference of Seventh-Day Adventists as Amicus Curiae on Motion for Rehearing, September 1942, 1–13.

70. Records, *Jones v. Opelika,* Brief of the General Conference of Seventh-Day Adventists as Amicus Curiae on Rehearing, March 1943, 10.

71. Louis H. Pollack, "Wiley Blount Rutledge: Profile of a Judge," *Six Justices,* ed. Rotunda, 177–211.

72. 319 U.S. 105 (1943); 319 U.S. 157 (1943); and 318 U.S. 624 (1943). Rutledge in particular urged Douglas to soften his language in replying to Jackson. Wiley B. Rutledge Papers, Box 95, Manuscript Division, Library of Congress, Washington, D.C. Douglas made the change. Douglas Papers, Box 78. Jackson argued that Witnesses were not isolated individuals expressing religious beliefs but members of a highly organized group that descended like locusts upon communities. Frankfurter strongly approved Jackson's opinion. Jackson Papers, Box 127.

73. 319 U.S. 105, 103 (1943). Box 78, Douglas Papers, contains extensive correspondence with Rutledge, shorter notes from Black, Murphy, and Stone, and numerous recirculations of Douglas's draft opinions in *Murdock.*

74. 319 U.S. 103, 117–33 (Reed, J., dissenting).

75. Ibid. at 134–40 (Frankfurter, J., dissenting).

76. Extensive clippings files in both the Murphy and Reed Papers reflect the widespread endorsement in the national press. For Alabama reactions see May 3, 1943, editions of the *Alabama Journal,* the *Birmingham News,* and the *Opelika Daily News;* May 4, 1943, edition of the *Montgomery Advertiser;* May 6 edition of the *Birmingham Post;* and the May 10 edition of the *Birmingham Age-Herald.* Relevant issues of the *Alabama Christian Advocate* are February 4 and June 10, 1943. The *Alabama Baptist* comment was made on May 13, 1943. It should be added that that Baptist publication on July 1, 1943, quoted the *Christian Century's* endorsement of the June 1943 decision overturning the flag-salute requirement, *West Virginia v. Barnette.* The Methodist journal gave its own strong approval of that decision on June 24, 1943.

Chapter 5. *Marsh v. Alabama*

1. A "company servant" was the director of a congregation. Marsh interview, 2; Marsh, "Biography," 1–4; Marsh to Newton, July 14, 1991.

2. Marsh, "Biography," 4.

3. Marsh, "Biography," 4; Marsh interview, 3, 8.

4. Marsh, "Biography," 4–5. Harold would later attend the Witness training at Brooklyn Bethel.

5. Marsh, "Biography," 5–7. Persons who did not condone violence were often afraid to assist the Witnesses. The owner of the property on which Marsh's trailer was parked at the time the mob encircled it had been friendly until that

night. When Marsh asked if he could help them, he replied, "I'm sorry, lady. All I want you to do is move your trailer off my property as soon as you can." Officials often winked at, or even participated in, the harassment. As the crowd grew, Marsh appealed to two policemen at a nearby service station but was told that no one could protect them from the mob. When she called the FBI in Jackson, Mississippi, she was advised to leave town.

6. Marsh states that District Attorney T. C. Barlow, Chief of Police Obb Smith, the mayor, and a deputy were involved in the raid. Ibid., 7–8; Marsh interview, 2.

7. Marsh, "Biography," 8; Marsh interview, 2. They used property because they feared that cash would not be returned, Marsh stated.

8. Marsh, "Biography," 8–9; Marsh interview, 2. Widespread distrust of other clergy existed among the Witnesses. Many Witnesses came to expect the established institutions—whether clergy or government institutions—to conspire to control them. See above, chap. 3, n. 5.

9. Marsh, "Biography," 8–10; Marsh interview, 2. Marsh's accounts of mob violence and of uncaring, frightened, or promob officials are very similar to those documented by the U.S. Justice Department and the 1941 ACLU study, *Persecution*. Ten prominent clergymen—Catholic, Protestant, and Jewish—signed the ACLU statement of concern. See also Cole, *Jehovah's Witnesses*, 111–12, and Penton, *Apocalypse*, 132–38.

Grace Marsh's physical deterioration during the Mississippi experience was confirmed under oath in court by an established physician, Dr. G. C. Kilpatrick, in Marsh's suit against Gulf Shipbuilding, Records, *Marsh v. Gulf*, 109–11. Kilpatrick stated that she had all the "signs of pulmonary tuberculosis active."

10. Marsh, "Biography," 2. The tribulations of Babin and Marsh are noted in Victor V. Blackwell, *O'er the Ramparts They Watched* (New York: A Hearthstone Book, Carlton Press, 1976), 144–47.

11. Marsh, "Biography," 10–11; *Marsh v. Gulf*, 128–31.

12. Marsh, "Biography," 15–16. The Stephenses' marriage apparently suffered from the multiple pressures associated with Aileen's Witnessing, particularly after she was arrested.

13. Smith, *History of Chickasaw*.

14. *Marsh v. Alabama*, 326 U.S. 501, 501–502 (1946).

15. Marsh, "Biography," 12. Among the women who assisted in working Chickasaw were Alberta Rouse, Cora Smith, Mittie Williamson, and Ruby Dalton. Grace Marsh's son, Harold, also joined the group on occasion. Marsh interview, 4. Even the staunchest liberals on the U.S. Supreme Court had found against the Witnesses in 1941 when they had used "fighting words" (*Chaplinsky*

v. New Hampshire, 315 U.S. 568 [1942]), while by mid-1943 the majority of the Court upheld their right to distribute literature and to refuse to salute the flag. It is not clear how much the Witness change in tactics was determined by the legal aspects and how much by the change in administration.

16. Testimony given by Chatham and that given by Marsh and Stephens conflict on several particulars. Records, *Marsh v. Alabama,* Alabama Proceedings, 11–13 (Chatham) and 61–68 (Marsh).

17. Peebles's account and that of the Witnesses differ on details. Ibid., (Peebles) 31–60 and (Marsh) 61–68.

18. Records, *Marsh v. Alabama,* Alabama Proceedings, (Chatham) 11–31 and (notice) 49; *Mobile Register,* December 26, 1943.

19. *Marsh v. Alabama,* 1–2; *Marsh v. Gulf,* 49. When Witness arrests continued on the business block, they shifted to Craft Highway, not a part of the company town, standing on the "turtle back" that separated the ongoing from the oncoming traffic. Chatham also removed them from the public highway on orders from Peebles, who was advised by the company attorney, Francis Inge, that he could do so on grounds of traffic safety. They may also have been arrested in the residential areas of Chickasaw. Testimony in *Marsh v. Gulf* is conflicting— Marsh maintained that the charge on January 19 was trespassing, not legally applicable to a public road. The deputy argued that the trespassing charge was for canvassing in the residential section of the village, that the Witnesses had been removed from the highway on a different date.

The battle of wills between the Witnesses, led by Marsh and Stephens, and Gulf Shipbuilding, led by E. B. Peebles, continued for months while the original case worked its way to the U.S. Supreme Court. After many arrests and many bonds Marsh and Stephens decided to reverse roles: they filed suit on February 24, 1944, against Gulf Shipbuilding, E. B. Peebles, and Mobile County Sheriff W. H. Holcombe in District Court of the United States for the Southern District, John McDuffie, judge. McDuffie, an Alabama Presbyterian with a law degree from The University of Alabama, had also served in the U.S. House of Representatives and had supported Franklin D. Roosevelt, who then appointed him to the federal district court. Marsh found McDuffie "fair," unlike Touart or Edington. Owen, *History,* 4:349–50; Marsh, "Biography," 16.

Marsh and Stephens contended that the defendants had conspired to hinder their work, had prosecuted them maliciously, and had maltreated them during their imprisonment in the Mobile County Jail, violating their civil rights. They asked for $5,000 for injuries to each woman. The cases were tried jointly as civil actions 445 and 446 before a jury in February 1945. A mistrial was declared after the jury could not reach a unanimous verdict. A second trial occurred October

17–18, 1945, with the jury finding for the defendants *(Marsh v. Gulf)*. During the February 1945 trial, Marsh states in "Biography," 16, Francis Inge used a tactic revealing appeal to the xenophobia of southerners. "He called us rich women here from New York who were robbing people with our magazine racket. 'No wonder,' he said, 'they can wear fur coats.'"

The Witnesses filed for an appeal but dropped the case in February 1946 after the U.S. Supreme Court ruling in *Marsh v. Alabama*. The countersuit produced the desired results, Marsh states in "Biography," 14. After "we filed suit there were no more arrests. We were able to go into our territory anywhere in Chickasaw and work. . . . We found many people who were in sympathy with us and wraught [*sic*] up by the way we had been treated. They felt as if they were being denied their freedom by Mr. Peebles and I am sure because of this we were able to start many bible studies. . . . What a pleasure to work in this once forbidden little town."

20. Owen, *History,* 4:499; David R. Coley, Jr., Surname Files; Alabama Bar, *Proceedings: Sixty-Fourth,* 13–14. The author's efforts to obtain information regarding Coley's willingness to take such a case produced no clue. Grace Marsh maintained, "Mr. Coley took great pride in defending us. . . . He told me, 'I'm not good enough for that work. I could never do it, but I guarantee you that I'll fight for your right to do it.'" Marsh interview, 5, 8.

21. Marsh interview, 7; Records, *Marsh v. Gulf,* 100–101, includes a discussion of one bond's being raised to $750. Inge, attorney for Gulf Shipbuilding, suggested that it was because the Witnesses continued to defy the Court. For information about Klumpp, see *Fairhope Courier,* October 21, 1946.

22. Records, *Marsh v. Gulf,* 109–15.

23. Ibid., (Sheriff Holcombe) 201–205, (Matron Cammack) 210–27, and (Weston) 254–60.

24. *Blue Book,* 274–75; Carl Booth and Francis Inge, Surname Files; *Martindale-Hubbell,* 1952, 1:44.

25. Records, *Marsh v. Alabama,* Alabama Proceedings, 3–11.

26. Ibid., 11–13.

27. Ibid., 31–49. In the civil suit that Marsh later brought against Gulf Shipbuilding, Peebles admitted that the contract with the Mobile newspapers was only an oral agreement transacted by telephone and that the women had called to explain the nature of their work. When Powell asked if he offered to give the women a permit, the following dialogue occurred:

Peebles: They denied me that right. They told me they would not accept one.
Powell: They said, "We won't accept any permit"? Is that the way they said it?

Peebles: No, they told me they did not have to have a permit. . . .

Powell: . . . in a nice, lady-like manner?

Peebles: Yes, I have no criticism of that.

Powell pursued a line of questioning to the effect that Peebles identified himself as a religious man, yet was hostile from the beginning to the Witnesses, never implying in any way that he would assist them, since they were doing ministerial work. He then asked, "You did not tell them 'I want to promote your work'?" and Peebles replied, "We do promote a great deal of religious activity out there in Chickasaw." Powell seized upon that statement, asking, "Were you promoting Christian activity when you caused their arrest?" Records, *Marsh v. Gulf,* 153–58.

28. Records, *Marsh v. Alabama,* Alabama Proceedings, 31–55.

29. Ibid., 55–60.

30. Ibid., 61–68.

31. Ibid., 68–71.

32. Ibid., 71–81.

33. Ibid., 82–90.

34. Ibid., 7–10; 21 So.2d 558 (Ala. 1945).

35. *Mobile Press,* January 28, 1944; *Mobile Register,* January 28, 1944.

36. Alabama, *Statistical Register,* 1947, pp. 142–43.

37. 21 So.2d at 559.

38. Ibid. at 561.

39. Ibid. at 563. Rice quoted from an annotation following *Massachusetts v. Richardson,* 146 A.L.R. 648, 656 (1943), citing *State v. Martin,* 199 La. 39, 5 So.2d 377, 380 (1941).

40. Records, *Marsh v. Alabama,* 150–66; 21 So.2d 558; 66 S.Ct. 26 (1945). (Swayze had Alabama connections. Sarah Wiggins to Merlin Owen Newton, summer 1991 [in possession of author]).

41. Owen, *History,* 5:976; Alabama, *Statistical Register,* 1935, pp. 109–10; William W. Callahan and John O. Harris, Surname Files.

The "Scottsboro Boys" trials provide a flagrant example of the racial inequity in the judicial system of Alabama in the 1930s. *Powell v. Alabama,* 287 U.S. 53 (1932); when several of the cases were retried in Decatur, somewhat west of Scottsboro, Callahan was the presiding judge. *Norris v. Alabama,* 294 U.S. 587 (1935). See also Dan T. Carter, *Scottsboro: A Tragedy of the American South* (Baton Rouge: Louisiana State University Press, 1979).

42. "We sued them in order to clear the work," Marsh stated. Marsh interview, 5. See above, chap. 5, n. 19, regarding *Marsh v. Gulf.*

43. Mary Francis Berry, *Stability, Security and Continuity: Mr. Justice Burton*

and Decision-Making in the Supreme Court, 1945–1958 (Westport, Conn.: Greenwood Press, 1978), 24–25.

44. Records, *Marsh v. Alabama,* Petition for Appeal, 157–66, and Statement as to Jurisdiction, 1–5.

45. Ibid., Statement Opposing Jurisdiction and Motion to Dismiss or Affirm, 1–10. Peebles had testified that the company had been issuing notices for more than a year prior to the Witnesses' presence. Nowhere does he state explicitly that he had posted notices earlier, and other testimony indicates that the "permits" were informal oral agreements. See ibid., Alabama Proceedings, 31–60.

46. For example, *Jamison v. Texas,* 318 U.S. 413 (1943), had overruled a Texas statute forbidding the distribution of handbills, and *Thornhill v. Alabama,* 310 U.S. 88 (1940), had recognized picketing by employees on privately owned company property.

47. Records, *Marsh v. Alabama,* Jurisdictional Statement on Appeal, 17–26.

48. Records, *Marsh v. Alabama,* Jurisdictional Statement on Appeal, 27–36. The brief cites *Busey v. District of Columbia,* 78 App. D.C. 189, 138 F.2d 592 (D.C. Cir. 1943), which quotes *Palko v. Connecticut,* 302 U.S. 319, 325 (1937).

49. Ibid., Brief for Appellee, 1–18.

50. Ibid., citing *Gobitis,* 310 U.S. 586, 594 (1940), and *Murdock,* 319 U.S. 105, 116 (1943).

51. 326 U.S. 501 (1946).

52. 326 U.S. at 502–506. The Black Papers, container 281, reveal notes of support from Douglas, Murphy, and Rutledge and include agreement—"Yes, sir!"—from Frankfurter.

53. *Marsh v. Alabama,* 326 U.S. 501, 506–507 (1946).

54. Ibid., at 510–11 (Frankfurter, J., concurring). Frankfurter did not agree with Black that the citizen's right to disseminate ideas was analogous to his right to commerce, with which the person owning property over which a road ran may not unconstitutionally interfere. First Amendment limitations applied to government at all levels, he argued, while the commerce clause involved a relationship between state and national levels of government.

55. Ibid. at 511–16 (Reed, J., dissenting).

56. *Birmingham News,* January 9, 1946; *Mobile Press* and *Mobile Register,* January 8, 1946.

57. *New York Times,* January 8, 1946, sec. 25, p. 2; *New Republic,* January 21, 1946, p. 69.

58. Marsh, "Biography," 18; Marsh interview, 1. Many years later, after Herbert had died, Grace remarried. Her second husband, George Horne, was one of her converts.

Chapter 6. The Impact of *Jones* and *Marsh*

1. Cole, *Jehovah's Witnesses*, 110, quoting Covington and American Bar Association, *The Bill of Rights Review*, 1942.

2. Ibid., 109–16. From 1935 to 1950 "Witnesses in the United States suffered ten thousand arrests," the attorney stated, as well as 2,500 mobbings in which they also suffered beatings and other violence. ACLU and Justice Department studies confirm maltreatment.

3. Olin R. Moyle had served as legal counsel from 1935 to 1939, when a dispute with Rutherford erupted. Penton, *Apocalypse*, 80–81. *Gitlow v. New York*, 268 U.S. 652 (1925), had begun the practice of incorporation, defining freedom of speech and press as fundamental liberties protected from impairment by the states. By the early 1930s the Court had extended the mantle of the due process clause to cover the First Amendment guarantees of speech (*Fiske v. Kansas*, 274 U.S. 380 [1927]) and press (*Near v. Minnesota*, 283 U.S. 697 [1931]; see Fred W. Friendly, *Minnesota Rag: The Dramatic Story of the Landmark Supreme Court Case That Gave New Meaning to Freedom of Press* [New York: Random House, 1981]), as well as the Sixth Amendment right to counsel (in capital cases, *Powell v. Alabama*, 287 U.S. 45 [1932]). Abraham, *Freedom and the Court*, 72.

4. *Cantwell v. Connecticut*, 310 U.S. 296 (1940). *Cox v. New Hampshire*, 312 U.S. 569 (1941); *Minersville Sch. Dist. v. Gobitis*, 310 U.S. 586 (1940); and *Chaplinsky v. New Hampshire*, 315 U.S. 568 (1942). Harrison, *Visions*, 50, quoting Covington.

5. See Freyer, *Hugo Black and the Dilemma*, 98–102. Black formally developed his view that history supported the incorporation of the first eight amendments into the due process clause of the Fourteenth Amendment in an elaborately researched appendix accompanying his dissent in *Adamson v. California*, 332 U.S. 46, 68 (Black, J., dissenting), 92 (appendix) (1947). Professor Charles Fairman of Stanford Law School soon challenged his interpretation of history in "Does the Fourteenth Amendment Incorporate the Bill of Rights? The Original Understanding," *Stanford Law Review* 2 (December 1949): 5–139.

6. *Washington Post*, June 10, 1942; *Collier's* editorial, July 18, 1942, p. 70; *Birmingham News*, June 10, 1942.

7. [Unsigned]. "Notes and Comments: Constitutional Law, Another Jehovah's Witness Case," *Indiana Law Journal* 17 (August 1942): 555–60; Adler, "Comments"; Robert Walsh, "Recent Decisions," *Michigan Law Review* 41 (October 1942): 316–27; Haenssler, "Decisions"; Rotman and Folsom, "Recent Restrictions," 1055; L.C.E., "Recent Cases: Constitutional Law—Freedom of

Religion, Press and Speech—Licensing Ordinances," *George Washington Law Review* 11 (December 1942): 114–16.

8. Hayden Covington to Roger Baldwin, June 20, 1942; Osmond Fraenkel to Hayden Covington, June 25, 1942; Hayden Covington to Osmond Fraenkel, August 19, 1942; ACLU Correspondence, 1942: *Jones v. Opelika*, vol. 2403, ACLU Files. For Jones's stands at the William Byrd Hotel, see above, chap. 3.

9. Leo Pfeffer, *God, Caesar, and the Constitution* (Boston: Beacon Press, 1975), 144.

10. *Murdock*, 319 U.S. 105 (1943); *Jones*, 319 U.S. 103 (1943); *Martin v. Struthers*, 319 U.S. 141 (1943). *Martin* involved an ordinance prohibiting door-to-door canvassing of any kind, justified on the grounds that many of the employees of the town's mills worked a night shift. Black phrased "his opinion more in free-speech than in free-exercise terms," noting that the liberty to disseminate information was essential to a free society and thus in a preferred position. While some regulation might be acceptable, the ordinance in question was overly broad. Murphy concurred, emphasizing the free exercise clause, while Jackson dissented. Jackson saw in the majority opinion "a contradiction of the establishment clause in any special exemption of religiously motivated behavior from otherwise valid secular regulations." Richard E. Morgan, *The Supreme Court and Religion* (New York: Free Press, 1972), 65–67. Irving Dillard, "About Face to Freedom," *New Republic*, May 24, 1943, pp. 693–95.

The Legal Tender Cases were a series of cases decided by the Court in 1870 and 1871 in which the Court reversed its stand in *Hepburn v. Griswold*, 8 Wall. 603 (1870), in *Knox v. Lee* and *Parker v. Davis*, 12 Wall. 457 (1871), with the rapid nature of the reversal leading some to charge that President Grant had "packed" the Court. Edward F. Waite, "The Debt of Constitutional Law to Jehovah's Witnesses," *Minnesota Law Review* 28 (March 1944): 246.

11. See Stanley Ingber, "The Marketplace of Ideas: A Legitimizing Myth," *Duke Law Journal* (February 1984): 32–89; and Leila Sadat-Keeling, "Notes, Constitutional Law: Supreme Court Finds First Amendment a Barrier to Taxation of the Press," *Tulane Law Review* 58 (1984): 1073–89.

12. *West Virginia v. Barnette*, 318 U.S. 624 (1943). See Douglas Papers, Box 78; Jackson Papers, Box 127; Rutledge Papers, Box 95; and Stone Papers, Box 72.

13. 326 U.S. 501, 506–507 (1946). A companion case, *Tucker v. Texas*, 326 U.S. 517 (1946), set aside a trespass conviction for a similar reason. Navigation Village in Hondo, Texas, was a housing project wholly owned by the government. The manager had ordered Witnesses to cease going door to door. In *Munn v. Illinois*, 94 U.S. (4 Otto) 113 (1877), the Court upheld the right of the state in

the public interest to regulate privately owned grain elevators, which were in effect public utilities. James D. Barnett, writing in the *Oregon Law Review* 25 (February 1946): 132–35, saw in *Marsh* an expansion of *Munn*. Such an interpretation may be questioned, however. Although both involved the conflict between private and public rights, Munn was concerned with the overall community good and not with the personal liberties of the individual. For the quotation re Black, see Lawrence H. Tribe, *American Constitutional Law* (Mineola, N.Y.: Foundation Press, 1978), 1165–66.

14. *New Republic,* January 1946, p. 69. National studies in the 1920s had indicated that personal liberties had been notoriously violated in many mining company towns, as well as in some such villages associated with textiles and steel manufacturing and in lumbering, turpentine, and plantation types of agricultural industries. Conditions had improved dramatically by the late 1940s, but how much the improvement sprang from the Wagner Act and increased union activity and how much effect *Marsh* might have had is not clear. *Michigan Law Review* 83 (October 1984): 19.

15. The *Marsh* rationale was applied in several state or lower federal court cases but was not cited by the U.S. Supreme Court until 1968. *People v. Barisi,* 193 Misc. 934, 86 N.Y.S.2d 277 (Magis. Ct. 1948), allowed First Amendment activity in a railroad station; *In re Hoffman,* 67 Cal.2d 845, 434 P.2d 353, 64 Cal. Rptr. 96 (1967), sanctioned leaflet distribution at Union Station. *Wolin v. Port of New York Auth.,* 392 F.2d 83 (2d Cir. 1968), *cert. denied,* 393 U.S. 940 (1968), permitted distribution of leaflets by antiwar activists in a bus terminal.

16. 391 U.S. 308, 332 (1968) (Black, J., dissenting).

17. 391 U.S. at 308. Justice Lewis Powell wrote for the Court in *Lloyd Corp. v. Tanner,* 407 U.S. 551 (1972), allowing a shopping center to deny the distribution of antiwar leaflets. Gerald Gunther, *Constitutional Law,* 11th ed. (Mineola, N.Y.: Foundation Press, 1985), 869. *Hudgens v. NLRB,* 424 U.S. 507 (1976). The case involved labor picketing. Marshall argued that in opening the property to the public, the shopping center owners had surrendered "a degree of privacy." Consumers with a complaint as well as employees with a grievance could most effectively make their objections public by protests at the site. "As far as these groups are concerned," he stated, "the shopping center owner has assumed the traditional role of the state in its control of historical First Amendment forums." Ibid. at 542–43.

For a discussion of the limits on the right to receive information, see Carl E. Schneider, "Free Speech and Corporate Freedom: A Comment on *First National Bank of Boston v. Bellotti,*" *California Law Review* 59 (September 1986): 1227–89. Schneider maintains that "*Marsh* is probably best understood as responding to the special history and circumstances of the Southern company town" (1247).

The public function doctrine was further limited in cases involving privately owned but publicly regulated utilities and warehouses; Justice William Rehnquist, writing for the Court, distinguished the latter cases from *Marsh* on the grounds that Gulf Shipbuilding had *exclusively* controlled the streets of Chickasaw. Thus the action of an electrical company cutting off electricity without a hearing had no close nexus to a state function and was not held to state limits. *Jackson v. Metropolitan Edison Co.*, 419 U.S. 345 (1974); *Flagg Bros., Inc. v. Brooks*, 436 U.S. 149 (1978).

18. *Pruneyard Shopping Center v. Robins*, 447 U.S. 74 (1980). Thomas Patrick Monaghan found *Marsh* relevant to the claim that sidewalk counseling regarding abortion should be allowed as free speech right in a public forum area. "Sidewalk Counseling: A First Amendment Right," *Catholic Lawyer* 31 (1987): 50–76. Michael J. Hudock III applied the "public function" question to the issue of employee-employer relations and drug testing in "Behind the Hysteria of Compulsory Drug Screening in Employment: Urinalysis Can Be a Legitimate Tool for Helping Resolve the Nation's Drug Problem If Competing Interests of Employer and Employee Are Equitably Balanced," *Duquesne Law Review* 25 (Summer 1987): 597–957.

19. In *Niemotko v. Maryland*, 340 U.S. 268 (1951), and *Fowler v. Rhode Island*, 345 U.S. 67 (1953), the Court found for the Witnesses. The Witnesses' claims as conscientious objectors during World War II had resulted in the imprisonment of thousands. The society continued to campaign against government action on this front, with a series of limited victories in the postwar era. Cole, *Jehovah's Witnesses*, 111, 182–83, and 200–206.

20. Kenneth R. O'Brien and Daniel E. O'Brien, "Cases and Studies: Freedom of Religion in Restatement of Inter-Church-and-State Common Law," *Jurist* 6 (October 1946): 502–23. Jackson had addressed the same issue in his dissent in *Martin v. Struthers* and concurrence in *Jeanette*, 319 U.S. 157, 166 (Jackson, J., dissenting and concurring).

21. *Engel v. Vitale*, 370 U.S. 421 (1963); *Abington School District v. Schempp*, 374 U.S. 203 (1963); *United States v. Seeger*, 380 U.S. 163 (1965); *Welsh v. United States*, 398 U.S. 333 (1970). *Yates v. United States*, 354 U.S. 298 (1957), upheld the right to advocate theoretically the overthrow of the government; *New York Times v. Sullivan*, 376 U.S. 254 (1964); limited libel to "malicious" (deliberate, knowing) falsity where public officials were concerned; *New York Times v. United States*, 403 U.S. 713 (1971), protected the press from prior restraint in publishing classified documents concerning the Vietnam War; *Tinker*

v. Des Moines Sch. Dist., 393 U.S. 503 (1969), upheld the right of school children
to wear black armbands symbolically protesting the Vietnam War. *Miller v.
California,* 413 U.S. 15 (1973), attempted to rely on local community standards
in determining obscenity, but *Texas v. Johnson,* 491 U.S. 397 (1989), ruled 5–4
that the First Amendment protected the right of an individual to burn a U.S. flag
as a political protest. Regarding religious issues, *Goldman v. Weinberger,* 475
U.S. 503 (1986), upheld the Air Force regulation preventing an Orthodox Jewish
serviceman from wearing his yarmulke with his uniform; *Employment Div.,
Dep't of Human Resources of Oregon v. Smith,* 110 S.Ct. 1595 (1990), ruled
against the use of peyote in the religious ceremonies of the Native American
Indian church. On the other hand, *Wallace v. Jaffre,* 472 U.S. 38 (1985), overturned an Alabama law establishing a moment of silent prayer in the public
schools, but with three dissents, and *Lee v. Wiesmann,* 112 S.Ct. 2649 (1992), in
a 5–4 decision, declared that the use of prayer at a graduation ceremony in the
public schools violated the establishment clause. New rulings in the summer of
1993 appear to indicate more flexibility, but a clear trend has not been established.

22. NAACP Files, Group II, Manuscript Division, Library of Congress, Washington, D.C. Papers regarding organization are found in Box C5. Box B1 contains
information indicating that the Reverend John Haynes Holmes served on the
board of both the NAACP and the ACLU, and NAACP records include a press
release from the ACLU following the unfavorable ruling in *Jones* in June 1942,
but nothing manifests any reaction by the NAACP. See also Dorothy Autrey,
"The National Association for the Advancement of Colored People in Alabama,
1913–1952" (Ph.D. diss., Notre Dame University, 1985).

The organization was approached by the Committee on Educational Aid for
Released Conscientious Objectors in 1946; in 1949 a similar committee urged
Thurgood Marshall, chief counsel for the NAACP, to support a petition to
President Truman regarding assistance to the objectors, though the papers in-
clude no replies. Furthermore, the committee specifically excluded Jehovah's
Witnesses from the category of those it intended to assist (Box B12).

The NAACP did consider backing a challenge to the draft on racially discriminatory grounds, *Lynn v. Downer,* 140 F.2d 397 (2d Cir. 1944), *cert. denied on
grounds of mootness,* 322 U.S. 756 (1944). But even in this case, Mark Tushnet,
professor of law at Georgetown University Law Center, states, "patriotism, and
Democratic party affiliations, of NAACP leaders pulled them the other way."
Mark Tushnet to Merlin Owen Newton, January 10, 1991 (in possession of the
author).

Professor Jack Greenberg, dean of Columbia College, Columbia University of the City of New York, states that he is "unaware of any NAACP involvement" in *Jones* or *Marsh*. Jack Greenberg to Merlin Owen Newton, January 22, 1991 (in possession of the author). Thelma Jones with Merlin Owen Newton, unrecorded telephone conversation, February 1991; Thelma Jones to Merlin Owen Newton, February 24, 1991 (in possession of the author).

23. "Well, in a sense I was considered a leader, and they thought if they arrested me, they could stop the movement. But that didn't matter; they were all leaders." Marsh interview, 4. Mrs. Nellie Cammack, the matron at the Mobile County Jail, did not win her favor, but she had kind words about Mr. Jackson, the jailer at Brookhaven, Mississippi.

24. By January 12, 1952, the *Opelika Daily News* listed the Kingdom Hall with other local churches.

25. Public Information Subject Files, Mobile County: Chickasaw. Manuscript Collections, Department of Archives and History, Montgomery, Ala. Listings for Kingdom Halls in Mobile and Whistler appear regularly in the *Mobile City Directory* after 1948. See, for example, the directories for 1949–1950, p. 519; 1955, p. 404; 1960, p. 375; and 1965, p. 192. As late as 1984 the *Mobile North Suburban Area Directory* carried no listing for the Witnesses in Chickasaw, nor in 1990 did the telephone directory for the Mobile area. By 1971, however, the *Chickasaw News Herald* included the hall in Saraland, an adjacent community, in its listing of local churches. Marsh interview, 6–9.

Selected Bibliography

Primary Sources

Unpublished Works

American Civil Liberties Union Correspondence. 1941: Alabama: Jehovah's Witnesses, vol. 2306; *Jones v. Opelika,* vol. 2317. 1942: *Jones v. Opelika,* vol. 2403. 1943: *Jones v. Opelika,* vol. 2519. ACLU Files, Seeley G. Mudd Library, Princeton University, Princeton, N.J.

Black, Hugo L. Papers. Manuscript Division, Library of Congress, Washington, D.C.

Douglas, William O. Papers. Manuscript Division, Library of Congress, Washington, D.C.

Eskridge, Ben, and Eskridge, Betty. Interview by the author, August 17, 1990. Transcription of tape recording in possession of the author.

Frankfurter, Felix. Papers. Manuscript Division, Library of Congress, Washington, D.C. (microfilm).

Grace Marsh v. Gulf Shipbuilding et al. Records of case, with briefs, supporting documents, transcripts, as presented to the U.S. District Court in Mobile, October 18, 1944. National Archives—Regional Center, East Point, Ga.

Grace Marsh v. State of Alabama. Records of case, with briefs, supporting documents, transcripts, as presented to the U.S. Supreme Court, October term, 1945. University of Alabama Law School, Tuscaloosa, Ala. (microfiche).

Greenberg, Jack, to Merlin Owen Newton, January 25, 1991. In possession of the author.

Harrell, David E., to Merlin Owen Newton, January 28, 1992. In possession of the author.

Jackson, Robert H. Papers. Manuscript Division, Library of Congress, Washington, D.C.

Jones, Rosco. "Putting Kingdom Interest First in My Life." Unpublished manuscript in possession of the author (photocopy).

Jones, Thelma. Interview by the author, March 27, 1991. Transcription of tape recording in possession of author.

———. "Leaving All Things Behind to Follow in the Footsteps of Christ Jesus: True Life Story." Unpublished manuscript in possession of the author (photocopy).

——— to Merlin Owen Newton, February 24, March 1, 7, 14, and 28, 1991. In possession of the author.

——— with Merlin Owen Newton, February 1, 1991. Telephone conversation, unrecorded.

Marsh, Grace. Interview by the author, July 25, 1990. Transcription of tape recording in possession of the author.

———. "My Biography." Unpublished manuscript in possession of the author (photocopy).

——— to Merlin Owen Newton, July 14 and December 24, 1991. In possession of the author.

Murphy, Frank. Papers. Michigan Historical Collection, Bentley Historical Library, University of Michigan, Ann Arbor, Mich.

National Association for the Advancement of Colored People (NAACP) Files, Group II. Manuscript Division, Library of Congress, Washington, D.C.

Newton, Wesley P., to Merlin Owen Newton, August 1, 1991. In possession of the author.

Public Information Subject Files, Mobile County: Chickasaw. Manuscript Collections, Department of Archives and History, Montgomery, Ala.

Reed, Stanley. Papers. Special Collections, University of Kentucky Libraries, Lexington, Ky.

Rosco Jones v. City of Opelika. Records of case, with briefs, supporting documents, transcripts, as presented to U.S. Supreme Court, October term, 1945. University of Alabama Law School, Tuscaloosa, Ala. (microfiche).

Rutledge, Wiley B. Papers. Manuscript Division, Library of Congress, Washington, D.C.

Simpson, James E., to Merlin Owen Newton, January 8, 1991. In possession of the author.

Stone, Harlan Fiske. Papers. Manuscript Division, Library of Congress, Washington, D.C.

Surname Files. Miscellaneous clippings and other information on some prominent Alabamians, alphabetically arranged by surname (microfilm). Alabama Department of Archives and History, Montgomery, Ala.

The Thirteen. Unpublished manuscript collection. Manuscript Collections, Alabama Department of Archives and History, Montgomery, Ala.

Thomas, William Holcombe. "College Men." An Address to Alumni at Emory University, Ga., 1906. Thomas Addresses. Alabama Pamphlets File, Alabama Department of Archives and History, Montgomery, Ala.

————. "Law and License." Thomas Addresses. Alabama Pamphlets File, Alabama Department of Archives and History, Montgomery, Ala.

————. "The New South—An Inside View." Thomas Addresses. Alabama Pamphlets File, Alabama Department of Archives and History, Montgomery, Ala.

Tushnet, Mark, to Merlin Owen Newton, January 10, 1991. In possession of the author.

Vollmer, Richard W., to Merlin Owen Newton, May 14, 1991. In possession of the author.

Wiggins, Sarah Woolfolk, to Merlin Owen Newton, summer 1991. In possession of author.

Published Works

Cases

Abington School District v. Schempp, 374 U.S. 203 (1963).

Adamson v. California, 332 U.S. 46 (1947).

Amalgamated Food Employees Local 590 v. Logan Valley Plaza, Inc., 391 U.S. 308 (1968).

Bridges v. California, 314 U.S. 252 (1941).

Brown v. Board of Education I, 347 U.S. 483 (1954).

Busey v. District of Columbia, 78 App. D.C. 189 (1942).

Cantwell v. Connecticut, 310 U.S. 296 (1940).

Chaplinsky v. New Hampshire, 315 U.S. 568 (1942).

Cox v. New Hampshire, 312 U.S. 569 (1941).

Coyle v. City of Fort Smith [consolidated as *Bowden and Sanders v. Fort Smith* in *Jones v. Opelika*, 316 U.S. 584 (1942)].

Douglas v. Jeannette, 319 U.S. 157 (1943).

Employment Division, Department of Human Resources of Oregon v. Smith, 110 S.Ct. 1595 (1990).

Engel v. Vitale, 370 U.S. 421 (1963).

Fiske v. Kansas, 274 U.S. 380 (1927).

Flagg Bros., Inc. v. Brooks, 436 U.S. 149 (1978).

Gitlow v. New York, 268 U.S. 652 (1925).

Goldman v. Weinberger, 475 U.S. 503 (1986).

Grosjean v. American Press Co., 297 U.S. 233 (1936).

Hamilton v. Regents of the University of California, 293 U.S. 245 (1934).

Haseltine v. Central Bank of Springfield, Missouri, 183 U.S. 130 (1901).

Hepburn v. Griswold, 8 Wall. 603 (1870).

In re Hoffman, 67 Cal.2d 845, 434 P.2d 353, 64 Cal. Rptr. 96 (1967).

Hudgens v. NLRB, 424 U.S. 507 (1976).

Jackson v. Metropolitan Edison Co., 419 U.S. 345 (1974).

Jamison v. Texas, 318 U.S. 413 (1945).

Jones v. Opelika, 30 Ala. App. 274 (1940).

Jones v. Opelika, 316 U.S. 584 (1942), 319 U.S. 103 (1943).

Knox v. Lee, 12 Wall. 457 (1871).

Korematsu v. United States, 323 U.S. 214 (1944).

Lee v. Wiesmann, 112 S.Ct. 2649 (1992).

Lloyd Corp. v. Tanner, 407 U.S. 551 (1972).

Lovell v. Griffin, 303 U.S. 444 (1938).

Lynn v. Downer, 140 F.2d 397 (2d Cir. 1944), *cert. denied*, 322 U.S. 756 (1944).

Marsh v. Alabama, 326 U.S. 501 (1946).

Martin v. Struthers, 319 U.S. 141 (1943).

Massachusetts v. Richardson, 48 N.E.2d 678 (1943).

Miller v. California, 413 U.S. 15 (1973).

Minersville School District v. Gobitis, 310 U.S. 586 (1940).

Minneapolis Star v. Minnesota Commiss'r of Revenue, 460 U.S. 575 (1983).

Munn v. Illinois, 94 U.S. (4 Otto) 113 (1877).

Murdock v. Pennsylvania, 319 U.S. 105 (1943).

Near v. Minnesota, 283 U.S. 697 (1931).

New York Times v. Sullivan, 376 U.S. 254 (1964).

New York Times v. United States, 403 U.S. 713 (1971).

Niemotko v. Maryland, 340 U.S. 268 (1951).

Norris v. Alabama, 294 U.S. 587 (1935).

Palko v. Connecticut, 302 U.S. 319 (1937).
People v. Barisi, 193 Misc. 934, 86 N.Y.S.2d 277 (Magis. Ct. 1948).
Powell v. Alabama, 287 U.S. 45 (1932).
Pruneyard Shipping Center v. Robins, 447 U.S. 74 (1980).
Schneider v. Irvington, New Jersey, 308 U.S. 147 (1939).
State v. Martin, 199 La. 39, 5 So.2d 377 (1941).
Texas v. Johnson, 491 U.S. 397 (1989).
Thornhill v. Alabama, 310 U.S. 88 (1940).
Tinker v. Des Moines School District, 393 U.S. 503 (1969).
Tucker v. Texas, 326 U.S. 517 (1946).
Twining v. New Jersey, 211 U.S. 78 (1908).
United States v. Carolene Products, 304 U.S. 144 (1938).
United States v. Seeger, 380 U.S. 163 (1965).
Wallace v. Jaffre, 472 U.S. 38 (1985).
Watson v. Jones, 80 U.S. 679 (1871).
Welsh v. United States, 398 U.S. 333 (1970).
West Virginia v. Barnette, 318 U.S. 624 (1943).
White v. Crook, 251 Fed. Supp. 401 (M.D. Ala. 1966).
Wolin v. Port of New York Authority, 392 F.2d 83 (2d Cir. 1968), *cert. denied*, 393 U.S. 940 (1968).
Yates v. United States, 354 U.S. 298 (1957).

Other

Alabama Blue Book and Social Register. Birmingham, Ala.: Blue Book Publishing, 1929.
Alabama Department of Archives and History. *Official and Statistical Register, 1935, 1939, 1943, 1947*. Wetumpka, Ala.: Wetumpka Printing, 1936–1948.
Alabama Legislative Reference, Alabama State Capitol. *Alabama Courts*. Montgomery, Ala.: n.p., December 15, 1954. Typewritten pamphlet.
Alabama State Bar Association. *Proceedings*. Sixty-Third Annual Meeting, 1940, and Sixty-Fourth Annual Meeting, 1941. n.p.
American Civil Liberties Union. *Annual Reports*, vols. 3 (July 1937–June 1944) and 4 (July 1944–December 1950). New York: Arno Press and *New York Times*, 1970.
———. *The Persecution of Jehovah's Witnesses: The Record of Violence Against a Religious Organization Unparalleled in America Since the Attack on the Mormons*. New York: ACLU, January 1, 1941. Pamphlet.
Black, Hugo. *A Constitutional Faith*. New York: Knopf, 1968.

Madison, James. *"The Federalist* Number 10.*"* In James MacGregor Burns, J. W. Petalson, and Thomas E. Cronin, *Government by the People.* National, state, and local version. 13th alt. ed. Englewood Cliffs, N.J.: Prentice-Hall, 1989.

Martindale-Hubbell Law Directory, 1942, 1952, 1966. New York: Martindale-Hubbell Publishers, 1942–1966.

Mobile City Directory. 1949–1950; 1955; 1960; 1965.

Mobile North Suburban Area Directory. 1984.

Plato. "The Trial of Socrates," from *Apology.* In *Aspects of Western Civilization: Problems and Sources in History,* ed. Perry M. Rogers. Vol. 1. Englewood Cliffs, N.J.: Prentice-Hall, 1988.

U.S. Department of Commerce, Jesse H. Jones, Secretary. Bureau of the Census. *Religious Bodies: 1936,* vol. 1. Washington, D.C.: U.S. Government Printing Office, 1941.

Secondary Sources

Books and Dissertations

Abraham, Henry J. *Freedom and the Court: Civil Rights and Liberties in the United States.* 5th ed. New York: Oxford University Press, 1988.

———. *Justices and Presidents: A Political History of Appointments to the Supreme Court.* New York: Oxford University Press, 1974.

Allen, Lee N. "The Woman Suffrage Movement in Alabama, 1910–1920." In *From Civil War to Civil Rights: Alabama, 1860–1960, An Anthology from the* Alabama Review, ed. Sarah Woolfolk Wiggins. Tuscaloosa: University of Alabama Press, 1987.

Autrey, Dorothy. "The National Association for the Advancement of Colored People in Alabama, 1913–1952." Ph.D. diss., Notre Dame University, 1985.

Bailey, Kenneth K. *Southern Protestantism in the Twentieth Century.* New York: Harper & Row, 1964.

Barnard, William. *Democrats and Dixiecrats: Alabama Politics, 1942–1950.* University: University of Alabama Press, 1974.

———. "The Old Order Changes: Graves, Sparks, Folsom, and the Gubernatorial Election of 1942." In *From Civil War to Civil Rights: Alabama, 1860–1960, An Anthology from the* Alabama Review, ed. Sarah Woolfolk Wiggins. Tuscaloosa: University of Alabama Press, 1987.

Beckford, James A. *The Trumpet of Prophecy.* New York: Halsted Press, 1975.

Bergman, Jerry. *Jehovah's Witnesses and Kindred Groups: A Historical Compen-*

dium and Bibliography. Garland Reference Service of Social Science, vol. 180. New York: Garland Publishing, 1984.

Berry, Mary Francis. *Stability, Security, and Continuity: Mr. Justice Burton and Decision-Making in the Supreme Court, 1945–1958*. Westport, Conn.: Greenwood Press, 1978.

Black, Hugo L., Jr. *My Father: A Remembrance*. New York: Random House, 1975.

Blackwell, Victor V. *O'er the Ramparts They Watched*. New York: A Hearthstone Book, Carlton Press, 1976.

Blum, John M., William S. McFeely, Edmund S. Morgan, Arthur M. Schlesinger, Jr., Kenneth M. Stampp, and C. Vann Woodward. *The National Experience: A History of the United States*. 7th ed. San Diego: Harcourt Brace Jovanovich, 1988.

Botting, Heather, and Botting, Gary. *The Orwellian World of Jehovah's Witnesses*. Toronto: University of Toronto Press, 1984.

Bruner, David. "Owen J. Roberts." In *The Justices of the United States Supreme Court, 1789–1969: Their Lives and Major Opinions*, ed. Leon Friedman and Fred L. Israel. New York: Chelsea House Publishers and R. R. Bowker, 1969.

Carlson, Jody. *George C. Wallace and the Politics of Powerlessness*. New Brunswick: Transaction Books, 1991.

Carter, Dan T. *Scottsboro: A Tragedy of the American South*, rev. ed. Baton Rouge: Louisiana State University Press, 1979.

Cash, W. J. *The Mind of the South*. New York: Knopf, 1941.

Cole, Marley. *Jehovah's Witnesses: The New World Society*. New York: Vantage Press, 1955.

Committee on History of Alabama Division of American Association of University Women. *A Half Century of AAUW in Alabama, 1927–1977*. Tuscaloosa, Ala.: Drake Printers, 1975.

Conrad, David Eugene. *The Forgotten Farmers: The Story of Sharecroppers in the New Deal*. Westport, Conn.: Greenwood Press, 1965.

Converse, Philip E. "The Nature of Mass Belief Systems in Mass Publics." In David Apter, ed., *Ideology and Dissent*. London: Press of Glencoe, 1964.

Cooper, Lee R. " 'Publish or Perish': Negro Jehovah's Witnesses in the Ghetto." In *Religious Movements in America*, ed. Irving I. Zaretsky and Mark P. Leone. Princeton: Princeton University Press, 1975.

Countryman, Vern. "Justice Douglas and Freedom of Expression." In *Six Justices on Civil Rights*. David C. Baum Memorial Lectures, ed. and with an introduction by Ronald D. Rotunda. New York: Oceana Publications, 1983.

Curry, Melvin Dotson. "Jehovah's Witnesses: The Effects of Millenarianism on the Maintenance of a Religious Sect." Ph.D. diss., Florida State University, Tallahassee, 1985.

Dabbs, James McBride. *Who Speaks for the South?* New York: Funk & Wagnalls, 1964.

Daniel, Pete. *Standing at the Crossroads: Southern Life Since 1900.* New York: Hill & Wang, 1986.

Degler, Carl N. *Place over Time: The Continuity of Southern Distinctiveness.* Baton Rouge: Louisiana State University Press, 1977.

Dillard, Irving. "The Flag Salute Cases." In *Quarrels That Have Shaped the Constitution,* ed. John A. Garraty. Rev. ed. New York: Harper & Row, 1987.

Ducat, Craig R., and Harold W. Chase. *Constitutional Interpretation.* 4th ed. St. Paul: West Publishing, 1988.

Durr, Virginia Foster. *Outside the Magic Circle: The Autobiography of Virginia Foster Durr,* ed. Hollinger F. Barnard. University: University of Alabama Press, 1986.

Dworkin, Ronald. "Taking Rights Seriously: Constitutional Cases." In Walter F. Murphy, James E. Fleming, and William F. Harris. *American Constitutional Interpretation.* Mineola, N.Y.: Foundation Press, 1986.

Encyclopaedia Britannica, 1965 ed. s.v. "Alabama," by Charles G. Summersell.

Farmer, Hallie. *The Legislative Process in Alabama.* University, Ala.: Bureau of Public Administration, University of Alabama, 1949.

Flynt, J. Wayne. "Alabama." *Encyclopedia of Religion in the South,* ed. Samuel S. Hill. Macon, Ga.: Mercer University Press, 1984.

————. "Religion in the Urban South: The Divided Religious Mind of Birmingham, 1900–1930." In *From Civil War to Civil Rights: Alabama, 1860–1960, An Anthology from the* Alabama Review, ed. Sarah Woolfolk Wiggins. Tuscaloosa: University of Alabama Press, 1987.

————. "Spindle, Mine, and Mule: The Poor White Experience in Post-Civil War Alabama." In *From Civil War to Civil Rights: Alabama, 1860–1960, An Anthology from the* Alabama Review, ed. Sarah Woolfolk Wiggins. Tuscaloosa: University of Alabama Press, 1987.

Freyer, Tony. *Hugo L. Black and the Dilemma of American Liberalism.* Glenview, Ill.: Scott Foresman/Little, Brown Higher Education, 1990.

————. *The Little Rock Crisis: A Constitutional Interpretation.* Westport, Conn.: Greenwood Press, 1984.

Friendly, Fred W. *Minnesota Rag: The Dramatic Story of the Landmark Supreme Court Case That Gave New Meaning to Freedom of the Press.* New York: Random House, 1981.

Frye, Robert J. *The Alabama Supreme Court: An Institutional View.* University:

Bureau of Public Administration, University of Alabama, 1969.

Gilbert, William E. "Bibb Graves as a Progressive, 1927–1930." In *From Civil War to Civil Rights: Alabama, 1860–1960, An Anthology from the* Alabama Review, ed. Sarah Woolfolk Wiggins. Tuscaloosa: University of Alabama Press, 1987.

Goodwyn, John L. "The Supreme Court at Work." *Alabama Lawyer: Official Organ State Bar of Alabama* 21 (January 1960): 6–10.

Goodwyn, Lawrence. *Democratic Promise: The Populist Moment in America.* New York: Oxford University Press, 1976.

Grafton, Carl, and Anne Permaloff. *Big Mules and Branchheads: James E. Folsom and Political Power in Alabama.* Athens: University of Georgia Press, 1985.

Grove, Frank A. *Library of Alabama Lives.* Hopkinsville, Ky.: Historical Record Association, 1961.

Gunther, Gerald. *Constitutional Law.* 11th ed. Mineola, N.Y.: Foundation Press, 1985.

Hackney, Sheldon. *Populism to Progressivism in Alabama.* Princeton: Princeton University Press, 1969.

Hamilton, Virginia van der Veer. *Alabama: A History.* New York: W. W. Norton, 1984.

———. *Hugo Black: The Alabama Years.* Baton Rouge: Louisiana State University Press, 1972.

———. *Lister Hill: Statesman from the South.* Chapel Hill: University of North Carolina Press, 1987.

Harrell, David Edwin, Jr. "Evolution of Plain-Folk Religion in the South, 1835–1920." In *Varieties of Southern Religious Experience,* ed. Samuel S. Hill. Baton Rouge: Louisiana State University Press, 1988.

———. "The South: Seedbed of Sectarianism." In *Varieties of Southern Evangelicalism,* ed. David Edwin Harrell, Jr. Macon, Ga.: Mercer University Press, 1981.

Harrison, Barbara. *Visions of Glory: A History and Memory of Jehovah's Witnesses.* New York: Simon & Schuster, 1978.

Hill, Samuel S. *Religion and the Solid South.* Nashville, Tenn.: Abingdon Press, 1972.

Hoekma, Anthony A. *The Four Major Cults.* Grand Rapids, Mich.: William B. Eerdmans, 1963.

Hofstadter, Richard. *The Age of Reform: From Bryan to FDR.* New York: Vintage Books, 1955.

———. *The Paranoid Style in American Politics and Other Essays.* New York: Vintage Books, 1967.

Howard, J. Woodford, Jr. *Mr. Justice Murphy: A Political Biography*. Princeton: Princeton University Press, 1968.

Irons, Peter. *The Courage of Their Convictions: Sixteen Americans Who Fought Their Way to the Supreme Court*. New York: Free Press, 1988.

———. *Justice at War*. New York: Oxford University Press, 1983.

Jones, Allen W. "Political Reforms of the Progressive Era." In *From Civil War to Civil Rights: Alabama, 1860–1960, An Anthology from the* Alabama Review, ed. Sarah Woolfolk Wiggins. Tuscaloosa: University of Alabama Press, 1987.

Kaplan, William. "The World War II Ban of the Jehovah's Witnesses in Canada: A Study of the Development of Civil Rights." J.S.D. thesis, Stanford University, 1988.

Key, V. O., Jr. *Southern Politics in State and Nation*. New York: Knopf, 1949.

Knovitz, Milton R. *Religious Liberty and Conscience: A Constitutional Inquiry*. New York: Viking Press, 1968.

Kousser, J. Morgan. *The Shaping of Southern Politics: Suffrage Restriction and the Establishment of the One-Party South, 1880–1910*. New Haven: Yale University Press, 1974.

Kurland, Philip B. "Justice Robert H. Jackson—Impact on Civil Rights and Civil Liberties." In *Six Justices on Civil Rights*, David C. Baum Memorial Lectures, ed. and with an introduction by Ronald D. Rotunda. New York: Oceana Publications, 1983.

Lash, Joseph P. *From the Diaries of Felix Frankfurter*. New York: W. W. Norton, 1975.

McGill, Ralph. *The South and the Southerner*. Boston: Little, Brown, 1959.

McMillan, Malcolm C. *Constitutional Development in Alabama, 1798–1901: A Study in Politics, the Negro, and Sectionalism*. Chapel Hill: University of North Carolina Press, 1955.

Manwaring, David R. *Render unto Caesar: The Flag Salute Controversy*. Chicago: University of Chicago Press, 1962.

Martin, David L. *Alabama's State and Local Governments*. 2d ed. University: University of Alabama Press, 1985.

Mason, Adolpheus T. *Harlan Fiske Stone: Pillar of the Law*. New York: Archon Books, 1968.

Matthews, C. E., and Anderson Brown. *Highlights of 100 Years in Mobile*. Mobile, Ala.: Powers, 1965.

Moore, Albert B. *History of Alabama and Her People*, vols. 2–3. Chicago: American Historical Society, 1927.

Morgan, Richard E. *The Supreme Court and Religion*. New York: Free Press, 1972.

Murphy, Walter F. *Elements of Judicial Strategy*. Chicago: University of Chicago Press, 1964.

Norrell, Robert J. *Reaping the Whirlwind: The Civil Rights Movement in Tuskegee*. New York: Knopf, 1985.

Nunn, Alexander, ed. *Lee County and Her Forebears*. Montgomery, Ala.: Herff Jones, 1983.

Owen, Marie Bankhead. *The Story of Alabama: A History of the State*. Vols. 1–5. New York: Lewis Publishing, 1949.

Parrish, Michael E. *Felix Frankfurter and His Times: The Reform Years*. New York: Free Press, 1982.

Penton, M. James. *Apocalypse Delayed: The Story of the Jehovah's Witnesses*. Toronto: University of Toronto Press, 1985.

———. *Jehovah's Witnesses in Canada: Champions of Freedom of Speech and Worship*. Toronto: Macmillan of Canada, 1976.

Pfeffer, Leo. *Church, State, and Freedom*. rev. ed. Boston: Beacon Press, 1967.

———. *God, Caesar, and the Constitution*. Boston: Beacon Press, 1975.

Pollak, Louis H. "Wiley Blount Rutledge: Profile of a Judge." In *Six Justices on Civil Rights*, David C. Baum Memorial Lectures, ed. and with an introduction by Ronald D. Rotunda. New York: Oceana Publications, 1983.

Pritchett, C. Herman. "Stanley Reed." In *The Justices of the United States Supreme Court, 1789–1969: Their Lives and Major Opinions*, ed. Leon Friedman and Fred L. Israel. New York: Chelsea House Publishers and R. R. Bowker, 1979.

Rehnquist, William. "The Notion of a Living Constitution." In Walter F. Murphy, James E. Fleming, and William F. Harris II, *American Constitutional Interpretation*. Mineola, N.Y.: Foundation Press, 1986.

Rogerson, Alan T. *Millions Now Living Will Die*. London: Constable, 1969.

Salisbury, W. Seward. *Religion in American Culture*. Homewood, Ill.: Dorsey Press, 1964.

Sayers, John W., comp. *Who's Who in Alabama*. Vols. 1, 2. Birmingham, Ala.: Sayers Enterprises, 1965–1967.

Schuman, Howard, et al. *Racial Attitudes in America*. Cambridge, Mass.: Harvard University Press, 1985.

Simon, James E. *The Antagonists: Hugo Black, Felix Frankfurter, and Civil Liberties in Modern America*. New York: Simon & Schuster, 1989.

Sims, George E. *The Little Man's Big Friend: James E. Folsom in Alabama Politics, 1946–1958*. University: University of Alabama Press, 1985.

Smith, L. J. *A Brief Sketch of the History of Chickasaw*. N.p.: Chickasaw Chamber of Commerce, 1958.

Stroup, Herbert Hewitt. *The Jehovah's Witnesses*. New York: Columbia University Press, 1945.

Summersell, Charles G. *Alabama History for Schools*. Birmingham, Ala.: Colonial Press, 1957.

Thornton, J. Mills. "Alabama Politics, J. Thomas Heflin, and the Expulsion Movement of 1929." In *From Civil War to Civil Rights: Alabama, 1860–1960, An Anthology from the* Alabama Review, ed. Sarah Woolfolk Wiggins. Tuscaloosa: University of Alabama Press, 1987.

———. "Challenge and Response in the Montgomery Bus Boycott of 1955–1956." In *From Civil War to Civil Rights: Alabama, 1860–1960, An Anthology from the* Alabama Review, ed. Sarah Woolfolk Wiggins. Tuscaloosa: University of Alabama Press, 1987.

———. "Hugo Black and the Golden Age." In *Justice Hugo Black and Modern America*, ed. Tony Freyer. Tuscaloosa: University of Alabama Press, 1990.

Tindall, George B. *The Emergence of the New South, 1913–1945*. Baton Rouge: Louisiana State University Press, 1967.

Tribe, Lawrence H. *American Constitutional Law*. Mineola, N.Y.: Foundation Press, 1978.

Urofsky, Melvin I. *A March of Liberty: A Constitutional History of the United States*. New York: Knopf, 1988.

Walker, Samuel. *In Defense of American Liberties: A History of the ACLU*. New York: Oxford University Press, 1990.

Watch Tower Bible and Tract Society of Pennsylvania. *Jehovah's Witnesses in the Twentieth Century*. Brooklyn: Watchtower Bible and Tract Society of New York, 1979.

———. *Yearbook of the Jehovah's Witnesses, 1975*. Brooklyn: Watchtower Bible and Tract Society of New York, 1976.

———. *You Can Live Forever in Paradise on Earth*. Brooklyn: Watchtower Bible and Tract Society of New York, 1982.

Wiebe, Robert. *Search for Order, 1877–1920*. New York: Hill & Wang, 1967.

Woodward, C. Vann. *Origins of the New South, 1877–1913*. Baton Rouge: Louisiana State University Press, 1951.

Wyatt-Brown, Bertram. "Ethical Background of Hugo Black's Career: Thoughts Prompted by the Essays of Sheldon Hackney and Paul L. Murphy." In *Justice Hugo Black and Modern America*, ed. Tony Freyer. Tuscaloosa: University of Alabama Press, 1990.

Yarbrough, Tinsley. *Judge Frank Johnson and Human Rights in Alabama*. University: University of Alabama Press, 1981.

Journals and Newspapers

Adler, G. "Comments: Licensing the Distribution of Religious Pamphlets." *Chicago-Kent Law Review* 20 (September 1942): 349–54.

Alabama Baptist. October 30, 1941–July 31, 1943.

Alabama Christian Advocate (Methodist). 1939–1943.

Alabama Journal. June 9, 1942; May 3, 1943.

Alabama: The News Magazine of the Deep South. 1937–1947.

Atkins, Leah Rawls. "Senator James A. Simpson and Birmingham Politics of the 1930s: His Fight Against the Spoilsmen and the Pie-Men." *Alabama Review* 41 (January 1988): 3–29.

Atlanta Constitution, June 22, 1942.

Barnet, James D. "Note and Comment: Constitutional Law—First and Fourteenth Amendments—Freedom of Religion and Press." *Oregon Law Review* 25 (February 1946): 132–35.

Bay City Times (Michigan). June 10, 1942.

Birmingham Age-Herald (Alabama). May 22, 23, 1941; June 9, 1942; May 4, 1943.

Birmingham News (Alabama). May 22, 1941; May 3, 1943; January 9, 1946; May 2, 1976.

Birmingham Post (Alabama). May 6, 1943.

Birmingham Post-Herald (Alabama). April 13, 1965.

"A Blow to Religious Freedom." *St. Louis Post-Dispatch.* June 9, 1942.

Boston Traveler. June 11, 1942.

Braunhut, Herman Jay. "Farm Labor Wage Rates in the South, 1909–1948." *Southern Economic Journal* 16 (October 1949): 189–99.

Chicago Daily News. June 11, 1942.

Chicago Daily Tribune. June 10, 1942.

Chickasaw News-Herald (Alabama). 1971.

Choper, Jesse H. "Consequences of Supreme Court Decisions Upholding Individual Constitutional Rights." *Michigan Law Review* 83 (1984): 4–212.

Collier's (Editorial), July 18, 1942, p. 70.

Dauer, Manning J. "Recent Political Thought." *Journal of Politics* 10 (May 1948): 327–53.

Dillard, Irving. "About Face to Freedom." *New Republic,* May 24, 1943, pp. 693–95.

E., L.C. "Recent Cases: Constitutional Law—Freedom of Religion, Press and Speech—Licensing Ordinances." *George Washington Law Review* 11 (December 1942): 114–16.

Fairhope Courier (Alabama). January 7, 1943–May 8, 1947.

Fairman, Charles. "Does the Fourteenth Amendment Incorporate the Bill of Rights? The Original Understanding." *Stanford Law Review* 2 (December 1949): 5–139.

Fraser, Hugh Russell. "A Black Day in Court." *Madison Progressive* (Wisconsin). June 21, 1942.

Grafton, Carl. "Community Power Methodology and Alabama Politics." *Alabama Historical Quarterly* (Winter 1976): 271–90.

Grafton, Samuel. "I'd Rather Be Right." *New York Post*. June 11, 1942.

Greene, Lee S. "The Southern State Judiciary." *Journal of Politics* 10 (August 1948): 441–64. (Part of a series, "The Southern Political Scene, 1938–1948.")

Haenssler, Edward E. "Decisions." *Brooklyn Law Review* 12 (October 1942): 71–75.

Ingber, Stanley. "The Marketplace of Ideas: A Legitimizing Myth." *Duke Law Journal* 1 (February 1984): 32–89.

Jacksonville Journal (Florida). June 16, 1942.

"Jehovah's Witnesses, Who Refuse to Salute U.S. Flag, Hold Their National Convention." *Life*, August 1940, pp. 20–21.

Jones, Walter B. "The Alabamian's Creed." *Alabama Lawyer: Official Organ State Bar of Alabama* 2 (January 1942): 118.

Kendrick, Alexander. "Alabama Goes on Strike." *Nation*, August 29, 1934, pp. 233–34.

Lazare, Monroe M. "State Licensing of the Distribution of Literature and Freedom of the Press and of Religion." *Fordham Law Review* 11 (1942): 230–33.

Lexington Leader. June 17, 1942.

Mobile Press (Alabama). January 8, 1946.

Mobile Register (Alabama). December 26, 1943; January 8, 1946; May 16, 1974.

Montgomery Advertiser (Alabama). May 22, 23, 1941; June 23, 1942; May 4, 1943.

New Republic. January 21, 1946, p. 69.

New York Daily News. June 12, 1942.

New York Times. January 8, 1946, sec. 25, p. 2.

Nixon, H. C. "Southern Legislatures and Legislation." *Journal of Politics* 10 (May 1948): 410–17. (Part of a series, "The Southern Political Scene, 1938–1948.")

Norrell, Robert J. "Labor at the Ballot Box: Alabama Politics from the New Deal to the Dixiecrat Movement." *Journal of Southern History* 42 (May 1991): 201–34.

"Notes and Comments: Constitutional Law, Another Jehovah's Witness Case." *Indiana Law Journal* 17 (August 1942): 555–60.

O'Brien, Kenneth R., and Daniel E. O'Brien. "Cases and Studies: Freedom of Religion in Restatement of Inter-Church-and-State Common Law." *Jurist* 6 (October 1946): 503–23.

Opelika Daily News (Alabama). 1930–1943; 1948–January 12, 1952.

Pettengill, Samuel. "Religious Freedom." *Hartford Times* (Connecticut). June 20, 1942.

Philadelphia Presbyterian Guardian. June 25, 1942, p. 179.

"Religion." *Newsweek*, March 22, 1943, pp. 68–69.

Richmond Times-Dispatch. June 12, 1942.

Rotman, Victor W., and F. G. Folsom, Jr. "Recent Restrictions upon Religious Liberty." *American Political Science Review* 36 (December 1942): 53–68.

Sadat-Keeling, Leila. "Notes, Constitutional Law: Supreme Court Finds First Amendment a Barrier to Taxation of the Press." *Tulane Law Review* 58 (1984): 1073–89.

Schneider, Carl E. "Free Speech and Corporate Freedom: A Comment on *First National Bank of Boston v. Bellotti.*" *California Law Review* 59 (September 1986): 1227–89.

South Bend Tribune (Indiana). June 11, 1942.

Thomas, William Holcombe. "The Layman in Religious Life." *Alabama Christian Advocate*, June 10, 1908, pp. 2–4.

Time, June 22, 1942, p. 55.

Waite, Edward F. "The Debt of Constitutional Law to Jehovah's Witnesses." *Minnesota Law Review* 28 (March 1944): 246.

Walsh, Robert. "Recent Decisions." *Michigan Law Review* 41 (October 1942): 316–27.

Watchman Examiner (New York; Baptist). July 1, 1942, p. 656.

Weiner, Jonathan M. "Class Structure and Economic Development in the American South, 1865–1955." *American Historical Review* 84 (October 1979): 970–92.

Index

Gobitis, Lillian, 6, 76, 174 (n. 6)
Gobitis, Walter, 6, 77
Gobitis, William, 6, 76
God, 10, 11, 26, 27, 29–30, 35, 37, 38,
  57, 88, 100, 121, 141
"God and State," (speech), 108
Golden Age, 28, 38, 40, 166 (n. 13). *See
  also Consolation*
Goldsmith, Jackson, & Brock, 85
Good Hope Baptist Church, 29
Gospel, 38, 61
Grace, Bishop, 39
Grafton, Sam, 97
Graves, Bibb, 15, 16
Great Depression, 13, 15
Great multitude, 37
Griffin, Georgia, 41–42, 47, 66, 67. *See
  also Lovell v. Griffin*
Grosjean v. American Press Company, 91
Gulf Shipbuilding Company, 23;
  boundaries of property unclear, 130;
  and Chickasaw business block, 118,
  120, 121, 123, 150; dedication issue,
  116, 118; de facto municipal
  corporation, 127, 128; trespass issue,
  127–28

Haenssler, Edward E., 136, 180 (n. 58)
Halloween, 26
*Hamilton v. Regents of the University of
  California*, 5
Harris, John O., 124
Hell(fire), Witness view of, 26, 44
Hill, Hill, Whiting, and Harris, 124
Hill, Lister: and elections, 13–16, 85;
  pro-labor position of, 17
Hitler, Adolf, 6, 21, 76, 107
Holiness (Church), 12, 31
Holmes, Oliver Wendell, Jr., 77, 166
  (n. 31)
Horne, George, 187 (n. 58)

Howell, T. O., 116
Hughes, Charles Evans, 7, 78, 79

Incorporation, constitutional concept of, 5.
  See also Bill of Rights; First Amend-
  ment; Fourteenth Amendment
Indiana Law Journal, 135
Inferior Court of Mobile County, 114
Inge, Francis, 23, 116, 119, 125, 146, 184
  (n. 19)
International Bible Students. *See* Bible
  Students
Intolerance, and the U.S. Supreme Court,
  76, 79. *See also* Japanese ancestry;
  Minersville School District v. Gobitis
Isaiah (26:4), 54

Jackson, Irving, 34
Jackson, Mr. (jailer), 109–10, 193 (n. 23)
Jackson, Robert, 1, 2; and *Douglas v.
  Jeanette*, 103, 141; does not participate
  in *Marsh v. Alabama*, 125; dissents in
  Murdock v. Pennsylvania, 103; at
  Nuremberg trials in Germany, 125; and
  West Virginia v. Barnette, 103, 139; sees
  Witnesses as intruders of privacy, 80,
  92, 95, 125, 139, 182 (n. 72). *See also*
  U.S. Supreme Court
Jacksonville Journal (Florida), 97
Jacksonville State Teachers' College
  (Alabama), 20
James River, 32
Japanese ancestry, treatment of persons of,
  8, 155 (n. 25), 156 (n. 29), 181 (n. 66)
Jehovah: and Armageddon, 144; divine
  plan of, 56; final judge, 100; instruments
  of, 23–24, 38, 107; triumph of, 73, 105,
  132; aids Witnesses, 10, 40, 44, 115
Jehovah's Witnesses: abuse of, 7, 21, 46,
  50, 52–53, 59–60, 64–65, 79–80, 81,
  85, 88–89, 108–10, 182 (n. 5), 188
  (n. 2); abrasive approach of, 4, 71, 155

About the Author

MERLIN OWEN NEWTON is Associate Professor of History and Political Science at Huntingdon College, Alabama. She received her bachelor's degree from Huntingdon College, her master's from Tulane University, and her doctorate from The University of Alabama where she earned awards for outstanding graduate student and best dissertation.

DATE DUE

JUL 2 8 1998			